The Fashion Knitting Book

WHSMITH
EXCLUSIVE
· BOOKS ·

Contents

Contents

BEACH AND SPORTSWEAR

6 super styles for fun in the sun

EVENING SPECIALS

4 sophisticated styles for night-time elegance

QUICK AND EASY KNITS

5 fashionable designs for easy knitting

Notes and Abbreviations

Tension

For best result always read the complete instructions and check the tension before starting work. If the tension piece measures **less** than the required width try a size larger needle or hook. If the tension piece measures **more** than the required width try a size smaller needle or hook. Where tensions are given over st st for a patterned garment, check your tension in st st. If you have to use a different needle size to obtain this tension a similar adjustment must be made to the needle sizes used in the patterns. A proper fit and correct size of finished garment is only possible with the correct tension.

Notes

Figures in round brackets refer to the larger sizes. Figures or instructions in square brackets, [ ], should be repeated as stated after the brackets.

The quantities of yarn stated in this publication are based on average requirements and are therefore approximate.

Abbreviations

Alt = alternate; beg = beginning; ch = chain; cms = centimetres; dec = decrease; dc = double crochet; garter stitch = every row knit; inc = increase; ins = inches; k = knit; p = purl; psso = pass slipped stitch over; rep = repeat; sl = slip; ssk = slip 1, knit 1, pass slipped stitch over; st = stitch; sts = stitches; st st = stocking stitch (1 row knit, 1 row purl); tbl = through back of loop; tog = together; tr = treble; wyib = with yarn in back; wyif = with yarn in front; yb = yarn back; yf = yarn forward; yfon = yarn forward and over needle; yfrn = yarn forward and round needle; yo = yarn over; yrn = yarn round needle.

Crochet Terms

Important: In all crochet, pick up both the top threads of each stitch unless otherwise stated.

Chain (ch) = make a slip knot, insert hook, *take yarn over, draw yarn through loop*. Rep from * to * for each additional chain.

Slip stitch (sl st) = insert hook into next st, yo and draw through st and loop on hook, (1 sl st made).

Double crochet (dc) = insert hook into next st, yo and draw loop through, yo and draw this loop through the 2 loops on hook (1 dc made).

Picked Up Edgings

It is easier to pick up a large number of stitches evenly along an edge (for example along the front edge of a cardigan), if you work as follows: lay the garment flat on a table and make sure that the edge is laying straight. Measure the length and place a pin halfway along this length at right angles to the material. Now halve the length above and below this and then halve these distances again so that the length is divided into eighths. Now divide the required number of stitches by 8 and pick up approximately that number of stitches in each section to total stated number.

Pressing

Always press each piece on wrong side of work avoiding ribbing.

Wool: Using a hot iron and a damp cloth, steam each piece thoroughly without allowing the weight of the iron to rest on the work. While the knitting is still damp pin out, then press lightly again and allow to dry.

Synthetic yarns: Press lightly on wrong side using a warm iron and a dry cloth (avoiding ribbings) **except** when label states that yarn should not be pressed.

TABLE OF APPROXIMATE KNITTING NEEDLE EQUIVALENTS

Imperial	14	13	12	11	10	9	8	7	6	5	4	3	2	1
Metric (in mm)	2	2¼	2¾	3	3¼	3¾	4	4½	5	5½	6	6½	7	7½

This is an international collection of knitting and crochet designs, therefore many of these patterns were originally knitted in yarns which are not necessarily available in exactly the same colours. For these designs, comparable yarns which are widely available have been used, but there may be occasional discrepancies with the colours in the photographs.

If you have any difficulty in obtaining yarn, contact the following spinners.

	U. K.	AUSTRALIA	NEW ZEALAND	SOUTH AFRICA
PATONS	Patons & Baldwins Ltd. P.O. Box, McMullen Road, Darlington, Co. Durham DL1 1YQ.	Coats Patons (Australia) Ltd., PO Box 110, Ferntree Gully Road, Nr. Waverley, Vic. 3149	Coats Patons (N.Z.) Ltd, PO Box 50, 140 Ellsdon Perirua, Wellington	Coats Patons (S.A.) Ltd., PO Box 33, Randfontein 1760
COATS	Coats Domestic Marketing Division 39 Durham Street, Kinning Park, Glasgow G41 1BS			
JAEGER	Jaeger Handknitting McMullen Road, Darlington, Co. Durham DL1 1YQ.			
COPLEY	L. Copley-Smith & Sons Limited PO Box 46, Darlington, Co. Durham DL1 1YW.	———	———	———
ANNY BLATT	Anny Blatt (UK) Ltd. Bull Bridge Road, Ambergate, Derby DE5 2EY.	The Countryside Yarns Co., 26 Punch Street, Artarmon, N.S.W. 2064	———	———
BERGER DU NORD	Berger Du Nord Viking Wools Ltd., Rothay Holme, Rothay Road, Ambleside, Cumbria LA22 0HQ.	Woolcraft Pty. Ltd., 16 The Mall, 3081 West Heidelberg, Victoria	———	———
SCHEEPJESWOL	Scheepjeswol (UK) Ltd. 7 Colemeadow Road, Redditch, Worcs., B98 9NZ.	Thorobred Scheepjeswol Ltd., PO Box 52-028, Kingsland, Auckland 3, New Zealand		———

Sweater
Spectaculars

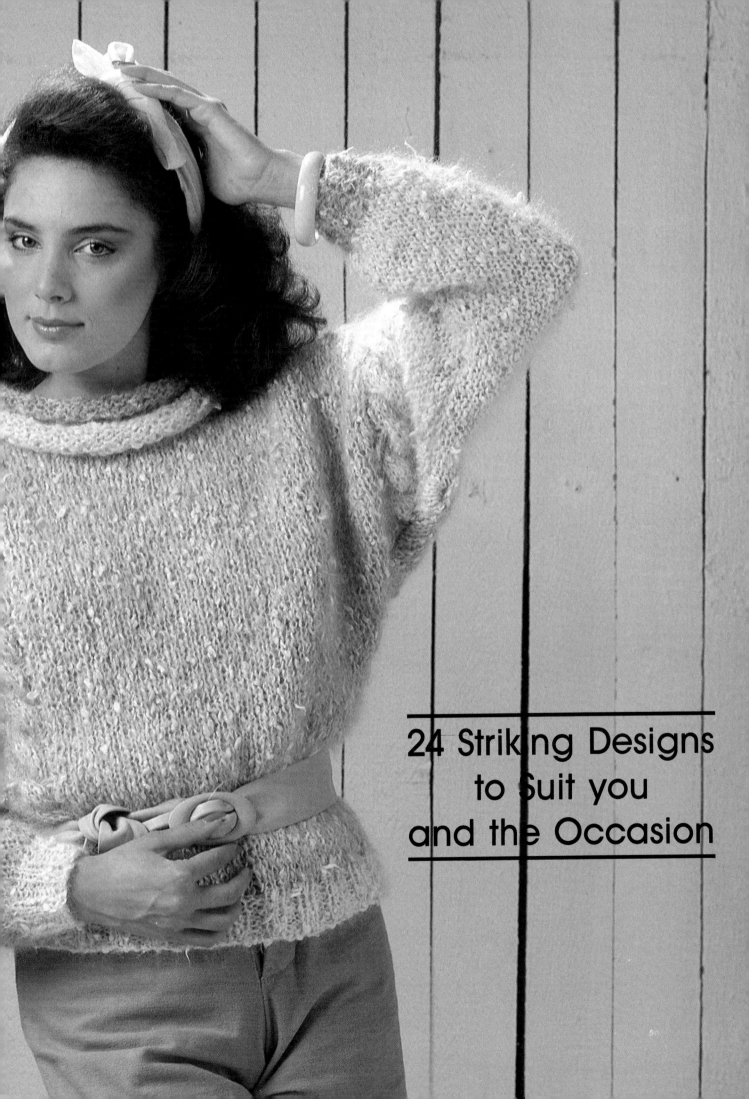

24 Striking Designs
to Suit you
and the Occasion

Mohair Jacket

MEASUREMENTS

To fit bust sizes 80(85-90-95-100-105) cms [32(34-36-38-40-42 ins]. Finished measurement 94(98-104-108-112-118) cms [37½(39-41½-43-45-47) ins]. Length to shoulder 64 cms [25¼ ins] all sizes. Sleeve length 45 cms [17¾ ins] all sizes.

MATERIALS

Patons Visions 50g balls: 6(6-6-6-7-7) balls Colour A, 5(5-5-6-6-6) balls each in Colours B and C. Pair needles each size 5mm (No 6) and 4mm (No 8). 4 buttons.

TENSION

18 sts and 24 rows = 10 cms [4 ins] square measured over st st using larger needles.

BACK

Using smaller needles and A cast on 78(82-86-90-94-98) sts. **1st row** (right side): K2, *p2, k2; rep from * to end. **2nd row:** P2, *k2, p2; rep from * to end.
Rep the last 2 rows until rib measures 8 cms [3 ins] ending with a wrong side row.
Next row (increase): Rib 1(3-2-2-4-1), *inc in next st, rib 4; rep from * to last 2(4-4-3-5-2) sts, inc in each of next 1(1-2-1-1-1) sts, rib to end. 94(98-104-108-112-118) sts.
Change to larger needles and knit 1 row. Joining in B and C as required, commence pattern:
1st row: Using B k4(6-2-4-6-2), sl 2 purlwise, *k12, sl 2 purlwise; rep from * to last 4(6-2-4-6-2) sts, knit to end. **2nd row:** Using B p4(6-2-4-6-2), sl 2 purlwise, *p12, sl 2 purlwise; rep from * to last 4(6-2-4-6-2) sts, purl to end.
Rep the last 2 rows 3 times more. Using A knit 2 rows.
11th row: Using C k11(13-9-11-13-9), sl 2 purlwise, *k12, sl 2 purlwise; rep from * to last 11(13-9-11-13-9) sts, knit to end. **12th row:** Using C p11(13-9-11-13-9), sl 2 purlwise, *p12, sl 2 purlwise; rep from * to last 11(13-9-11-13-9) sts, purl to end.
Rep the last 2 rows 3 times more. Using A knit 2 rows.
These 20 rows form the pattern. Continue in pattern until back measures 64 cms [25¼ ins] ending with a wrong side row.
Shape Shoulders: Keeping pattern correct cast off 30(32-34-36-37-40) sts at beg of next 2 rows. 34(34-36-36-38-38) sts remain.
Back collar: Change to smaller needles and continuing in A only knit 1 row increasing 2 sts evenly spaced for 3rd and 4th sizes only. 34(34-38-38-38-38) sts. Work 32 rows in k2, p2 rib as given for Back. Cast off in rib.

POCKET LININGS (Make 2)

Using larger needles and A cast on 22 sts and work 11 cms [4¼ ins] in st st, starting knit (right side), and increasing 2 sts evenly spaced on last row. 24 sts. Break yarn and slip sts onto a holder.

LEFT FRONT

Note: Figures or instructions in italics are for use when working Right Front.
Using smaller needles and A cast on 34(38-38-42-42-46) sts and work 8 cms [3 ins] in k2, p2 rib as given for Back ending with a wrong side row.
Next row (increase): Rib 2(3-2-2-2-2), *inc in next st, rib 3(5-3-5-4-4); rep from * to last 4(5-4-4-5-4) sts, inc in each of next 2(2-2-2-3-1) sts, rib to end. 43(45-48-50-52-55) sts.
Change to larger needles and knit 1 row. Commence pattern:
1st row: Using B k4(6-2-4-6-2) *9(9-2-2-2-9)*, sl 2 purlwise, *k12, sl 2 purlwise; rep from * to last 9(9-2-2-2-9) *4(6-2-4-6-2)* sts, knit to end. **2nd row:** Using B p9(9-2-2-2-9) *4(6-2-4-6-2)*, sl 2 purlwise, *p12, sl 2 purlwise; rep from * to last 4(6-2-4-6-2) *9(9-2-2-2-9)* sts, purl to end.
Rep the last 2 rows 3 times more. Using A knit 2 rows.
11th row: Using C k11(13-9-11-13-9) *2(2-9-9-9-2)*, sl 2 purlwise, *k12, sl 2 purlwise; rep from * to last 2(2-9-9-9-2) *11(13-9-11-13-9)* sts, knit to end. **12th row:** Using C p2(2-9-9-9-2) *11(13-9-11-13-9)*, sl 2 purlwise, *p12, sl 2 purlwise; rep from * to last 11(13-9-11-13-9) *2(2-9-9-9-2)* sts, purl to end.
Rep the last 2 rows 3 times more. Using A knit 2 rows. Work 14 more rows in pattern.
Place Pocket
1st row: Work 7(9-12-14-16-19) *12* sts, slip next 24 sts onto a holder, work in pattern across sts of one pocket lining, work to end. 43(45-48-50-52-55) sts.
Continue in pattern until front measures 24 cms [9½ ins] ending with a wrong side row.
Shape Front
Note: When decreasing or increasing in pattern on rows where sl sts are at shaped edge, work the decrease or increase in the nearest sts in B or C.
Keeping pattern correct dec 1 st (see Note above) at end *beg* (front edge) of next and same edge of every following 9th(9th-8th-8th-8th-8th) row until 30(32-34-36-37-40) sts remain. Work straight until front measures same as back to shoulder ending at side edge. Cast off.

RIGHT FRONT

Work as given for Left Front reversing pattern and shaping by *following figures or instructions in italics where indicated.*

SLEEVES

Using smaller needles and A cast on 34(38-38-42-42-46) sts and work 7 cms [2¾ ins] in k2, p2 rib as given for Back ending with a wrong side row.
Next row (increase): Rib 3(5-5-7-7-8), inc in every st to last 3(5-5-7-7-8) sts, rib to end. 62(66-66-70-70-76) sts.
Change to larger needles and knit 1 row. Work 4 rows in pattern as given for 3rd(1st-1st-2nd-2nd-3rd) size on Back. Keeping pattern correct and bringing extra sts into pattern inc 1 st at each end of next and every following 5th(5th-5th-5th-4th-5th) row until there are 100(104-108-112-116-120) sts. Work straight until sleeve measures 45 cms [17¾ ins] or required sleeve length ending with a wrong side row. Cast off.

FINISHING AND BANDS

Press according to instructions on ball band.
Pocket Edgings: Using smaller needles and A and with right side of work facing, knit across sts of one pocket opening increasing 2 sts evenly spaced. 26 sts. Work 7 rows in k2, p2 rib as given for Back starting with the 2nd row. Cast off in rib.
Work other pocket edging in the same way.
Left Front Band and Collar: Using smaller needles and A, with right side of work facing, and starting at top of shoulder, pick up and k86 sts evenly along shaped front edge to first neck dec, and 50 sts along straight edge to cast on edge. 136 sts.
1st row: *P2, k2; rep from * to end. Keeping rib correct shape collar as follows: **2nd row:** Rib 56 sts, turn. **3rd and every alt row:** Sl 1, rib to end. **4th row:** Rib 59 sts, turn. **6th row:** Rib 62 sts, turn.
Continue to work 3 sts more in rib on every alt row until the row 'rib 86 sts, turn' has been worked. **Next row:** Sl 1, rib to end. Work 9 rows in rib across all 136 sts. Cast off in rib.
Right Front Band and Collar: Using smaller needles and A, with right side of work facing, and starting at cast on edge, pick up and k50 sts evenly along straight edge of front to first neck dec, and 86 sts along shaped edge to shoulder. 136 sts.
1st row: *K2, p2; rep from * 13 times more, turn. **2nd and every alt row:** Sl 1, rib to end. Bringing extra sts into rib continue to shape collar as follows: **3rd row:** Rib 59 sts, turn. **5th row:** Rib 62 sts, turn.
Continue to work 3 sts more in rib on every alt row until the row 'rib 86 sts, turn' has been worked.
Next row: Sl 1, rib to end. Work 4 rows in rib across all 136 sts.
Next row (buttonholes): Rib to last 48 sts, *cast off next 2 sts in rib, rib until there are 12 sts on right-hand needle after casting off; rep from * twice more, cast off next 2 sts in rib, rib to end.
Work 5 more rows in rib, casting on 2 sts over each buttonhole on first of these rows. Cast off in rib.
Join shoulder seams and collar, reversing seam on outside half of collar. Fold sleeves in half lengthways and mark centre of cast off edge. Sew sleeve to side edge placing centre at shoulder seam. Note: armholes should measure approximately 25(26-27-28-29-30) cms [10(10¼-10¾-11-11½-11¾) ins]. Join side and sleeve seams. Sew pocket linings and edgings in place. Sew on buttons.

Block Pattern Cardigan

MEASUREMENTS

To fit bust sizes 81/86(91-96/101) cms [32/34(36-38/40) ins]. Finished measurement at underarm (buttoned) 102(107.5-112.5) cms [40½(42½-44½) ins]. Length 63.5(63.5-68.5) cms [25(25-27) ins]. Sleeve width at upper arm 50(50-54) cms [20(20-22) ins].

MATERIALS

Patons Diploma Double Knitting 50g balls: 4(5-5) balls Colour A, 2(3-3) balls colour B, 3(3-3) balls Colour C, 2(2-2) balls colour D and 6(6-6) balls Colour E. Pair needles size 3¾mm (No 9). 3.00mm crochet hook. 6 buttons. Shoulder pads (optional).

TENSION

22 sts and 30 rows = 10 cms [4 ins] over st st using 3¾mm needles. **Note:** After making a tension piece, steam lightly, stretching the piece to its maximum. Allow to dry completely. Take measurements over blocked piece.

PATTERN STITCHES

St st = With A k on right side, p on wrong side.

Reverse st st = With D p on right side, k on wrong side.

Garter st = With C k every row.

Sl st pattern = With B work as follows:

1st row (right side): *K1, sl 1 wyib; rep from * to end.

2nd row: Purl.

3rd row: *Sl 1 wyib, k1; rep from * to end.

4th row: Purl.

Rep 1st to 4th rows for sl st pattern.

Moss st = With E work as follows:

1st row (right side): *K1, p1; rep from * to end.

2nd row: K the purl sts and p the knit sts.

Rep 2nd row for moss st.

NOTES

When changing colours, twist yarns on wrong side to prevent holes.

Use separate bobbins for each block of colour.

BACK

Using C cast on 112(118-124) sts and work 2 rows in garter st.

Commence Block Pattern

1st row (right side): Using E work moss st over first 5 sts, using A work st st over next 25(27-27) sts, using D work reverse st st over next 10 sts, using B work sl st pattern over next 32(34-40) sts, using D work reverse st st over next 10 sts, using A work st st over next 25(27-27) sts, using E work moss st over last 5 sts.

Continue in colours and patterns as set for 13 rows more, ending with a wrong side row.

15th row (right side): Using B work sl st pattern over first 11(13-13) sts, using E work moss st over next 40 sts, using A work st st over next 10(12-18) sts, using E work moss st over next 40 sts, using B work sl st pattern over last 11(13-13) sts.

Continue in colours and patterns as set for 14 rows more.

30th to 32nd rows: Using C work garter st for 3 rows.

Rep 1st to 32nd rows for block pattern for a total of 6 reps. 192 rows. Rep 1st to 14th rows for 0(0-1) times more — piece measures approx 63.5(63.5-68.5) cms [25(25-27) ins] from beg. Cast off.

LEFT FRONT

Using C cast on 65(68-71) sts and work 2 rows in garter st.

Commence Block Pattern

1st row (right side): Using B work sl st pattern over first 15(17-19) sts, using D work reverse st st over next 10 sts, using A work st st over next 25(27-27) sts, using E work moss st over next 10 sts, using A work st st over last 5(4-5) sts.

Continue in colours and patterns as set for 13 rows more.

15th row (right side): Using A work st st over first 7(6-7) sts, using E work moss st over next 40 sts, using B work sl st pattern over last 18(22-24) sts.

Block Pattern Cardigan

Continue in colours and patterns as set for 14 rows more.

30th to 32nd rows: Using C work garter st for 3 rows.

Rep 1st to 32nd rows for block pattern until piece measures 57(57-62) cms [22½(22½-24½) ins] from beg, ending with a right side row.

Shape Neck

Next row (wrong side): Cast off 14(15-16) sts (neck edge), work to end.

Continue to cast off at neck edge 3 sts 3 times, 2 sts twice, 1 st 3 times. 35(37-39) sts. If necessary work straight until same number of rows as for back.

Cast off all sts for shoulder.

RIGHT FRONT

Using C cast on 56(59-62) sts and work 2 rows in garter st.

Commence Block Pattern

1st row (right side): Using E work moss st over first 6(5-6) sts, using A work st st over next 25(27-27) sts, using D work reverse st st over next 10 sts, using B work sl st pattern over last 15(17-19) sts.

Continue in colours and patterns as set for 13 rows more.

15th row (right side): Using B work sl st pattern over first 10(11-14) sts, using E work moss st over next 40 sts, using A work st st over last 6(8-8) sts.

Continue in colours and patterns as set for 14 rows more.

30th to 32nd rows: Using C work garter st for 3 rows.

Rep 1st to 32nd rows for block pattern until same length as left front to neck, ending with a wrong side row.

Shape Neck

Next row (right side): Cast off 5(6-7) sts (neck edge), work to end.

Continue to cast off at neck edge 3 sts 3 times, 2 sts twice, 1 st 3 times. 35(37-39) sts. If neces-

sary, work straight until same number of rows as for back.

Cast off all sts for shoulder.

SLEEVES

Using C cast on 60(60-66) sts and work 2 rows in garter st.

Commence Block Pattern

1st row (right side): Using A work st st over first 4(3-3) sts, using D work reverse st st over next 10 sts, using B work sl st pattern over next 32(34-40) sts, using D work reverse st st over next 10 sts, using A work st st over last 4(3-3) sts.

Continuing in colours and patterns as set, inc 1 st each end every 4th row 15(15-21) times, then every 6th row 10(10-6) times **at the same time,** continue colours and patterns as for centre back, working inc sts into pattern. Work straight on 110(110-120) sts until 127 rows have been worked from beg, piece measures approx 42 cms [17 ins]. Cast off.

FINISHING

Press pieces according to instructions on ball band. Sew shoulder seams. Mark 25(25-27) cms [10(10-11) ins] on front and back down from shoulder seam for armholes. Fold top of sleeve in half and sew to front and back between markers. Sew side and sleeve seams.

Outside Edging: With right side facing, crochet hook and C and starting at lower left side seam, work a row of dc along lower edge of back, right front, neck and left front edges, working 3 dc into corners and spacing sts to keep edge flat. Join with sl st to first dc. Working from left to right, work 1 backwards dc in each dc. Fasten off.

Work edging in same way along lower edge of sleeves.

Sew buttons 5 cms [2 ins] from centre left front edge, placing top button 1.5 cms [½ inch] from neck edge, lower button 7.5 cms [3 ins] from lower edge, other 4 buttons spaced evenly between. On right front, work crochet loops opposite buttons.

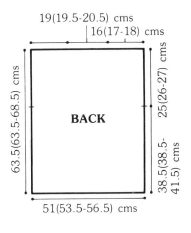

19(19.5-20.5) cms
16(17-18) cms
63.5(63.5-68.5) cms
25(26-27) cms
BACK
38.5(38.5-41.5) cms
51(53.5-56.5) cms

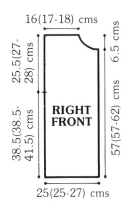

16(17-18) cms
6.5 cms
25.5(27-28) cms
RIGHT FRONT
57(57-62) cms
38.5(38.5-41.5) cms
25(25-27) cms

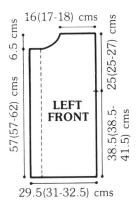

16(17-18) cms
6.5 cms
25(25-27) cms
LEFT FRONT
57(57-62) cms
38.5(38.5-41.5) cms
29.5(31-32.5) cms

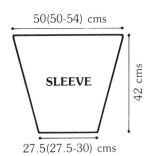

50(50-54) cms
SLEEVE
42 cms
27.5(27.5-30) cms

Cabled Sweater

MEASUREMENTS

To fit bust sizes 80(85-90-95-100) cms [32(34-36-38-40) ins]. Finished measurement 90(96-100-106-110) cms [36(38½-40-42½-44) ins]. Length to shoulder 59(60-61-62-63) cms [23(23½-24-24¼-24¾) ins]. Sleeve seam 45 cms [17¾ ins].

MATERIALS

Patons Promise Double Knitting 40g balls: 9(9-9-10-10) balls. Pair needles each size 4mm (No 8) and 3¼mm (No 10). Cable needle.

TENSION

20 sts and 38 rows = 10 cms [4 ins] square measured over garter st using larger needles.

SPECIAL ABBREVIATIONS

Slip marker = make a slip knot in a short length of contrasting yarn and place on needle where indicated. On the following rows slip the marker from one needle to the other until the pattern is established and the marker is no longer required.

MB (Make Bobble) = knit into front, back and front of next st, turn and p3, turn and k3, turn and p3, turn and sl 1, k2tog, psso.

C8F (Cable 8 Front) = slip next 4 sts onto cable needle and hold at front of work, knit next 4 sts from left-hand needle, then knit sts from cable needle.

CABLE PANEL (Worked across 16 sts between markers)

1st row: K16.
2nd and every alt row: K4, p8, k4.
3rd row: K16.
5th row: MB, k3, C8F, k3, MB.
7th row: K16.
9th row: K16.
11th row: MB, k14, MB.
12th row: K4, p8, k4.
These 12 rows form the Cable Panel.

DIAMOND PANEL (Worked across 13 sts between markers)

1st row: K6, yf, k2tog tbl, k5.
Work 3 rows in garter st (every row knit).
5th row: K4, k2tog, yf, k1, yf, k2tog tbl, k4.
Work 3 rows in garter st.
9th row: K3, k2tog, yf, k3, yf, k2tog tbl, k3.
Work 3 rows in garter st.
13th row: K2, k2tog, yf, k5, yf, k2tog tbl, k2.
Work 3 rows in garter st.
17th row: K1, k2tog, yf, k7, yf, k2tog tbl, k1.
Work 3 rows in garter st.
21st row: K2tog, yf, k9, yf, k2tog tbl.
Work 3 rows in garter st.
25th row: Yf, k2tog tbl, k9, yf, k2tog, yf.
Work 3 rows in garter st.
29th row: K1, yf, k2tog tbl, k7, k2tog, yf, k1.

Work 3 rows in garter st.
33rd row: K2, yf, k2tog tbl, k5, k2tog, yf, k2.
Work 3 rows in garter st.
37th row: K3, yf, k2tog tbl, k3, k2tog, yf, k3.
Work 3 rows in garter st.
41st row: K4, yf, k2tog tbl, k1, k2tog, yf, k4.
Work 3 rows in garter st.
45th row: K5, yf, sl 1, k2tog, psso, yf, k5.
Work 3 rows in garter st.
These 48 rows form the Diamond Panel.

BACK

Using 3¼mm needles cast on 91(97-101-107-111) sts.
1st row (right side): K1, *p1, k1; rep from * to end.
2nd row: P1, *k1, p1; rep from * to end.
Rep the last 2 rows until rib measures 10 cms [4 ins] ending with a right side row.
Next row (increase): Rib 21(22-23-24-25), inc in next st, rib 47(51-53-57-59), inc in next st, rib to end. 93(99-103-109-113) sts.
Change to larger needles and commence pattern:
1st row: K14(15-16-17-18), slip marker (see Special Abbreviations), work 1st row of Cable Panel across next 16 sts, slip marker, k10(12-13-15-16), slip marker, work 1st row of Diamond Panel across next 13 sts, slip marker, k10(12-13-15-16), slip marker, work 1st row of Cable Panel across next 16 sts, slip marker, k14(15-16-17-18).
2nd row: K14(15-16-17-18), work 2nd row of Cable Panel, k10(12-13-15-16), work 2nd row of Diamond Panel, k10(12-13-15-16), work 2nd row of Cable Panel, k14(15-16-17-18).
Keeping the 48 rows of Diamond Panel and 12 rows of each Cable Panel correct between markers, rep the last 2 rows until back measures 41 cms [16 ins] or required length to armholes ending with a wrong side row.

Shape Armholes

Keeping pattern correct cast off 3(4-4-5-5) sts at beg of next 2 rows. Dec 1 st at each end of next 5 rows, then every alt row until 69(73-75-79-81) sts remain ★. Work straight until armholes measure 18(19-20-21-22) cms [7(7½-8-8¼-8¾) ins] measured straight from start of armhole shaping and ending with wrong side row.

Shape Shoulders

Keeping pattern correct cast off 5(6-6-6-6) sts at beg of next 6 rows, then 6(5-5-7-7) sts at beg of following 2 rows.
Slip remaining 27(27-29-29-31) sts onto a holder for neckband.

FRONT

Work as given for Back to ★. Work straight until front is 19(21-23-25-27) rows shorter than back to start of shoulder shaping thus ending with a right side row.

Shape Neck

1st row: Work 30(32-32-34-34) sts, turn and complete this side first.
★★ Keeping pattern correct dec 1 st at neck edge on next 5 rows, then following 4 alt rows. 21(23-23-25-25) sts remain. Work 6(8-10-12-14) rows straight (work 1 row less here for 2nd side), thus ending at armhole edge.

Shape Shoulder

Cast off 5(6-6-6-6) sts at beg of next and following 2 alt rows. Work 1 row. Cast off remaining 6(5-5-7-7) sts.
Slip next 9(9-11-11-13) sts at centre onto a holder for neckband. With wrong side of work facing rejoin yarn to neck edge of remaining sts and work to end.
Complete to match first side from ★★ to end, reversing shaping by working 1 row less where indicated.

SLEEVES

Using smaller needles cast on 45(47-49-51-53) sts and work 8 cms [3 ins] in k1, p1 rib as given for Back ending with a wrong side row and increasing 1 st at centre of last row. 46(48-50-52-54) sts.
Change to larger needles and commence pattern:
1st row: K15(16-17-18-19), slip marker, work 1st row of Cable Panel across next 16 sts, slip marker, k15(16-17-18-19).
2nd row: K15(16-17-18-19), work 2nd row of Cable Panel, k15(16-17-18-19).
Keeping the 12 rows of Cable Panel correct work 14 more rows. Bringing extra sts into garter st, inc 1 st at each end of next and every following 14th(12th-11th-10th-9th) row until there are 62(66-70-74-78) sts. Work straight until sleeve measures 45 cms [17¾ ins], or required seam length ending with a wrong side row.

Shape Top

Keeping pattern correct, cast off 3(4-4-5-5) sts at beg of next 2 rows. Dec 1 st at each end of next 3 rows, then every following 4th row until 34(36-38-40-42) sts remain, then every alt row until 24(26-28-30-32) sts remain. Dec 1 st at each end of next 3 rows. Cast off 5 sts at beg of next 2 rows. Cast off remaining 8(10-12-14-16) sts.

FINISHING AND NECKBAND

Press pieces according to instructions on ball band. Join left shoulder seam.
Neckband: Using smaller needles and with right side of work facing, knit across sts on holder at back neck decreasing 1 st at centre, pick up and k20(22-24-26-28) sts down left front slope, knit across sts on holder at centre front and pick up and k20(22-24-26-28) sts up right front slope. 75(79-87-91-99) sts.
Work 8 rows in k1, p1 rib as given for Back starting with the 2nd row. Cast off in rib.
Join right shoulder seam and ends of neckband. Join side and sleeve seams. Insert sleeves.

Summer Stripes

MEASUREMENTS

To fit bust sizes 81(86-96) cms [32(34-36) ins]. Finished bust measurement at underarm 117(122-127) cms [46(48-50) ins]. Sleeve width at upperarm 40.5(43-46) cms [16(17-18) ins].

MATERIALS

Patons Cotton Perlé 50g balls: 7 balls Colour A, 5(6-7) balls Colour B, 4 balls Colour C and 2(3-4) balls Colour D. Pair needles each size 3¼mm (No 10) and 3¾mm (No 9). Circular needle size 3¼mm (No 10).

TENSION

24 sts and 32 rows = 10 cms [4 ins] over st st using size 3¾mm needles.

NOTES

Sweater design is oversized. If closer fit is required, follow directions for smaller size OR use one size smaller knitting needles.

Each block of colour on front is knitted using separate ball of yarn. To make working easier, wind yarn onto separate bobbins. When changing colours, twist yarns on wrong side to prevent holes.

BACK

Using smaller needles and A cast on 90(96-102) sts.

1st row (right side): *K1, p1; rep from * to end.

Rep this row for 4.5 cms [1¾ ins], ending with a wrong side row.

Change to larger needles and B and knit next row increasing 12 sts evenly across. 102(108-114) sts.

Working in st st, inc 1 st at each end of every 4th row 14 times, at each end of every 8th row 4 times and **at the same time,** work colour stripes as follows: work *12 rows B, 12 rows A; rep from * for stripe pattern until there are 102 stripe rows (8½ stripes) and back measures 37 cms [14½ ins] from beg.

There are 138(144-150) sts after all increases. Place markers at each end of last row for underarm.

Cap Sleeeve

Continuing in stripe pattern as set, inc 1 st at each end of every 4th row 15 times. 168(174-180) sts. Work straight until cap sleeve measures 20.5(21.5-23) cms [8(8½-9) ins] from markers, ending with a wrong side row.

Shape Shoulder and Neck

Keeping to pattern, cast off 4 sts at beg of next 12 rows.

Next row: Cast off 4 sts, knit until there are 38(41-44) sts on needle, join 2nd ball of yarn and cast off centre 36 sts, knit to end.

Continue to work each side with separate balls of yarn and cast off 3 sts at each neck edge 6 times and **at the same time,** cast off 4 sts at beg of next 11(7-3) rows, 5 sts at beg of next 0(2-4) rows, 6 sts at beg of next 0(2-4) rows.

FRONT

Cast on and work rib as given for Back. Change to larger needles.

Next row (right side): Using B k37(40-43) increasing 5 sts evenly spaced, place first marker, using C k27 increasing 3 sts, [using B k5, inc 1 st, using A k5, inc 1 st] twice, using B k6, using D k0(3-6). 102(108-114) sts.

Working in st st and carrying marker, inc 1 st (in D on right side, in colour-pattern on left side) at each end of every 4th row 14 times, every 8th row 4 times and **at the same time,** work colour-pattern as follows: work 11 more rows in colour-pattern as set.

Next 12 rows: Work sts before first marker in A, work 12 more rows in colour-patterns.

Next row (right side): Work sts to first marker in D, work 12 more sts in D, place 2nd marker, work remaining sts in colour patterns as set. Work 59 more rows as last row.

Next row (right side): Work sts to first marker

in A, next 30 sts in C and remove 2nd marker, work patterns as set to end.

Continue in this way to work stripe pattern on sts before first marker as for Back and remaining sts in pattern as set until front has same number of rows as Back to underarm.

Cap Sleeve

Continuing in pattern as set, inc 1 st at each end of every 4th row 15 times. Work straight until cap sleeve measures 19(20.5-21.5) cms [7½(8-8½) ins].

Shape Neck

Next row (right side): Knit to centre 24 sts, join 2nd ball of yarn and cast off centre 24 sts, knit to end.

Continue to work each side with separate balls of yarn, casting off 2 sts at each neck edge 12 times and **at the same time,** when cap sleeve measures 20.5(21.5-23) cms [8(8½-9) ins], cast off 4 sts at each shoulder edge 12(10-8) times, 5 sts 0(1-2) times, 6 sts 0(1-2) times.

FINISHING

Press pieces according to instructions on ball band. Sew shoulder seams.

Using smaller needles and A pick up and k112(118-124) sts along right sleeve edge. Work 5 rows in st st.

Next row: Knit to last 8 sts, slip these sts onto a holder.

Next row: Purl to last 8 sts, slip these sts onto a holder.

Rep last 2 rows once more.

Next row: Knit all sts including sts from holders.

Knit 2 more rows for garter st band. Cast off. Using C work edge on left sleeve as for right sleeve.

Neckband: Using circular neeedle and A pick up and knit sts evenly around neck edge. Purl 8 rows. Do not cast off. Fold band to right side and weave band, working through each st on needle, to neck edge.

Batwing Sweater

MEASUREMENTS

One size to fit bust sizes 80-105 cms [32-42 ins]. Width from wrist to wrist (approximately) 133 cms [53¼ ins]. Length to shoulder (approximately) 62 cms [24¾ ins].

MATERIALS

Copley Sonata Double Knitting 100g balls: 2 balls Colour A, 1 ball Colour B and 2 balls Colour C. Pair needles each size 4mm (No 8) and 3¼mm (No 10). Row counter.

TENSION

22 sts and 30 rows = 10 cms [4 ins] square measured over st st using larger needles.

SPECIAL NOTE

Twist yarns together on wrong side of work when changing colour to avoid making a hole.

BACK

Using smaller needles and A cast on 101 sts.
1st row (right side): K1, *p1, k1; rep from * to end.
2nd row: P1, *k1, p1; rep from * to end.
Rep the last 2 rows until rib measures 5 cms [2 ins] ending with a right side row (work 1 row less here for Front).
Next row (increase): Rib 5, *inc in next st, rib 9; rep from * to last 6 sts, inc in next st, rib 5. 111 sts ★.

★ ★ Change to larger needles and commence pattern:
1st row: Knit 29C, 53B, 29A.
2nd row: Purl 29A, 53B, 29C.
3rd row: Knit 30C, 51B, 30A.
4th row: Purl 30A, 51B, 30C.
5th row: Knit 31C, 80A.
6th row: Purl 80A, 31C.
7th row: Using C inc in first st, k31, using A knit to last 2 sts, inc in next st, k1.
8th row: Purl 80A, 33C.
9th row: Knit 34C, 79A.
10th row: Purl 79A, 34C.
11th row: Using C inc in first st, k34, k43B,

using A knit to last 2 sts, inc in next st, k1.
12th row: Purl 36A, 43B, 36C.
13th row: Knit 37C, 41B, 37A.
14th row: Purl 37A, 41B, 37C.
15th row: Using C inc in first st, k37, using A knit to last 2 sts, inc in next st, k1.
16th row: Purl 78A, 39C.
17th row: Knit 40C, 77A.
18th row: Purl 77A, 40C.
19th row: Using C inc in first st, k40, using A knit to last 2 sts, inc in next st, k1.
20th row: Purl 77A, 42C.
21st row: Knit 43C, 33B, 43A.
22nd row: Purl 43A, 33B, 43C.
23rd row: Using C inc in first st, k43, k31B, using A knit to last 2 sts, inc in next st, k1.
24th row: Purl 45A, 31B, 45C.
25th row: Knit 46C, 75A.
26th row: Purl 75A, 46C.
27th row: Using C inc in first st, k46, using A knit to last 2 sts, inc in next st, k1.
28th row: Purl 75A, 48C.
29th row: Knit 49C, 74A.
30th row: Purl 74A, 49C.
31st row: Using C inc in first st, k49, k23B, using A knit to last 2 sts, inc in next st, k1.
32nd row: Purl 51A, 23B, 51C.
33rd row: Knit 52C, 21B, 52A.
34th row: Purl 52A, 21B, 52C.
35th row: Using C inc in first st, k52, using A knit to last 2 sts, inc in next st, k1.
36th row: Purl 73A, 54C.
37th row: Knit 55C, 72A.
38th row: Purl 72A, 55C.
39th row: Using C inc in first st, k55, using A knit to last 2 sts, inc in next st, k1.
40th row: Purl 72A, 57C.
41st row: Knit 58C, 13B, 58A.
42nd row: Purl 58A, 13B, 58C.
43rd row: Using C inc in first st, k58, k11B, using A knit to last 2 sts, inc in next st, k1.
44th row: Purl 60A, 11B, 60C.

Batwing Sweater

45th row: Knit 61C, 70A.

46th row: Purl 70A, 61C.

47th row: Using C inc in first st, k61, using A knit to last 2 sts, inc in next st, k1.

48th row: Purl 70A, 63C.

49th row: Knit 64C, 69A.

50th row: Purl 69A, 64C.

51st row: Using C inc in first st, k64, k3B, using A knit to last 2 sts, inc in next st, k1.

52nd row: Purl 66A, 3B, 66C.

53rd row: Knit 67C, 1B, 67A.

54th row: Purl 67A, 1B, 67C.

55th row: Using C inc in first st, k66, using A knit to last 2 sts, inc in next st, k1. 137 sts.

56th row: Purl 69A, 68C.

57th row: Using C inc in first st, k66, k68A, using B inc in next st, k1.

58th row: Purl 3B, 68A, 68C.

59th row: Using C inc in first st, k66, k69A, using B k1, inc in next st, k1.

60th row: Purl 4B, 69A, 68C.

61st row: Using C inc in first st, k66, k69A, using C k3, inc in next st, k1.

62nd row: Purl 6C, 69A, 68C.

63rd row: Using C inc in first st, k66, k69A, using C k5, inc in next st, k1.

64th row: Purl 8C, 69A, 68C.

65th row: Using C inc in first st, k66, using A knit to last 2 sts, inc in next st, k1.

66th row: Purl 79A, 68C.

67th row: Using C inc in first st, k66, using A knit to last 2 sts, inc in next st, k1.

68th row: Purl 81A, 68C.

69th row: Using C inc in first st, k66, using A knit to last 2 sts, inc in next st, k1.

70th row: Purl 83A, 68C.

71st row: Using A inc in first st, knit 66C, 69A, using B k13, inc in next st, k1.

72nd row: Purl 16B, 69A, 66C, 2A.

73rd row: Using A inc in first st, k1, knit 65C, 69A, using B k15, inc in next st, k1.

74th row: Purl 18B, 69A, 65C, 3A.

75th row: Using C inc in first st, k66, k69A, using C k17, inc in next st, k1.

76th row: Purl 20C, 69A, 68C.

77th row: Using C inc in first st, k66, k69A, using C k19, inc in next st, k1.

78th row: Purl 22C, 69A, 68C.

79th row: Using C inc in first st, k66, k69A, using C k21, inc in next st, k1.

80th row: Purl 24C, 69A, 68C.

81st row: Using B inc in first st, k9, k57C, using A knit to last 2 sts, inc in next st, k1.

82nd row: Purl 95A, 57C, 11B.

83rd row: Using B inc in first st, k11, k55C, using A knit to last 2 sts, inc in next st, k1.

84th row: Purl 97A, 55C, 13B.

85th row: Using B inc in first st, k13, k53C, 69A, using B k27, inc in next st, k1. 167 sts.

86th row: Using B inc in first st, p29, purl 69A, 53C, using B p13, inc in next st, p1.

87th row: Using B inc in first st, k16, knit 51C, 69A, using B k30, inc in next st, k1.

88th row: Using B inc in first st, p32, purl 69A, 51C, using B p16, inc in next st, p1.

89th row: Using B inc in first st, k19, knit 49C, 69A, using B k33, inc in next st, k1.

90th row: Using B inc in first st, p35, purl 69A, 49C, using B p19, inc in next st, p1.

91st row: Using A inc in first st, k22, knit 47C, 69A, using C k36, inc in next st, k1.

92nd row: Using C inc in first st, p38, purl 69A, 47C, using A p22, inc in next st, p1.

93rd row: Using A inc in first st, k25, knit 45C, 69A, using C k39, inc in next st, k1.

94th row: Using C inc in first st, p41, purl 69A, 45C, using A p25, inc in next st, p1.

95th row: Using C inc in first st, k71, using A knit to last 2 sts, inc in next st, k1.

96th row: Using A inc in first st, p113, using C purl to last 2 sts, inc in next st, p1.

97th row: Using C inc in first st, k72, using A knit to last 2 sts, inc in next st, k1.

98th row: Using A inc in first st, p116, using C purl to last 2 sts, inc in next st, p1.

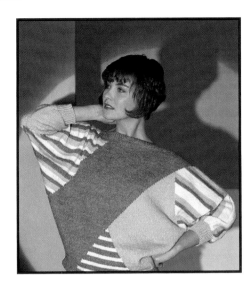

99th row: Using C inc in first st, k73, using A knit to last 2 sts, inc in next st, k1.

100th row: Using A inc in first st, p119, using C purl to last 2 sts, inc in next st, p1.

101st row: Using B inc in first st, k37, knit 37C, 69A, using B k51, inc in next st, k1.

102nd row: Using B inc in first st, p53, purl 69A, 37C, using B p37, inc in next st, p1.

103rd row: Using B inc in first st, k40, knit 35C, 69A, using B k54, inc in next st, k1.

104th row: Using B inc in first st, p56, purl 69A, 35C, using B p40, inc in next st, p1.

105th row: Using B inc in first st, k43, knit 33C, 69A, using C k57, inc in next st, k1.

106th row: Using C inc in first st, p59, purl 69A, 33C, using B p43, inc in next st, p1.

107th row: Using B inc in first st, k46, knit 31C, 69A, using C k60, inc in next st, k1.

108th row: Using C inc in first st, p62, purl 69A, 31C, using B p46, inc in next st, p1.

109th row: Using B inc in first st, k49, knit 29C, 69A, using C k63, inc in next st, k1.

110th row: Using C inc in first st, p65, purl 69A, 29C, using B p49, inc in next st, p1.

111th row: Using A inc in first st, k52, k27C, using A knit to last 2 sts, inc in next st, k1C.

112th row: Using C inc in first st, purl 137A, 27C, using A p52, inc in next st, p1.

113th row: Using A inc in first st, k55, knit 25C, 137A, using C k1, inc in next st, k1.

114th row: Using C inc in first st, p3, purl 137A, 25C, using A p55, inc in next st, p1.

115th row: Using C inc in first st, k81, knit 69A, 68B, using C k4, inc in next st, k1.

116th row: Using C inc in first st, p6, purl 68B, 69A, using C purl to last 2 sts, inc in next st, p1.

117th row: Using C inc in first st, k82, knit 69A, 68B, using C k7, inc in next st, k1.

118th row: Using C inc in first st, p9, purl 68B, 69A, using C purl to last 2 sts, inc in next st, p1. 233 sts.

119th row: Using C cast on 19 sts, knit these sts, then k84, knit 69A, 68B, 12C.

120th row: Using C cast on 19 sts, purl these sts, then p12, purl 68B, 69A, 103C. 271 sts.

121st row: Knit 85B, 17C, 69A, 100C.

122nd row: Purl 100C, 69A, 17C, 85B.

123rd row: Knit 86B, 15C, 69A, 101C.

124th row: Purl 101C, 69A, 15C, 86B.

125th row: Knit 87B, 13C, 137A, 34C.

126th row: Purl 34C, 137A, 13C, 87B.

127th row: Knit 88B, 11C, 137A, 35C.

128th row: Purl 35C, 137A, 11C, 88B.

129th row: Knit 89B, 9C, 137A, 36C.

130th row: Purl 36C, 137A, 9C, 89B.

131st row: Knit 90A, 7C, 69A, 68B, 37C.

132nd row: Purl 37C, 68B, 69A, 7C, 90A.

133rd row: Knit 91A, 5C, 69A, 68B, 38C.

134th row: Purl 38C, 68B, 69A, 5C, 91A.

135th row: Knit 95C, 69A, 107C.

136th row: Purl 107C, 69A, 95C.

137th row: Knit 94C, 69A, 108C.

138th row: Purl 108C, 69A, 94C.

139th row: Knit 93C, 69A, 109C.

140th row: Purl 109C, 69A, 93C.

141st row: Knit 92B, 137A, 42C.

142nd row: Purl 42C, 137A, 92B.

143rd row: Knit 91B, 137A, 43C.

144th row: Purl 43C, 137A, 91B.

145th row: Knit 90B, 69A, 68B, 44C.

146th row: Purl 44C, 68B, 69A, 90B.

147th row: Knit 89B, 69A, 68B, 45C.

148th row: Purl 45C, 68B, 69A, 89B.

149th row: Knit 88B, 69A, 68B, 46C.

150th row: Purl 46C, 68B, 69A, 88B.

151st row: Knit 156A, 115C.

152nd row: Purl 115C, 156A.

153rd row: Knit 155A, 116C.

154th row: Purl 116C, 155A.

155th row: Knit 85C, 137A, 49C.

156th row: Purl 49C, 137A, 85C.

157th row: Knit 84C, 137A, 50C.

158th row: Purl 50C, 137A, 84C.

159th row: Knit 83C, 137A, 51C.

160th row: Purl 51C, 137A, 83C.

161st row: K82B, using A k18, p1, [k1, p1] 35 times, knit 48B, 52C.

162nd row: Purl 52C, 48B, using A k1, [p1, k1] 35 times, p18, p82B.

163rd row: K81B, using A k19, p1, [k1, p1] 35 times, knit 47B, 53C.

164th row: Purl 53C, 47B, using A k1, [p1, k1] 35 times, p19, p81B.

165th row: K80B, using A k20, p1, [k1, p1] 35 times, k100C.

166th row: P100C, using A k1, [p1, k1] 35 times, p20, p80B.

167th row: K79B, using A k21, p1, [k1, p1] 35 times, k100C.

168th row: P100C, using A k1, [p1, k1] 35 times, p21, p79B.

169th row: K78B, using A k22, p1, [k1, p1] 35 times, k100C.

170th row: P100C, using A k1, [p1, k1] 35 times, p22, p78B.

Cast off in pattern.

FRONT

Work as given for Back to ★ working 1 row less where indicated.

Complete as given for Back from ★★ to end **but** reading knit for purl and purl for knit throughout.

FINISHING AND CUFFS

Press pieces according to instructions on ball band. Join shoulder seams leaving ribbing at centre open for neck.

Cuffs: Using smaller needles and C and with right side of work facing, pick up and k75 sts evenly along sleeve edge.

Next row (decrease): P1, k1, *p2tog, k1; rep from * to last st, p1. 51 sts remain.

Work 5 cms [2 ins] in k1, p1 rib as given for Back. Cast off in rib.

Join side and underarm seams and ends of cuffs. Press seams.

Sweater with Cable Panels

MEASUREMENTS

To fit bust sizes 80(85/90-95/100) cms [32(34/36-38/40) ins]. Finished measurement 89(98-107) cms [35½(39-43) ins]. Length to shoulder (approximately) 65(65-65) cms [26(26-26) ins]. Sleeve seam (approximately) 40(40-40) cms [16(16-16) ins].

MATERIALS

Coats 'Anchor' Knitting and Crochet Cotton No. 6 (50g) used double: 17(18-19) balls. Pair needles each size 4mm (No.8) and 3mm (No. 11). Cable needle.

Coats Maxi 'Pellicano' Knitting and Crochet Cotton No. 5 (200g) used double 5(5-5) balls. Pair needles each size 4½mm (No. 7) and 3¼mm (No. 10). Cable needle.

TENSION

With yarn used double: 22 sts and 30 rows = 10 cms [4 ins] square measured over st st using larger needles.

SPECIAL ABBREVIATIONS

M1 (Make 1 Stitch) = pick up horizontal strand of yarn lying between st just worked and next st and purl into front of it.

Inc 1K = knit into front and back of next st.

Inc 1P = purl into front and back of next st.

C2R (Cross 2 Right) = slip next st onto cable needle and hold at back of work, knit next st from left-hand needle, then knit st from cable needle.

T2L (Twist 2 Left) = slip next st onto cable needle and hold at front of work, purl next st from left-hand needle, then knit st from cable needle.

T2R (Twist 2 Right) = slip next st onto cable needle and hold at back of work, knit next st from left-hand needle, then purl st from cable needle.

C4F or C4B (Cable 4 Front or Back) = slip next 2 sts onto cable needle and hold at front (or back) of work, knit next 2 sts from left-hand needle, then knit sts from cable needle.

C10F or C10B (Cable 10 Front or Back) = slip next 5 sts onto cable needle and hold at front (or back) of work, knit next 5 sts from left-hand needle, then knit sts from cable needle.

T9 (Twist 9) = slip next 4 sts onto a cable needle and hold at front of work, k4, p1 from left-hand needle, then knit sts from cable needle.

C12B (Cross 12 Back) = slip next 8 sts onto cable needle and hold at back of work, knit next 4 sts from left-hand needle, slip the 2nd 4 sts from cable needle back onto left-hand needle and knit them, then k4 from cable needle.

C12F (Cross 12 Front) = slip next 8 sts onto cable needle and hold at front of work, knit next 4 sts from left-hand needle, slip the 2nd 4 sts from cable needle back onto left-hand needle and knit them, then k4 from cable needle.

Sweater with Cable Panels

PANEL A (Worked across 22 sts)
1st, 3rd, 7th and 9th rows: [K1, p2] twice, k10, [p2, k1] twice.
2nd and every alt row: [P1, k2] twice, p10, [k2, p1] twice.
5th row: [K1, p2] twice, C10F, [p2, k1] twice.
10th row: As 2nd row.
These 10 rows form Panel A.

PANEL B (Worked across 22 sts)
Work as given for Panel A but working C10B in place of C10F on 5th row.

PANEL C (Worked across 8 sts)
1st row: P2, k4, p2.
2nd row: K2, p4, k2.
3rd row: P2, C4F, p2.
4th row: As 2nd row.
These 4 rows form Panel C.

PANEL D (Worked across 8 sts)
Work as given for Panel C but working C4B in place of C4F on 3rd row.

PANEL E (Note: the number of sts varies in this panel)
1st row: [K4, p2] twice, k4, p1, k4, [p2, k4] twice. 33 sts.
2nd, 4th, 6th and 8th rows: [P4, k2] twice, p4, k1, p4, [k2, p4] twice.
3rd row: K4, p2, C4F, p2, k4, p1, k4, p2, C4B, p2, k4.

5th row: As 1st row.
7th row: K4, p2, C4F, p2, T9, p2, C4B, p2, k4.
9th row: M1, k4, [p2, k4] twice, M1, p1, M1, [k4, p2] twice, k4, M1. 37 sts.
10th row: K1, p4, [k2, p4] twice, k3, [p4, k2] twice, p4, k1.
11th row: P1, M1, k4, p2tog, C4F, p2tog, k4, M1, p3, M1, k4, p2tog, C4B, p2tog, k4, M1, p1.
12th row: K2, p4, [k1, p4] twice, k5, [p4, k1] twice, p4, k2.
13th row: P2, M1, k4, k2tog, k2, sl 1, k1, psso, k4, M1, p5, M1, k4, k2tog, k2, sl 1, k1, psso, k4, M1, p2.
14th row: K3, p12, k7, p12, k3.
15th row: P3, M1, k4, C4F, k4, M1, p7, M1, k4, C4B, k4, M1, p3. 41 sts.
16th, 18th and 20th rows: K4, p12, k9, p12, k4.
17th row: P4, C12B, p9, C12F, p4.
19th row: P4, k4, C4F, k4, p9, k4, C4B, k4, p4.
21st row: P3, *k2tog, k2, [Inc 1K, k3] twice, sl 1, k1, psso*, p7, rep from * to * once more, p3.
22nd row: K3, [p4, k1] twice, p4, k7, [p4, k1] twice, p4, k3.
23rd row: P2, k2tog, k3, Inc 1P, C4F, Inc 1P, k3, sl 1, k1, psso, p5, k2tog, k3, Inc 1P, C4B, Inc 1P, k3, sl 1, k1, psso, p2.
24th row: [K2, p4] 3 times, k5, [p4, k2] 3 times.
25th row: P1, *k2tog, k3, p2, k4, p2, k3, sl

1, k1, psso*, p3, rep from * to * once more, p1. 37 sts.

26th row: As 10th row.

27th row: K2tog, k3, p2, C4F, p2, k3, sl 1, k1, psso, p1, k2tog, k3, p2, C4B, p2, k3, sl 1, k1, psso. 33 sts.

28th and 30th rows: As 2nd row.

29th row: [K4, p2] twice, T9, [p2, k4] twice.

31st row: As 3rd row.

32nd row: As 2nd row.

These 32 rows form Panel E.

SPECIAL NOTE
Yarn is used double throughout.

BACK AND FRONT (Both alike)
Using smaller needles cast on 114(126-138) sts.

1st row (right side): K2, *p2, k2; rep from * to end.

2nd row: P2, *k2, p2; rep from * to end.

Rep the last 2 rows until rib measures 5 cms [2 ins] ending with a right side row.

Next row (increase): Rib 2(4-5), *inc in next st, rib 4(5-5), inc in next st, rib 6(6-7); rep from * to last 4(5-7) sts, inc in next st, rib to end. 133(145-157) sts.

Change to larger needles and commence pattern:

1st row: [T2L, p4] 2(3-4) times, T2L, p6, work 1st row of Panel A across next 22 sts, 1st row of Panel C across next 8 sts, Panel E across next 33 sts, Panel D across next 8 sts, Panel B across next 22 sts, p6, [T2R, p4] 2(3-4) times, T2R.

2nd row: K1, [T2R, k4] 2(3-4) times, T2R, k5, work 2nd rows of Panels B, D, E, C then A, k5, [T2L, k4] 2(3-4) times, T2L, k1.

3rd row: P2, [T2L, p4] 3(4-5) times, work 3rd rows of Panels A, C, E, D then B, [p4, T2R] 3(4-5) times, p2.

4th row: K3, [T2R, k4] 2(3-4) times, T2R, k3, work 4th rows of Panels B, D, E, C then A, k3, [T2L, k4] 2(3-4) times, T2L, k3.

5th row: [P4, T2L] 3(4-5) times, p2, work next rows of Panels A, C, E, D then B, p2, [T2R, p4] 3(4-5) times.

6th row: K5, [T2R, k4] 1(2-3) times, T2R, k7, work next rows of Panels B, D, E, C then A, k7, [T2L, k4] 1(2-3) times, T2L, k5.

These 6 rows form the diagonal pattern at each side of panels. Keeping continuity of panels correct rep these 6 rows until the 32 rows of Panel E have been worked 4 times in all, then work the first 17 rows once more, thus ending with a 1st row of diagonal pattern, 5th row of Panels A and B and 1st row of Panels C and D. Work 1 more row increasing 1 st at centre for 1st and 3rd sizes only and decreasing 3 sts evenly spaced for 2nd size only. 142(150-166) sts.

Commence Yoke Pattern

1st row: P2, k2, p2, *C2R, p2, k2, p2; rep from * to end.

2nd row: K2, *p2, k2; rep from * to end.

These 2 rows form the yoke pattern. Rep these 2 rows until yoke measures 8 cms [3 ins] ending with a wrong side row. Cast off in pattern.

SLEEVES
Using smaller needles cast on 66 sts and work 5 cms [2 ins] in k2, p2 rib as given for Back and Front ending with a right side row.

Next row (increase): Rib 5, *inc in next st, work 1 st; rep from * to last 7 sts, inc in next st, rib to end. 94 sts.

Change to larger needles and commence pattern:

1st, 3rd, 7th and 9th rows: [P6, k2] twice, p4, k10, p4, [C2R, p2, k2, p2] 3 times, C2R, p4, k10, p4, [k2, p6] twice.

2nd, 4th, 6th and 8th rows: [K6, p2] twice, k4, p10, k4, [p2, k2] 6 times, p2, k4, p10, k4, [p2, k6] twice.

5th row: [P6, k2] twice, p4, C10F, p4, [C2R, p2, k2, p2] 3 times, C2R, p4, C10B, p4, [k2, p6] twice.

10th row: As 2nd row.

These 10 rows form the rib pattern either side of cable pattern. Bringing extra sts into rib pattern, inc 1 st at each end of next and every following 6th(5th-5th) row until there are 120(126-126) sts. Work straight until sleeve measures approximately 40 cms [16 ins] ending with an 8th row of pattern. Cast off in pattern.

TO MAKE UP
Press pieces according to instructions on ball band. Join shoulder seams leaving 18 cms [7 ins] at centre for neck opening. Fold sleeves in half lenthways and mark centre of cast off edge. Sew sleeve to side edge placing centre at shoulder seam. Join side and sleeve seams.

2-Colour Cardigan

MEASUREMENTS

To fit bust sizes 84/88(92/96) cms [33/35(36/38) ins]. Length 60(61) cms [23½(24) ins]. Sleeve seam 46 cms [18 ins].

MATERIALS

Patons Beehive Chunky Twirl 50g balls: 12(13) balls Main colour (M), 2 balls Contrast colour (C). Pair of needles size 7mm (No 2). Cable needle. 6 buttons.

TENSION

16 sts and 17 rows = 10 cms [4 ins] over pattern on back and fronts.

13 sts and 17 rows = 10 cms [4 ins] over pattern on sleeves.

SPECIAL ABBREVIATION

Cross 2 = take the needle behind the first st on left-hand needle and knit the 2nd st, then knit the first st, slip both sts off the needle together.

2-COLOUR CABLE PANEL

(Referred to as Cable Pattern 18)

Note: When using more than one colour use a separate ball of yarn for each part, and ensure that yarns are twisted together at back of work when changing colour to avoid holes.

1st and 3rd rows: Knit 12M, 6C.

2nd and 4th rows: Purl 6C, 12M.

5th row: Slip next 6 sts onto cable needle and hold at front, knit next 6 sts and then k6 sts from cable needle (C12F Cable 12 Front), then k6C.

Note: Where colours are not given, work sts in colour as previous row.

6th, 8th and 10th rows: Purl.

7th and 9th rows: Knit.

11th row: K6M, slip next 6 sts onto cable needle and hold at back, knit next 6 sts then k6 sts from cable needle using the thread from the left-hand M ball (C12B Cable 12 Back).

12th, 14th and 16th rows: Purl.

13th and 15th rows: Knit.

17th row: C12F, k6M.

18th, 20th and 22nd rows: Purl.

19th and 21st rows: Knit.

23rd row: K6C, C12B.

24th, 26th and 28th rows: Purl.

25th and 27th rows: Knit.

29th row: C12F, k6M.

30th, 32nd and 34th rows: Purl.

31st and 33rd rows: Knit.

35th row: K6M, C12B.

36th row: Purl.

These 36 rows form the pattern.

BACK

Using 7mm needles and M cast on 92(96) sts.

1st row: P1, k2, *p2, k2; rep from * to last st, p1.

2nd row: K1, p2, *k2, p2; rep from * to last st, k1.

Rep 1st and 2nd rows for 4 cms [1½ ins] ending with a 2nd row.

Continue in pattern:

1st row: K1, [Cross 2, p2] 3 times, cable pattern 18, [p2, Cross 2] 7(8) times, p2, cable pattern 18, [p2, Cross 2] 3 times, k1.

2nd row: K1, [p2, k2] 3 times, cable pattern 18, [k2, p2] 7(8) times, k2, cable pattern 18, [k2, p2] 3 times, k1.

These 2 rows form pattern for remainder of back. Continue with 2 cable panels and the remainder in pattern in this way. Work until the 24th(26th) row of the 3rd cable pattern has been completed (work should measure 56.5(58) cms [22¼(22¾) ins] from top of ribbing). Cast off loosely in pattern.

LEFT FRONT

Using 7mm needles and M cast on 44(46) sts.

1st size only: Work 4 cms [1½ ins] in rib as given for Back ending with a 2nd row.

Continue in pattern:

1st row: K1, [Cross 2, p2] 3 times, cable pattern 18, [p2, Cross 2] 3 times, k1.

2nd size only

1st row: P1, k2, *p2, k2; rep from * to last 3 sts, p2, k1.

Rep 1st row for 4 cms [1½ ins].

Continue in pattern:

1st row: K1, [Cross 2, p2] 3 times, cable pattern 18, [p2, Cross 2] 3 times, p2, k1.

All sizes: Continue in pattern as set. Work until the 13th(15th) row of the 3rd cable pattern has been completed.

Shape Neck

Keeping side edge straight cast off at beg of next and following alt rows 5(6) sts once, 3 sts once, 2 sts twice and 1 st once. Continue on remaining 31(32) sts until front measures same as back to shoulders. Cast off.

RIGHT FRONT

Using 7mm needles and M cast on 44(46) sts.

1st size only: Work 4 cms [1½ ins] in rib as given for Back.

Continue in pattern:

1st row: K1, [Cross 2, p2] 3 times, cable pattern 18, [p2, Cross 2] 3 times, k1.

2nd size only

1st row: K1, p2, *k2, p2; rep from * to last 3 sts, k2, p1.

2-Colour Cardigan

17.5(18.5) cms
8(8.5) cms

27(28) cms

½ BACK

29.5 cms

3.5 cms

├─ 26(27) cms ─┤

8(8.5) cms
17.5(18.5) cms

6 cms

½ FRONT

50.5(51.5) cms

3.5 cms

├─ 25.5(27) cms ─┤

Rep 1st row for 4 cms [1½ ins].

Continue in pattern:

1st row: K1, p2, [Cross 2, p2] 3 times, cable pattern 18, [p2, Cross 2] 3 times, k1.

All sizes: Complete to match left front, working 1 row more than left front to end at centre front edge before shaping neck.

SLEEVES

Using 7mm needles and M cast on 26(26) sts.

1st row: *P2, k2; rep from * to last 2 sts, p2.

2nd row: *K2, p2; rep from * to last 2 sts, k2.

Rep 1st and 2nd rows for 4 cms [1½ ins], ending with a 1st row (1 row more than back).

Next row: P1, now purl into front and back of each st to end. 51 sts.

Continue in pattern:

1st row: P1, k1, *p5, k1; rep from * to last st, p1.

2nd row: K1, p1, *k5, p1; rep from * to last st, k1.

3rd to 6th rows: Rep 1st and 2nd rows twice.

7th row: Inc in first st, *p1, k5; rep from * to last 2 sts, p1, inc in last st.

8th row: P2, *k1, p5; rep from * to last 3 sts, k1, p2.

9th row: K2, *p1, k5; rep from * to last 3 sts, p1, k2.

10th row: As 8th row.

11th and 12th rows: As 9th and 10th rows.

These 12 rows form the pattern. Bringing extra sts into pattern, inc 1 st at each end of next row, then every 6th row until there are 71(73) sts. Work until sleeve measures 46 cms [18¼ ins]

from beg. Cast off loosely.

MAKING UP

Press pieces according to instructions on ball band.

Buttonhole Band: Using 7mm needles and M knit up 76(78) sts evenly along right front edge.

1st row: P1(2), k2, *p2, k2; rep from * to last 1(2) sts, p1(2).

2nd row: K1(2), p2, *k2, p2; rep from * to last 1(2) sts, k1(2).

These 2 rows form rib. Work 1 more row.

Next row (buttonholes): Rib 5(6), cast off 1 st, *rib 15 including st on needle, cast off 1 st; rep from * 3 times more, rib to end.

Next row: Work in rib casting on 1 st over those cast off.

Work 3 more rows in rib. Cast off in rib.

Button Band: Work as given for Buttonhole Band omitting buttonholes.

Join shoulder seams.

Neckband: Using 7mm needles and M knit up 72(76) sts evenly along neck edge. Work in rib as given for 1st size of buttonhole band. Work 3 rows. Make buttonhole in next 2 rows exactly above 5th buttonhole. Work 6 rows. Make buttonhole in next 2 rows. Work 3 rows. Cast off in rib.

Fold neckband in half onto wrong side and slip stitch in position. Place a marker 27(28) cms [10¾(11) ins] on each side of shoulder seams to mark depth of armholes. Join cast off edge of sleeves to armhole edges. Join side and sleeve seams. Sew on buttons.

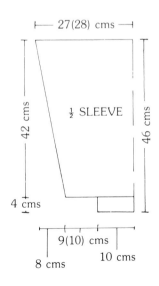

27(28) cms

½ SLEEVE

42 cms

46 cms

4 cms

9(10) cms

8 cms   10 cms

Cowl Neck Sweater

MEASUREMENTS

To fit bust sizes 87/92(95/99) cms [34/36(37/39) ins]. Length 57(59) cms [22½(23¼) ins]. Sleeve seam 47 cms [18½ ins].

MATERIALS

Patons Siberia 50g balls: 8(9) balls Main colour (M), 1(1) ball Contrast colour (C). 2 balls extra in Contrast colour (C) for separate collar. Pair needles size 6mm (No 4). 6mm (No 4) circular needle for collar. Cable needle.

TENSION

14 sts and 19 rows = 10 cms [4 ins] over main pattern.

SPECIAL ABBREVIATIONS

Cross 2 = take the needle behind the first st on left-hand needle and knit the 2nd st, now knit the first st, slip both sts off the needle together.

C12F (Cable 12 Front) = slip next 6 sts onto cable needle and hold at front, knit next 6 sts, then k6 sts from cable needle.

C12B (Cable 12 Back) = slip next 6 sts onto cable needle and hold at back, knit next 6 sts, then k6 sts from cable needle.

MAIN PATTERN

1st row: P1, k1, *p5, k1; rep from * to last st, p1.

2nd row: K1, p1, *k5, p1; rep from * to last st, k1.

3rd to 6th rows: Rep 1st and 2nd rows twice.

7th row: As 2nd row.

8th row: As 1st row.

9th to 12th rows: Rep 7th and 8th rows twice.

These 12 rows form the pattern.

FRONT

Using 6mm needles and M cast on 58(62) sts.

1st row: *P2, k2; rep from * to last 2 sts, p2.

2nd row: *K2, p2; rep from * to last 2 sts, k2.

Rep 1st and 2nd rows for 5 cms [2 ins], ending with a 2nd row and increasing 11(13) sts evenly spaced in last row by picking up loop from between needles and working into back of it. 69(75) sts.

Continue with M in main pattern: Work 8(6) rows ★.

Commence Panel in C

Use a separate ball of yarn for each part and ensure that yarns are twisted together at back of work when changing colour to avoid holes.

1st row: Using C p4, using M work in main pattern to end.

2nd row: Using M work in main pattern to last 4 sts, using C k4.

3rd row: Using C p7, using M work in main pattern to end.

4th row: Using M work in main pattern to last 7 sts, using C k7.

5th row: Using C p10, using M work in main pattern to end.

Continue to work 3 sts more in reverse st st and C and 3 sts less in main pattern on every alt row until 5 sts are left in M, ending with a wrong side row.

Next row: Using C purl.

Next row: Using C knit to end increasing 15 sts evenly spaced. 84(90) sts.

Break off C. Using M continue in pattern as follows:

1st row: K1(2), p2, Cross 2, p2, k18, [p2, Cross 2] 8(9) times, p2, k18, p2, Cross 2, p2, k1(2).

2nd row: P1(2), k2, p2, k2, p18, [k2, p2] 8(9) times, k2, p18, k2, p2, k2, p1(2).

3rd and 4th rows: As 1st and 2nd rows.

5th row: K1(2), p2, Cross 2, p2, C12F, k6, [p2, Cross 2] 8(9) times, p2, C12F, k6, p2, Cross 2, p2, k1(2).

6th row: As 2nd row.

7th to 10th rows: Rep 1st and 2nd rows twice.

11th row: K1(2), p2, Cross 2, p2, k6, C12B, [p2, Cross 2] 8(9) times, p2, k6, C12B, p2, Cross 2, p2, k1(2).

12th row: As 2nd row.

These 12 rows form the pattern. Work until the 10th(12th) row of the 3rd pattern has been completed.

Shape Neck

Next row: Pattern 33(35) sts, turn leaving remaining sts on spare needle.

Continue on these sts. Cast off at beg of next and following alt rows 3 sts once, 2 sts once and 1 st twice. Work 4 rows. Cast off remaining 26(28) sts.

Rejoin yarn to remaining sts at neck edge, cast off centre 18(20) sts, pattern to end. Work 1 row. Shape neck as other side. Work 3 rows. Cast off remaining 26(28) sts.

BACK

Work as given for Front to ★.

Commence Panel in C

1st row: Using M pattern to last 4 sts, using C p4.

2nd row: Using C k4, using M pattern to end.

3rd row: Using M pattern to last 7 sts, using C p7.

Continue in this way with C panel reversed.

When C panel is completed work increase row as for front, then continue with M in pattern as front. Work until back measures same as front to shoulders. Cast off.

SLEEVES

Using 6mm needles and M cast on 34 sts and work 5 cms [2 ins] in rib as given for Front, ending with a 2nd row and increasing 17 sts in last row. 51 sts.

Continue in main pattern. Work 8 rows. Bringing extra sts into pattern, inc 1 st at each end of next row, then every 8th row until there are 67(69) sts. Work until sleeve measures 47 cms [18½ ins] from beg. Cast off loosely.

MAKING UP

Press pieces according to instructions on ball band. Join right shoulder seam.

Neckband: With right side facing knit up 68(72) sts evenly round neck edge. Work 2½ cms [1 inch] in rib. Cast off in rib.

Join left shoulder seam. Place a marker 26(27) cms [10¼(10¾) ins] on each side of shoulder seams to mark depth of armholes. Join cast off edge of sleeves to armhole edges. Join side and sleeve seams.

Separate Collar

Using circular needle cast on 90 sts. Work in rounds of st st (every round knit) for 22 cms [8¾ ins].

Next round: Cast off 45 sts, knit to end.

Continue in st st, working backwards and forwards, starting with a purl row. Work 1 row. Dec 1 st at each end of next row, then every alt row until 3 sts remain ending with a purl row. K3tog and fasten off.

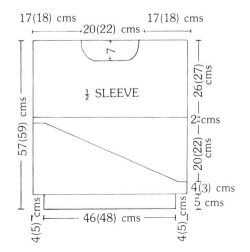

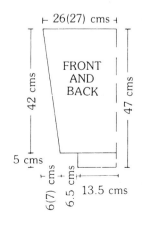

Patchwork Sweater with Separate Collar

MEASUREMENTS

To fit bust sizes 92/96 cms [36/38 ins]. Length from shoulder approximately 56 cms [22¼ ins]. Sleeve length approximately 50 cms [19¾ ins].

MATERIALS

Patons Visions 50g balls: 5 balls Main colour (M), 3 balls each in Contrast colours A, B, C, D and E. Pair needles each size 5mm (No 6) and 5½mm (No 5) and 5mm (No 6) circular knitting needle.

TENSION

14 sts and 20 rows = 10 cms [4 ins] over st st using 5½mm needles.

FRONT

Using 5mm needles and M cast on 66 sts. Work 6 cms [2½ ins] in k1, p1 rib, increasing 4 sts evenly spaced in last row. 70 sts.

Change to 5½mm needles and continue in st st, working colour pattern from chart. Use a separate ball of yarn for each part, and ensure that yarns are twisted together on the wrong side when changing colour to avoid holes.

Work until the 88th row of chart has been completed.

Shape Neck

Next row: K27, cast off 16 sts, knit to end. Continue on last set of sts. Dec 1 st at neck edge on next 10 rows. Work 1 row. Cast off remaining 17 sts.

Rejoin yarn to remaining sts at neck edge and complete to match other side.

BACK

Work as given for Front omitting neck. When back measures same as front to shoulders, cast off all sts.

SLEEVES

Using 5mm needles and M cast on 28 sts. Work 5 cms [2 ins] in k1, p1 rib increasing 12 sts evenly spaced in last row. 40 sts.

Change to 5½mm needles and continue in st st, working colour pattern from chart. Work 5 rows. Inc 1 st at each end of next row, then every 6th row until there are 64 sts, then every 4th row until there are 72 sts. Work 3 rows. Cast off.

MAKING UP

Press pieces according to instructions on ball band. Weave in loose ends. Join shoulder

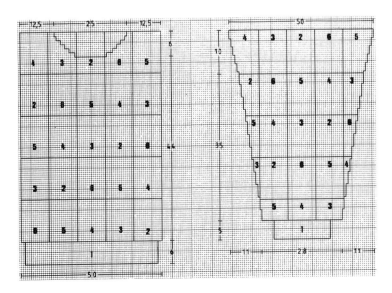

1 = M
2 = A
3 = B
3 = C
4 = D
5 = E

Note: Figures at side of chart refer to cms.

Patchwork Sweater with Separate Collar

seams. Join cast off edge of sleeves to armhole edges. Join side and sleeve seams.

Neck Edging: Using 5mm circular needle and M, knit up 82 sts along neck edge. Work 5 rounds in k1, p1 rib. Cast off in rib.

Separate Collar: Using 5mm circular needle and M cast on 84 sts. Work in rounds of st st (every round knit), until collar measures 24 cms [9½ ins].

Next round: Cast off 42 sts, knit to end of round.

Continue working backwards and forwards over remaining 42 sts. Work 3 rows. Continue as follows:

1st row: K2tog, knit to last 2 sts, k2tog.

Work 1 row.

3rd row: As 1st row.

Work 3 rows.

Rep last 6 rows until 2 sts remain. K2tog and fasten off.

Patchwork Sweater

MEASUREMENTS

To fit bust sizes 92/96 cms [36/38 ins]. Length (approximately) 53 cms [21 ins]. Sleeve length (approximately) 48 cms [19 ins].

MATERIALS

Patons Visions 50g balls: 5 balls Main colour (M), 3 balls each in Contrast colours A, B, C, D and E. Pair needles each size 5mm (No 6) and 5½mm (No 5). 5mm (No 6) circular needle, 50 cms [20 ins] long.

TENSION

14 sts and 20 rows = 10 cms [4 ins] over st st using 5½mm needles.

BACK

Using 5mm needles and M cast on 66 sts. Work 10 rows in st st, starting with a purl row.

Next row: Purl to end increasing 4 sts evenly spaced by picking up loop from between needles and purling into the back of it. 70 sts.

Change to 5½mm needles and continue in st st, working colour pattern from Chart 1. Use a separate ball of yarn for each part, and ensure that yarns are twisted together on the wrong side when changing colour to avoid holes. When chart is completed, cast off all sts.

FRONT

Work as given for Back until the 60th row of Chart 1 has been completed.

Continue for yoke:

Next row (1st row of Chart 2): K14 sts in B and 3 sts in C, turn and cast on 36 sts in M leaving remaining sts on a holder.

Continue working from Chart 2 until the 31st row has been completed.

Shape Neck

Next row: P10, cast off 16 sts, p27 sts to end.

Continue on last set of sts. Dec 1 st at neck edge on next 9 rows. Cast off remaining 18 sts.

Rejoin yarn to remaining sts at neck edge. Dec 1 st at neck edge on every row until 2 sts remain. K2tog and fasten off.

With right side facing rejoin yarn to sts left on holder.

Next row: K36 sts in M, 3 sts in E and 14 sts in A.

Continue working from chart until the 31st row has been completed.

Shape Neck

Next row: Purl to last 26 sts, cast off these sts. Break yarn. Turn and rejoin yarn to remaining sts at neck edge. Dec 1 st at neck edge on next 9 rows. Cast off remaining 18 sts.

SLEEVES

Using 5mm needles and M cast on 28 sts and work 10 rows in st st, starting purl.

Next row: Purl to end increasing 12 sts evenly spaced. 40 sts.

Change to 5½mm needles and continue in st st, working colour pattern from Chart 3. Work 5 rows. Inc 1 st at each end of next row, then every 6th row until there are 64 sts, then every 4th row until there are 72 sts. Work 3 rows. Cast off.

MAKING UP

Press pieces according to instructions on ball band. Weave in loose ends. Join shoulder seams. Sew cast on and side edge of first yoke piece in position. Place a marker in the centre of the 3rd square on each side of shoulder seams to mark depth of armholes.

Armhole Edgings: Using 5mm needles and M, knit up 80 sts evenly between the markers (approximately 4 sts for each 5 rows). Work 8 rows in st st, starting with a purl row. Cast off.

Sew cast off edge of sleeves to armhole edges. Join side and sleeve seams. Fold armhole edgings to wrong side and sew in position.

Collar: Using 5mm circular needle and M knit up 78 sts evenly along neck edge. Work 10 cms [4 ins] in rounds of k1, p1 rib. Cast off in rib.

Fold collar in half to wrong side and sew in position. Fold edgings at lower edges of front, back and sleeves in half to wrong side and sew in position.

1 = M
2 = A
3 = B
4 = C
5 = D
6 = E

Figures at side of chart refer to cms.

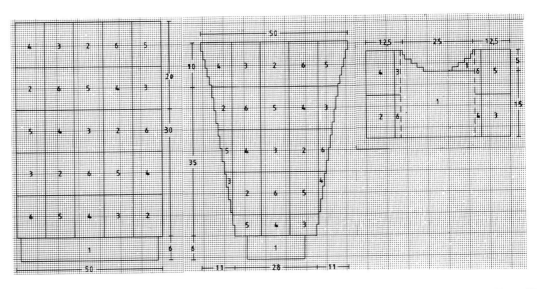

Textured Sweater

MEASUREMENTS

To fit bust sizes 84/89(91/96) cms [33/35(36/38) ins]. Length (approximately) 63 cms [25 ins]. Sleeve length (approximately) 50 cms [19½ ins].

MATERIALS

Patons Siberia 8(9) 50g balls (M), Patons Cotton Ribbon 1 50g ball (A) and Patons Cotton Top 2 50g balls (B). Pair needles each size 5½mm (No 5) and 6mm (No 4).

TENSION

12 sts and 19 rows = 10 cms [4 ins] over st st using 6mm needles.

NOTE

Ensure that yarns are twisted together on wrong side when changing colour or yarn to avoid holes.

FRONT

Using 5½mm needles and M cast on 60(64) sts. Work 6 cms [2½ ins] in k1, p1 rib.

Change to 6mm needles and continue working from chart. Note that chart is for smaller size, larger size will have 2 sts more at each side.

1st to 6th rows: Work in st st.

7th row (commence insertions): Using M k39(41), using B [p1, k1] 7 times, using M k7(9).

8th row: Using M p7(9), using B [k1, p1] 7 times, using M p39(41).

The last 2 rows form moss st pattern. Work 6 more rows in this way.

15th row: Using M k3(5), using A k24, using M k12, using B moss st 14, using M k7(9).

16th row: Using M p7(9), using B moss st 14, using M p12, using A k24, using M p3(5).

Continue working from chart with insertions as shown and the remainder in st st, until the 92nd row has been completed ★.

Shape Neck

Next row: Work 25(27) sts, turn leaving remaining sts on a spare needle.

Continue on these sts. Dec 1 st at neck edge on next 4 rows, then the 3 following alt rows. Work 3 rows. Dec 1 st at neck edge on next row. Work 1 row. Cast off.

Rejoin yarn to remaining sts at neck edge, cast off 10 centre sts, work to end. Complete to match other side.

BACK

Work as given for Front to ★. Work 14 more rows.

Shape Back of Neck

Next row: K17(19), turn leaving remaining sts on a spare needle.

Continue on these sts. Work 1 row. Cast off.

Rejoin yarn to remaining sts at neck edge, cast off 26 centre sts, knit to end. Complete to match other side.

SLEEVES

With 5½mm needles and M cast on 30 sts. Work 6 cms [2½ ins] in rib as given for Front, increasing 10 sts evenly spaced in last row by picking up loop from between needles and working into the back of it. 40 sts.

Change to 6mm needles and work from chart with insertions as shown and the remainder in st st.

Work 5 rows. Inc 1 st at each end of next row, then every 6th row until there are 66 sts. Work 4 rows. Cast off.

MAKING UP

Press pieces according to instructions on ball band. Sew in ends. Join right shoulder seam.

Collar: Using 5½mm needles knit up 80 sts round neck edge. Work 20 cms [8 ins] in k1, p1 rib. Cast off in rib.

Join left shoulder seam. Place a marker 27 cms [10½ ins] on each side of shoulder seams to mark depth of armholes. Join cast off edge of sleeves to armhole edges. Join side and sleeve seams. Tie in ribbon fringes as shown on front.

1 = Colour M, K1, p1 rib   3 = Colour A
2 = Colour M, st st   4 = Colour B

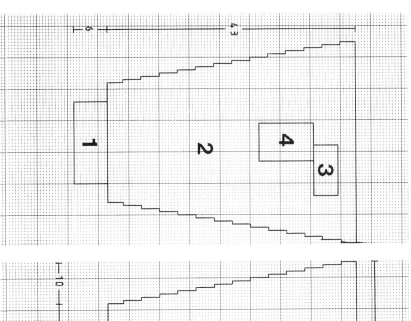

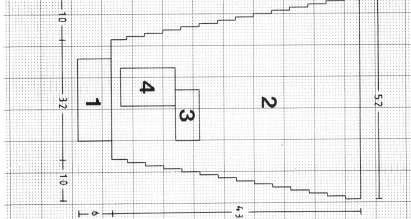

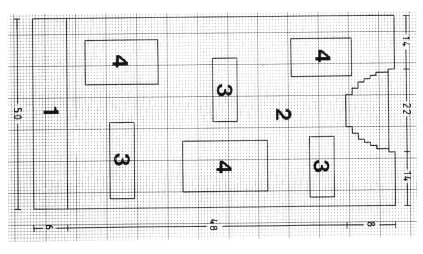

Sweater with Cables

MEASUREMENTS

To fit bust sizes 84/89(91/96) cms [33/35[36/38] ins. Length from shoulder 58(59) cms [23(23½) ins].

MATERIALS

Patons Siberia 50g balls: 4 balls in Colour A, 3 balls in Colour B and 2 balls in Colour C. Pair needles each size 5½mm (No 5) and 7mm (No 2). 7mm (No 2) circular knitting needle, 50 cms [20 ins] long. Cable needle.

TENSION

10 sts and 16 rows = 10 cms [4 ins] over st st using 7mm needles.

SPECIAL ABBREVIATION

Cable 8 Front = slip next 4 sts onto cable needle and hold at front, k4, then k4 from cable needle.

NOTE

Garment is worked in one piece, starting at front. Use a separate ball of yarn for each part, and ensure that yarns are twisted together on wrong side when changing colour to avoid holes.

Using 5½mm needles and C cast on 54(58) sts.

1st row: *P2, k2; rep from * to last 2 sts, p2.
2nd row: *K2, p2; rep from * to last 2 sts, k2.
Rep 1st and 2nd rows for 6 cms [2½ ins] ending with a 2nd row.

Change to 7mm needles and commence pattern:

1st row: Using A k39(41), p1, [k4A, 4B] for cable, using B p6(8).

2nd row: Using B k6(8), [p4B, 4A] for cable, using A k1, p39(41).

3rd and 4th rows: As 1st and 2nd rows.

5th row: Using A k39(41), p1, Cable 8 Front over A and B, using B p6(8).

6th row: As 2nd row, working over colours as previous row.

These 6 rows form the pattern. Continue until 4th row of 4th pattern has been completed. Now working new sts in st st or reversed st st as before cast on 1 st at beg of next 14 rows. Continue as follows:

1st row: Using A cast on 2 sts, k1, p1, pattern to end.

2nd row: Cast on 2 sts, pattern to last 2 sts, k1, p1.

3rd row: Using A cast on 2 sts, k3, p1, pattern to end.

4th row: Cast on 2 sts, pattern to end.

5th row: Cast on 1 st in A and 1 st in C, pattern to end.

6th row: As 4th row.

7th row: Using C cast on 2 sts, k3, using A k4, p1, pattern to end.

8th row: As 4th row.

9th row: Using C cast on 2 sts, p1, k4, using A k4, p1, pattern to end.

10th row: As 4th row.

11th row: Using C cast on 2 sts, p3, Cable 8 Front over C and A, pattern to end.

12th row: As 4th row.

Continue with 2 cables and the remainder in

pattern as set. Cast on 2 sts at beg of next 2 rows, 3 sts at beg of next 8 rows and 12 sts at beg of next 2 rows. 144(148) sts. Work 16(18) rows straight.

Shape Neck

Next row: Pattern 67(69) sts, cast off 10 sts, pattern to end.

Continue on last set of sts. Dec 1 st at neck edge on next 6 rows. Work 1 row. Break yarn and leave sts on a spare needle.

Rejoin yarn to remaining sts at neck edge. Dec 1 st at neck edge on next 6 rows. Work 1 row.

Commence Back

Next row: Work to end, cast on 22 sts then work across sts on spare needle.

Work 25(27) more rows. Cast off 12 sts at beg of next 2 rows, 3 sts at beg of next 8 rows and 2 sts at beg of next 14 rows. Cast off 1 st at beg of next 14 rows. Complete to match front.

MAKING UP

Press pieces according to instructions on ball band.

Left Cuff: Using 5½mm needles and B knit up 26(28) sts evenly along left sleeve edge. Work 6 cms [2½ ins] in k2, p2 rib. Cast off in rib.

Using C work Right Cuff the same.

Join side and sleeve seams.

Collar: Using circular needle and C knit up 78 sts evenly along neck edge. Work 12 rounds in st st (every row knit). Cast off.

Now along the same edge knit up 70 sts evenly in B. Work 12 rounds in st st. Allow collars to roll one over the other. Cast off.

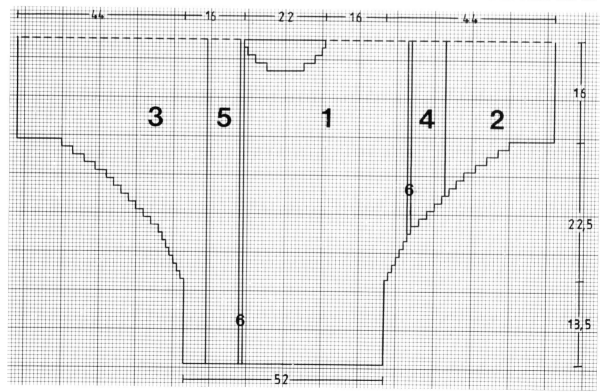

1 = Colour A, st st
2 = Colour B, reverse st st
3 = Colour C, reverse st st
4 = Colour B/A, cable
5 = Colour A/C, cable
6 = Garter st

Note: Figures at side of chart refer to cm.

Striped Dolman Sweater

MEASUREMENTS

To fit bust sizes 81/86(91-96) cms [32/34(36-38) ins]. Finished measurement from sleeve edge to sleeve edge (without cuffs) 102(105-107) cms [41(42-43) ins]. Finished length from back neck to lower edge of ribbing (approximately) 63(64.5-65.5) cms [25¼(25¾-26¼) ins].

MATERIALS

7(8-9) 50g balls Berger du Nord Lin et Coton in colour 8625 blue (A), 6(7-8) balls in colour 8397 green (B). Pair needles each size 3¾mm (No 9) and 4½mm (No 7).

TENSION

18 sts and 40 rows = 10 cms [4 ins] over stripe pattern using 4½mm needles. **Note:** To work tension piece cast on 26 sts and rep rows 1 to 4 of chart pattern (smallest size) to check tension.

NOTES

Body of pullover is worked in 2 pieces from sleeve edge to sleeve edge.

When changing colours at beg of right side rows, pick up new strand from under old strand.

Always knit first and last st of every row. These selvage sts aid in seaming and proper working of mosaic pattern. Note that selvage sts do not appear on chart.

Work increases in colour of row, incorporating new sts into pattern as established on next wrong side row.

FRONT PIECE

Using larger needles and A and beg at left sleeve edge cast on 26(28-30) sts and purl 1 row (wrong side). (**Note:** All chart rows are written for right side rows only. Work all wrong side rows following 2nd row of pattern. Selvage sts are not indicated on chart).

Commence Chart Pattern

1st and 3rd sizes only

1st row (right side): Using B k1 (selvage st), sl 1 wyib, k2, *sl 2 wyib, k2; rep from * ending sl 1, k1 (selvage st).

2nd and all wrong side rows: K1 (selvage st), *purl all the purl sts with colour of previous row and slip all the sl sts of previous row wyif; rep from * ending k1 (selvage st).

3rd row: Using A k1 (selvage st), k1, sl 2 wyib, *k2, sl 2; rep from * ending k1, k1 (selvage st).

2nd size only

1st row (right side): Using B k1 (selvage st), k1, *sl 2 wyib, k2; rep from * ending sl 1, k1 (selvage st).

2nd and all wrong side rows: K1 (selvage st), *purl all the purl sts with colour of previous row and slip all the sl sts of previous row wyif; rep from * ending k1 (selvage st).

3rd row: Using A k1 (selvage st), sl 1 wyib, *k2, sl 2; rep from * ending k1, k1 (selvage st).

All sizes

Continue to work chart pattern in this way, alternating 2 rows in B and 2 rows in A, **at the same time** increasing at shoulder edge (beg of right side rows as indicated on chart) 1 st every 6th row 14 times, **at the same time** increasing at underarm edge (beg of wrong side rows) 1 st every 4th row 4 times, every 6th row 6 times, every 4th row 8 times, every alt row 8 times, cast on 2 sts 8 times, 3 sts once, **at the same time** on 35th row of chart begin diagonal mosaic pattern with A.

After all increases have been worked at shoulder edge, work this edge straight. After all increases have been worked at underarm edge, there are 85(87-89) sts (including selvage sts) and piece measures approximately 30 cms [12 ins] from beg.

Work straight in chart pattern to 199th row. Work in stripe pattern following chart on all sts for a total of 54(66-74) rows.

253th(265th-273th) row (right side): Using B begin diagonal mosaic pattern following chart. Continue to follow chart pattern to 287th(299th-307th) row, ending with a right side row.

Next row (wrong side): Cast off 3 sts (underarm edge), work in pattern to end.

Continue to cast off at underarm edge 2 sts 8 times, dec 1 st every alt row 8 times, every 4th row 8 times, every 6th row 6 times, every 4th row 4 times **at the same time** at beg of chart row 325(337-345), dec 1 st (shoulder edge) and continue to dec at this edge every 6th row 13 times more. When all rows of chart have been worked and there are 26(28-30) sts, cast off all sts with A.

BACK PIECE

Starting with right sleeve edge work as given for Front.

BACK YOKE

Using smaller needles and A pick up and k108(114-120) sts evenly along centre top straight edge of back piece. Work in k1, p1 rib for 2 rows. Dec 1 st at each end of every alt row 24 times. 60(66-72) sts. Cast off sts in rib.

FRONT YOKE

Work as given for Back Yoke.

FINISHING

Press pieces according to instructions on ball band. Sew upper sleeve, shoulder and yoke seams, leaving cast off sts of yoke free for neck.

Sleeve Cuffs: With right side facing, using smaller needles and B, pick up and k47(51-55) sts along lower edge of sleeve. Work 4.5 cms [1¾ ins] in rib. Cast off in rib.

Lower Edge Band: With right side facing, smaller needles and B, pick up and k95(101-107) sts along lower edge of Back. Work 4.5 cms [1¾ ins] in rib. Cast off in rib.

Work band in same way along lower edge of front.

Sew side and underarm sleeve seams, including lower edge band. Fold 2 cms [¾ inch] of front neck to wrong side and sew in place.

Striped Dolman Sweater

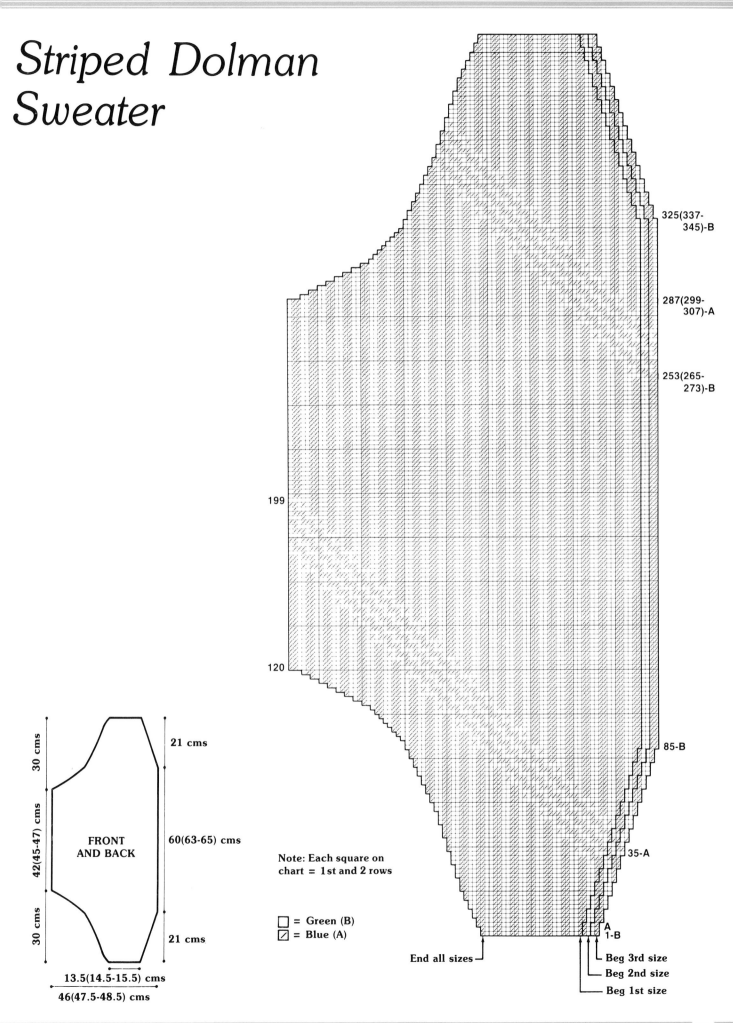

325(337-345)-B

287(299-307)-A

253(265-273)-B

199

120

85-B

21 cms

30 cms

30 cms

42(45-47) cms

60(63-65) cms

FRONT
AND BACK

35-A

Note: Each square on
chart = 1st and 2 rows

□ = Green (B)
⧄ = Blue (A)

21 cms

A
1-B

End all sizes

Beg 3rd size

Beg 2nd size

Beg 1st size

13.5(14.5-15.5) cms

46(47.5-48.5) cms

'Collar and Tie' Sweater

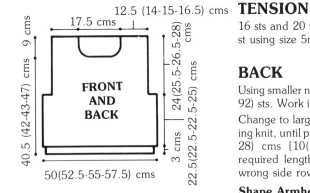

FRONT AND BACK

12.5 (14-15-16.5) cms
17.5 cms
9 cms
24(25.5-26.5-25) cms
40.5 (42-43-47) cms
22.5(22.5-22.5-25) cms
3 cms
50(52.5-55-57.5) cms

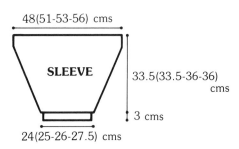

SLEEVE

48(51-53-56) cms
33.5(33.5-36-36) cms
3 cms
24(25-26-27.5) cms

MEASUREMENTS

To fit bust sizes 81(86-91-96) cms [32(34-36-38) ins]. Finished bust measurement at underarm 100(105-110-115) cms [40(42-44-46) ins]. Length 49.5(51-52-56) cms [19½(20-20½-22) ins]. Sleeve width at upper arm 48(51-53-56) cms [19(20-21-22) ins].

MATERIALS

Patons Cotton Top 50g balls: 7(8-9-10) balls Colour A, 2 balls each in Colours B and C. Pair needles each size 4mm (No 8) and and 5mm (No 6).

TENSION

16 sts and 20 rows = 10 cms [4 ins] over st st using size 5mm needles.

BACK

Using smaller needles and A cast on 80(84-88-92) sts. Work in k2, p2 rib for 3 cms [1¼ ins].
Change to larger needles. Work in st st, starting knit, until piece measures 25.5(25.5-25.5-28) cms [10(10-10-11) ins] from beg, or required length to underarm, ending with a wrong side row.

Shape Armholes

Cast off 6 sts at beg of next 2 rows. 68(72-76-80) sts. Work straight until armhole measures 24(25.5-26.5-28) cms [9½(10-10½-11) ins]. Cast off.

FRONT

Work as given for Back until armhole measures 15(16.5-17.5-19) cms [6(6½-7-7½) ins], ending with a wrong side row.

Shape Neck

Next row (right side): K24(26-28-30) sts, join 2nd ball of yarn and cast off centre 20 sts for neck, work to end.
Working both sides at same time with separate balls of yarn, dec 1 st at each neck edge every other row 4 times. 20(22-24-26) sts each side. Work straight until armhole measures same length as back. Cast off sts each side.

SLEEVES

Using smaller needles and A cast on 38(40-42-44) sts and work in k2, p2 rib for 3 cms [1¼ ins].
Change to larger needles. Work in st st, increasing 1 st each end alternately every 2nd and 4th row (therefore 4 sts are inc every 6 rows) until there are 76(80-84-88) sts. Work straight until piece measures 36.5(36.5-39-39) cms [14¼(14¼-15¼-15¼) ins] from beg. Cast off.

COLLAR

Using smaller needles and B cast on 23 sts and work in k1, p1 rib slipping first st on every row purlwise, for 45.5 cms [18 ins]. Cast off in rib.

TIE

Using smaller needles and C cast on 13 sts and work in k1, p1 rib for 43 cms [17 ins]. Cast off in rib.

MAKING UP

Press pieces according to instructions on ball band. Sew shoulder seams. Sew top of sleeve to straight edge of armhole, then sew last 4 cms [1½ ins] of sleeve to cast off sts of front and back. Sew side and sleeve seams. Sew collar around neck, making edges meet at centre front. Fold tie 5 cms [2 ins] from one end and sew tie under collar edges at centre front along this point, allowing short end to hang over long end at front. Bring corners of short end, one on either side, to back of long end and stitch corners tog underneath to simulate tie knot.

Designed by Tom Nuechterlein
Photographed by Naomi Kaltman

Dropped Shoulder Sweater

MEASUREMENTS

To fit bust sizes 86(91-96) cms [34(36-38) ins]. Finished measurement at underarm 93(100-107) cms [37(40-43) ins]. Length 60 cms [24 ins]. Sleeve width at upper arm 60 cms [24 ins].

MATERIALS

9(10-10) 100g balls of Anny Blatt Flirt'Anny in colour 671 blue. Pair needles size 4½mm (No 7). Cable needle.

TENSION

18 sts and 26 rows = 10 cms [4 ins] over cable pattern using size 4½mm needles.

Notes: To work test piece, cast on 22 sts with size 4½mm needles. Knit first and last 2 sts of every row and work centre 18 sts in cable pattern. Work for at least 32 rows or 4 pattern repeats. Cast off.

Because cotton or cotton blend yarns have a tendency to stretch, wet your test piece and block, stretching it as much as possible. Allow to dry. Then measure tension over blocked piece.

CABLE PATTERN (multiple of 6 sts)

1st row (right side): Knit.

2nd and all wrong side rows: Purl.

3rd row: *K2, sl next 2 sts to cable needle and hold to back of work, k next 2 sts, k2 from cable needle — back cable (BC); rep from * to end.

5th row: Knit.

7th row: *Sl next 2 sts to cable needle and hold to front of work, k next 2 sts, k2 from cable needle — front cable (FC), k2; rep from * to end.

8th row: Purl.

Rep these 8 rows for cable pattern.

BACK

Using size 4½mm needles cast on 84(90-96) sts. Work in k1, p1 rib for 6 rows.

Work the 8 rows of cable pattern until piece measures 56 cms [22½ ins] from beg, or 4 cms [1½ ins] less than required length. Work in k1, p1 rib for 8 rows. Cast off in rib.

FRONT

Work as given for Back.

SLEEVES

Using size 4½mm needles cast on 60 sts and work in k1, p1 rib for 6 rows.

Beg cable pattern, inc 1 st each side every 4th row as follows:

1st — 4th rows: Work straight in cable pattern.

5th row (increase): Inc 1 st, k to last st, inc 1 st (1 st inc each side). 62 sts.

6th row: Purl.

7th row: K1; rep from * of 7th pattern row, ending k3 instead of k2.

8th row: Purl.

9th row: Rep Increase row. 64 sts.

10th row: Purl.

11th row: K4, work BC; rep from * of 3rd pattern row, ending k2.

12th row: Purl.

13th row: Rep Increase row. 66 sts.

14th row: Purl.

15th row: K3; rep from * of 7th pattern row ending k5 instead of k2.

16th row: Purl.

17th row: Work Increase row. 68 sts.

18th row: Purl.

19th row: Work BC; rep from * of 3rd pattern row ending k4.

20th row: Purl.

21st row: Work Increase row. 70 sts.

22nd row: Purl.

23rd row: K5, rep from * of 7th pattern row, ending k1 instead of k2.

24th row: Purl.

25th row: Work Increase row. 72 sts.

26th row: Purl.

27th row: As 3rd pattern row.

28th row: Purl.

Rep 5th — 28th rows for pattern until there are 108 sts. Work straight in cable pattern until piece measures 43 cms [17 ins] from beg or required sleeve length. Cast off.

FINISHING

Press according to instructions on ball band. Sew first and last 18(22-24) sts at top of front and back tog for shoulder seams. Place markers 30 cms [12 ins] down from shoulder seam on front and back for armhole. Sew top of sleeve between markers. Sew side and sleeve seams.

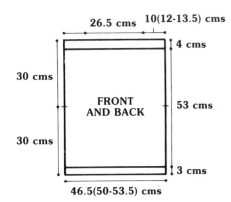

26.5 cms 10(12-13.5) cms
4 cms
30 cms
FRONT AND BACK
53 cms
30 cms
3 cms
46.5(50-53.5) cms

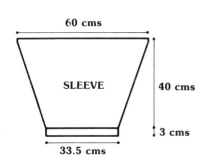

60 cms
SLEEVE
40 cms
3 cms
33.5 cms

Sweater with Horizontal Cables

MEASUREMENTS

To fit bust sizes 81/86(91-96/101) cms [32/34(36-38/40) ins]. Finished measurement at underarm 101(107-111) cms [40(42-44) ins]. Length 52.5(55-57.5) cms [21(22-23) ins]. Sleeve width at upper arm 45(48-50) cms [18(19-20) ins].

MATERIALS

Jaeger Monte Cristo 14(15-16) 50g balls. Pair needles size 4½mm (No 7). Crochet hook size 2.50mm. Cable needle.

TENSION

24 sts and 28 rows = 10 cms [4 ins] over cable pattern st using 4½mm needles. **Note:** To work tension piece cast on 24 sts and work first 14 rows, 1 additional rep and 2 rows (28 rows in total) as in cable pattern below. Cast off sts and press edges lightly before measuring.

CABLE PATTERN (over 24 sts)

1st row (right side): P12, k6, p6.

2nd row: K6, p6, k12.

3rd row: P6, sl next 6 sts to cable needle and hold to **front** of work, p next 6 sts, k6 sts from cable needle, p6.

4th row: As 2nd row.

5th to 14th rows: Rep 1st and 2nd rows five times.

Rep 3rd to 14th row for cable pattern st.

BACK AND SLEEVE PIECE

Starting at right sleeve edge, cast on 54(57-60) sts.

1st row (right side): P6(9-12), *p12, k6; rep from * to last 12 sts, p12.

2nd row: K12, *p6, k12; rep from * to last 6(9-12) sts, k6(9-12).

3rd row: P12(15-18), *sl next 6 sts to cable needle and hold to **front** of work, p next 6 sts, k6 sts from cable needle, p6; rep from * ending last rep p12.

4th row: As 2nd row.

5th to 14th rows: Rep 1st and 2nd rows five times.

Work straight in cable pattern as set until sleeve measures 25.5 cms [10 ins] from beg, ending with a right side row. Cast on 72(74-78) sts at end of this row for body. 126(131-138) sts.

Next row (wrong side): K12(14-18), *p6, k12; rep from * to last 6(9-12) sts, k6(9-12).

Work straight in cable pattern as set, over 4 more cables for body and continue with 2 cables on sleeve until piece measures 38(39.5-40.5) cms [15(15½-16) ins] from beg of sleeve, ending with a wrong side row.

Shape Neck

Dec 1 st at neck edge every alt row 4 times. Work straight in pattern for 20.5 cms [8 ins] more. Inc 1 st at neck edge every alt row 4 times. Work straight for 12.5(14-15) cms [5(5½-6) ins] from last neck inc, body measures approx 50.5(53.5-55.5) cms [20(21-22) ins], ending with a right side row.

Cast off 72(74-78) sts at beg of next row, work to end. Continue on 54(57-60) sts working straight for 25.5 cms [10 ins]. Cast off.

FRONT AND SLEEVE PIECE

Starting at left sleeve edge, work as given for Back until same length to neck.

Shape Neck

Cast off 3 sts at neck edge once then dec 1 st at neck edge every alt row 6 times. Work straight for 15 cms [6 ins] more. Inc 1 st at neck edge every alt row 6 times, then cast on 3 sts at neck edge once. Work remainder of front as given for back.

FINISHING

Press pieces according to instructions on ball band. Sew upper sleeve and shoulder seams. Sew side and underarm sleeve seams.

Neck Edge: With right side facing and crochet hook, work 1 round of dc evenly around neck edge. Turn and working from left to right, work l backwards dc in each dc.

Sleeve and Lower Edge: Work as given for Neck Edge.

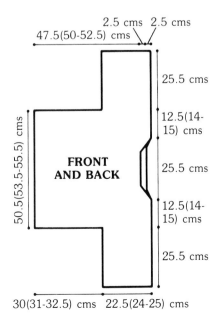

47.5(50-52.5) cms · 2.5 cms · 2.5 cms

50.5(53.5-55.5) cms

25.5 cms

12.5(14-15) cms

FRONT AND BACK

25.5 cms

12.5(14-15) cms

25.5 cms

30(31-32.5) cms · 22.5(24-25) cms

His and Her Sweater

MEASUREMENTS

To fit bust/chest sizes 86(91-96-101) cms [34(36-38-40) ins]. Finished measurement at underarm 99(105-111-117) cms [40(42-44½-47) ins]. Finished length 60 cms [24 ins]. Sleeve width at upper arm 45(48-48-50) cms [18(19-19-20) ins].

MATERIALS

Patons Cotton Perlé 50g balls: 7(8-8-9) balls Main colour (M), 2 balls each in Colours A and B, 1 ball each in Colours C, D, E, F, G and H. Pair needles each size 3¾mm (No 9) and 4½mm (No 7).

TENSION

20 sts and 24 rows = 10 cms [4 ins] over st st using size 4½mm needles.

NOTE

When changing colours, twist yarns on wrong side to prevent holes and carry yarn not in use loosely across back of work. To avoid excessively long loose strands or long 'floats' at back of work, weave or twist yarns not in use around working yarn every 3 or 4 sts.

BACK

Using smaller needles and M cast on 99(105-111-117) sts. Work in k1, p1 rib for 6.5 cms [2½ ins].

Change to larger needles. Beginning each size as indicated, work 1st to 8th rows of Chart 1 twice, 1st to 25th rows of Chart 2 once, 1st to 24th rows of Chart 3 once and 1st to 33rd rows of Chart 4 once.

Rep 1st to 12th rows of Chart 5, working contrasting colours (CC) in following sequence: 2 rows H, 2 rows C, 2 rows F, 2 rows A and 2 rows B, until 30 rows of chart have been worked. Piece measures approx 60 cms [24 ins] from beg.

Shape Shoulder

Cast off 15(16-17-18) sts at beg of next 2 rows, and 16(17-18-19) sts at beg of next 2 rows. Cast off remaining 37(39-41-43) sts for back neck.

FRONT

Work as given for Back until piece measures 52.5 cms [21 ins] from beg or 7.5 cms [3 ins] less than back to shoulder.

Shape Neck

Work 40(42-44-46) sts in pattern, join 2nd ball of yarn and cast off centre 19(21-23-25) sts for neck, work to end.

Working both sides at same time with separate balls of yarn, cast off from each neck edge 3 sts once, 2 sts once, 1 st 4 times. 31(33-35-37) sts each side.

Work straight until same length as back to shoulder. Shape shoulder as given for back.

SLEEVES

Using smaller needles and M cast on 43(47-47-49) sts. Work in k1, p1 rib for 6.5 cms [2½ ins] increasing 1(0-0-1) st at centre of last row. 44(47-47-50) sts.

Change to larger needles. Work 1st to 12th rows of Chart 5, working contrast colour sts in following sequence: 2 rows each of *B, E, D, G, H, C, F, A; rep from * for colour sequence, **at the same time,** inc 1 st at each end (working inc sts into pattern) every 4th row 23(24-24-25) times. 90(95-95-100) sts. Work straight until piece measures 47(48-48-51) cms [18½(19-19-20) ins] from beg or required sleeve length. Cast off.

FINISHING

Press pieces according to instructions on ball band. Weave in all loose ends.

Neckband: Sew left shoulder seam. With right side facing, smaller needles and M, pick up and k88(92-96-100) sts evenly spaced around neck edge. Work in k1, p1 rib for 2.5 cms [1 inch]. Cast off in rib.

Sew right shoulder seam including neckband. Place markers 22.5(24-24-25) cms [9(9½-9½-10) ins] down from shoulder seams on front and back for armhole. Sew top of sleeve between armhole markers. Sew side and sleeve seams.

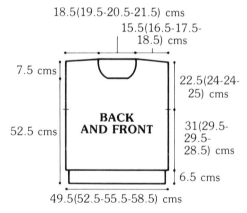

18.5(19.5-20.5-21.5) cms
15.5(16.5-17.5-18.5) cms
7.5 cms
22.5(24-24-25) cms
52.5 cms
BACK AND FRONT
31(29.5-29.5-28.5) cms
6.5 cms
49.5(52.5-55.5-58.5) cms

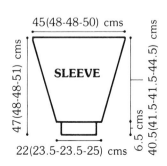

45(48-48-50) cms
47(48-48-51) cms
SLEEVE
6.5 cms
40.5(41.5-41.5-44.5) cms
22(23.5-23.5-25) cms

Designed by Donald Grover
Photographed by Mario Testino

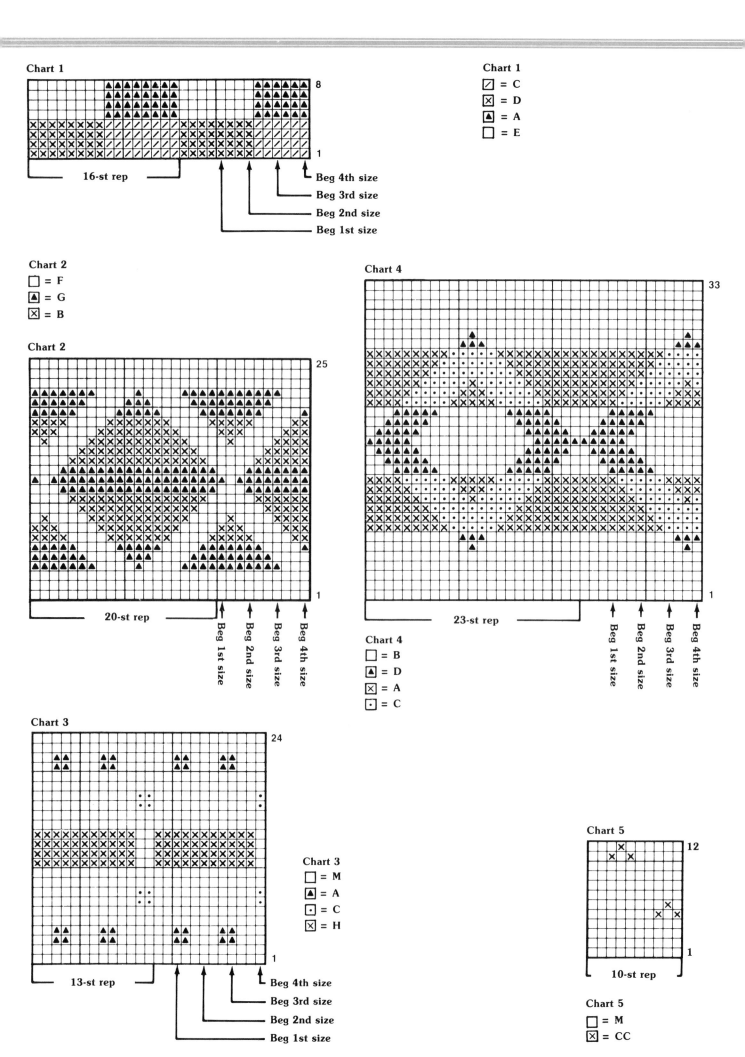

Chart 1

☑ = C
⊠ = D
▲ = A
☐ = E

16-st rep

Beg 4th size
Beg 3rd size
Beg 2nd size
Beg 1st size

Chart 2

☐ = F
▲ = G
⊠ = B

20-st rep

Beg 1st size
Beg 2nd size
Beg 3rd size
Beg 4th size

Chart 4

23-st rep

Beg 1st size
Beg 2nd size
Beg 3rd size
Beg 4th size

Chart 4

☐ = B
▲ = D
⊠ = A
⊡ = C

Chart 3

13-st rep

Beg 4th size
Beg 3rd size
Beg 2nd size
Beg 1st size

Chart 3

☐ = M
▲ = A
⊡ = C
⊠ = H

Chart 5

10-st rep

Chart 5

☐ = M
⊠ = CC

Flower Pattern Sweater

MEASUREMENTS

To fit bust sizes 81/86(91-96/101) cms [32/34(36-38/40) ins]. Finished measurement at underarm 104(110-116) cms [42(44-46) ins]. Length 63(63-65) cms [25(25-26) ins]. Sleeve width at upper arm 48(50-52) cms [19(20-21) ins].

MATERIALS

Patons Diploma Double Knitting 50g balls: 12(13-14) balls Main colour (M), 1 ball each in light blue (A), medium blue (B), pink (I), dusty pink (K), dusty olive (R) and forest green (S). Tapisserie wool or oddments: 2 skeins (15m) each in colours royal blue (C), aqua (D), teal (E), lilac (F), dark fuchsia (G), dark purple (H), medium purple (N), light olive (P), medium green (Q), 3 skeins (25m) each in light lilac (J), hot pink (L), medium green (T), 1 skein (10m) each in fuchsia (M), dusty purple (O) and gold (U). Pair needles each size 3¼mm (No 10) and 3¾mm (No 9). Shoulder pads (optional). Bobbins (optional). Tapestry needle.

TENSION

22 sts and 28 rows = 10 cms [4 ins] over st st using size 3¾mm needles.

NOTES

When working knit-in sections, use separate bobbins and twist colours on wrong side to prevent holes.

Since this pattern is done completely by chart, it is **essential** to get the correct row tension to obtain the proper sweater length.

BACK

Using smaller needles and M cast on 115(121-127) sts.
1st row: K1, *pl, kl; rep from * to end.
2nd row: P1, *k1, p1; rep from * to end.

Rep these 2 rows for 5 cms [2 ins], ending with a wrong side row.
Change to larger needles.

Commence Chart

1st row (right side): Following 1st row of chart from right to left and beginning as indicated for chosen size, knit across row, ending as indicated for chosen size.

2nd row (wrong side): Following 2nd row of chart from left to right, purl across row.

Continue in st st and chart as set until 162nd(162nd-168th) row has been completed, approx 63(63-65) cms [25(25-26) ins] from beg. Cast off.

FRONT

Work as given for Back until 148th(148th-154th) row has been completed.

Shape Neck

Next row (right side): Work across first 42(45-48) sts, join 2nd ball of yarn and cast off centre 31 sts, work to end.

Working both sides at same time with separate balls of yarn, cast off 1 st from each neck edge 6 times. 36(39-42) sts each side.

Work straight until same length as Back. Cast off.

SLEEVES

Using smaller needles and M cast on 53(59-65) sts and work in k1, pl rib for 5 cms [2 ins].

Next row: Purl, increasing 20 sts evenly across row. 73(79-85) sts.

Change to larger needles. Beginning chart pattern for sleeves **at the same time** inc 1 st each end every 6th row 16(15-15) times. 105(109-115) sts.

Work straight until 102nd(106th-112th) row has been completed, approx 41.5(43-45) cms [16½(17-18) ins] from beg. Cast off.

FINISHING

Press pieces according to instructions on ball band. Sew left shoulder seam.

Neckband: Beginning right neck edge, with right side facing, smaller needles and M, pick up and k103 sts evenly around neck. Work in k1, pl rib for 2.5 cms [1 inch]. Cast off loosely in rib.

Sew right shoulder including neckband. Place markers on front and back 24(25-26) cms [9½(10-10½) ins] down from shoulder seams. Fold sleeves in half and sew top of sleeves between markers. Sew side and sleeve seams.

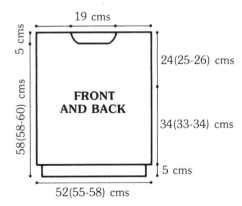

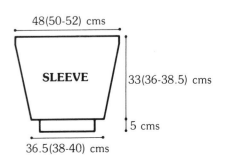

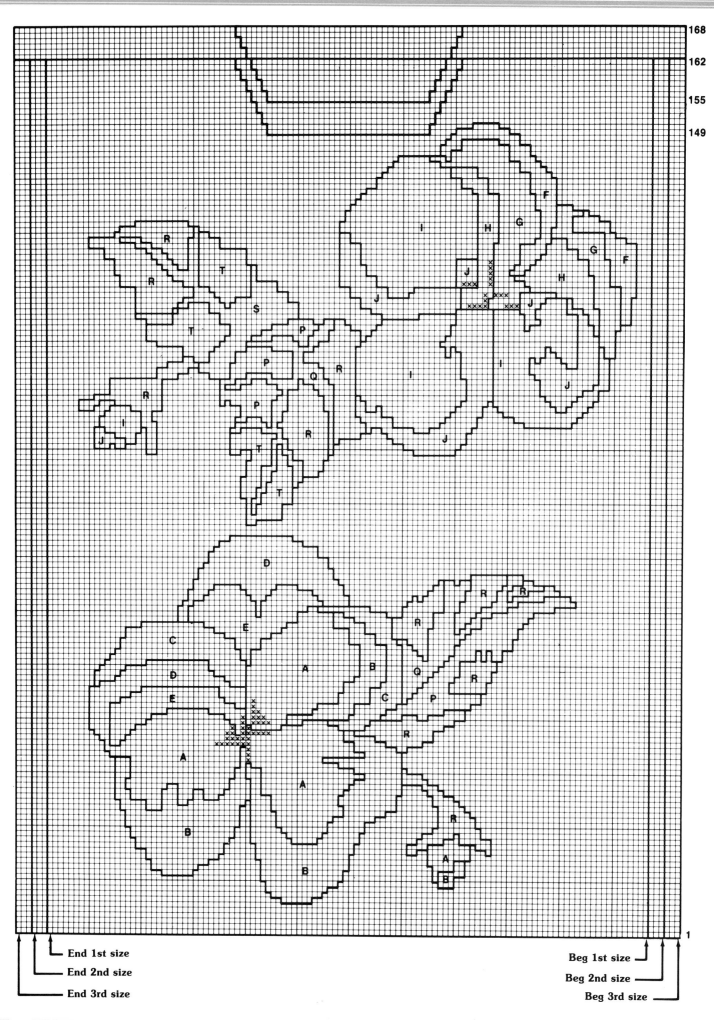

168

162

155

149

1

End 1st size

End 2nd size

End 3rd size

Beg 1st size

Beg 2nd size

Beg 3rd size

Geometric Pattern Sweater

p2, [k1, p2] 4 times, C4F, [p2, k1] 4 times, p1, using B p1, k1, p2, T13F, p2, [k1, p2] 4 times, using C [k1, p2] 5 times, C4F, [p2, k1] 3 times, p2, T13F, p2, k1, p1, using A p1, [k1, p2] 4 times, C4F, p2, [k1, p2] 4 times, T13F, p2, [k1, p2] 3 times.

40th row: Using A [k2, p1] 3 times, k2, p6, k1, p6, k2, [p1, k2] 4 times, p4, [k2, p1] 4 times, k1, using C k1, p1, k2, p6, k1, p6, k2, [p1, k2] 3 times, p4, k2, [p1, k2] 4 times, p2, using B k1, [p1, k2] 4 times, p6, k1, p6, k2, p1, k1, using A k1, [p1, k2] 4 times, p4, k2, [p1, k2] 4 times, p6, k1, p6, k2, [p1, k2] 3 times.

41st row: Using A [p2, k1] 3 times, p2, k6, p1, k6, p2, [k1, p2] 4 times, k4, [p2, k1] 4 times, p1, using B p1, k1, p2, k6, p1, k6, [p2, k1] 4 times, using C k3, p2, [k1, p2] 4 times, k4, p2, [k1, p2] 3 times, k6, p1, k6, p2, k1, p1, using A p1, [k1, p2] 4 times, k4, p2, [k1, p2] 4 times, k6, p1, k6, p2, [k1, p2] 3 times.

42nd row: Using A [k2, p1] 3 times, k2, p6, k1, p6, k2, [p1, k2] 4 times, p4, [k2, p1] 4 times, k1, using C k1, p1, k2, p6, k1, p6, k2, [p1, k2] 3 times, p4, k2, [p1, k2] 4 times, p4, using B k2, [p1, k2] 3 times, p6, k1, p6, k2, p1, k1, using A k1, [p1, k2] 4 times, p4, k2, [p1, k2] 4 times, p6, k1, p6, k2, [p1, k2] 3 times.

43rd row: Using A [p2, k1] 3 times, p2, k6, p1, k6, p2, [k1, p2] 4 times, C4F, [p2, k1] 4 times, p1, using B p1, k1, p2, k6, p1, k6, [p2, k1] 3 times, p1, using C p1, C4F, p2, [k1, p2] 4 times, C4F, p2, [k1, p2] 3 times, k6, p1, k6, p2, k1, p1, using A p1, [k1, p2] 4 times, C4F, p2, [k1, p2] 4 times, k6, p1, k6, p2, [k1, p2]

3 times.

Work 25 more rows in pattern as set, **at the same time** working T13F as before on 10th and 24th of these rows. Break yarns.

Commence 2nd pattern

1st row: Using C p2, [k1, p2] 3 times, k6, p1, k6, p2, [k1, p2] 4 times, k4, [p2, k1] 4 times, p1, using A p1, k1, p2, k6, p1, k6, *p2, [k1, p2] 5 times, k4; rep from * once more, [p2, k1] 6 times, p1, using C [p1, k6] twice, p2, [k1, p2] 4 times, k4, p2, [k1, p2] 7 times.

2nd row: Using C k2, [p1, k2] 7 times, p4, k2, [p1, k2] 4 times, [p6, k1] twice, using A k1, [p1, k2] 6 times, *p4, k2, [p1, k2] 5 times; rep from * once more, p6, k1, p6, k2, p1, k1, using C k1, [p1, k2] 4 times, p4, k2, [p1, k2] 4 times, p6, k1, p6, k2, [p1, k2] 3 times.

3rd row: Using D p1, using C p1, [k1, p2] 3 times, k6, p1, k6, p2, [k1, p2] 4 times, C4F, [p2, k1] 4 times, p1, using A p1, k1, p2, k6, p1, k6, *p2, [k1, p2] 5 times, C4F; rep from * once more, [p2, k1] 6 times, p1, using C [p1, k6] twice, p2, [k1, p2] 4 times, C4F, [p2, k1] 7 times, p1, using D p1.

4th row: Using D k2, using C [p1, k2] 7 times, p4, k2, [p1, k2] 4 times, [p6, k1] twice, using A k1, [p1, k2] 6 times, *p4, k2, [p1, k2] 5 times; rep from * once more, p6, k1, p6, k2, p1, k1, using C k1, [p1, k2] 4 times, p4, k2, [p1, k2] 4 times, p6, k1, p6, [k2, p1] 3 times, using D k2.

5th row: Using D p2, k1, using C p2, [k1, p2] twice, k6, p1, k6, p2, [k1, p2] 4 times, k4, [p2, k1] 4 times, p1, using A p1, k1, p2, k6, p1, k6, *p2, [k1, p2] 5 times, k4; rep from * once

more, [p2, k1] 6 times, p1, using C [p1, k6] twice, p2, [k1, p2] 4 times, k4, [p2, k1] 6 times, p2, using D k1, p2.

6th row: Using D k2, p2, using C k1, [p1, k2] 6 times, p4, k2, [p1, k2] 4 times, [p6, k1] twice, using A k1, [p1, k2] 6 times, *p4, k2, [p1, k2] 5 times; rep from * once more, p6, k1, p6, k2, p1, k1, using C k1, [p1, k2] 4 times, p4, k2, [p1, k2] 4 times, p6, k1, p6, [k2, p1] twice, k1, using D p2, k2.

7th row: Using D p2, k3, using C [k1, p2] twice, k6, p1, k6, p2, [k1, p2] 4 times, C4F, [p2, k1] 4 times, p1, using A p1, k1, p2, k6, p1, k6, *p2, [k1, p2] 5 times, C4F; rep from * once more, [p2, k1] 6 times, p1, using C [p1, k6] twice, p2, [k1, p2] 4 times, C4F, [p2, k1] 6 times, using D k3, p2.

8th row: Using D k2, p4, using C [k2, p1] 5 times, k2, p4, k2, [p1, k2] 4 times, [p6, k1] twice, using A k1, [p1, k2] 6 times, *p4, k2, [p1, k2] 5 times; rep from * once more, p6, k1, p6, k2, p1, k1, using C k1, [p1, k2] 4 times, p4, k2, [p1, k2] 4 times, p6, k1, p6, k2, p1, k2, using D p4, k2.

9th row: Using D p2, k5, using C p1, k1, p2, k6, p1, k6, p2, [k1, p2] 4 times, k4, [p2, k1] 4 times, p1, using A p1, k1, p2, k6, p1, k6, *p2, [k1, p2] 5 times, k4; rep from * once more, [p2, k1] 6 times, p1, using C [p1, k6] twice, p2, [k1, p2] 4 times, k4, [p2, k1] 5 times, p1, using D k5, p2.

10th row: Using D k2, p6, using C [p1, k2] 5 times, p4, k2, [p1, k2] 4 times, [p6, k1] twice, using A k1, [p1, k2] 6 times, *p4, k2, [p1, k2] 5 times; rep from * once more, p6,

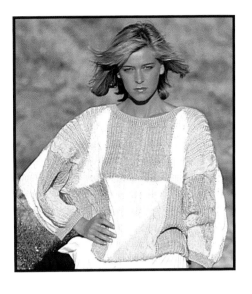

k1, p6, k2, p1, k1, using C k1, [p1, k2] 4 times, p4, k2, [p1, k2] 4 times, p6, k1, p6, k2, p1, using D p6, k2.

11th row: Using D p2, k6, p1, using C p2, k6, p1, k6, p2, [k1, p2] 4 times, C4F, [p2, k1] 4 times, p1, using A p1, k1, p2, k6, p1, k6, *p2, [k1, p2] 5 times, C4F; rep from * once more, [p2, k1] 6 times, p1, using C [p1, k6] twice, p2, [k1, p2] 4 times, C4F, [p2, k1] 4 times, p2, using D p1, k6, p2.

12th row: Using D k2, p6, k1, p1, using C k1, [p1, k2] 4 times, p4, k2, [p1, k2] 4 times, [p6, k1] twice, using A k1, [p1, k2] 6 times, *p4, k2, [p1, k2] 5 times; rep from * once more, p6, k1, p6, k2, p1, k1, using C k1, [p1, k2] 4 times, p4, k2, [p1, k2] 4 times, [p6, k1] twice, using D p1, k1, p6, k2.

13th row: Using D p2, k6, p1, k2, using C T13F, p2, [k1, p2] 4 times, k4, [p2, k1] 4 times, p1, using A p1, k1, p2, T13F, *p2, [k1, p2] 5 times, k4; rep from * once more, [p2, k1] 6 times, p1, using C p1, T13F, p2, [k1, p2] 4 times, k4, [p2, k1] 4 times, using D k2, p1, k6, p2.

14th row: Using D k2, p6, k1, p3, using C k2, [p1, k2] 3 times, p4, k2, [p1, k2] 4 times, [p6, k1] twice, using A k1, [p1, k2] 6 times, *p4, k2, [p1, k2] 5 times; rep from * once more, p6, k1, p6, k2, p1, k1, using C k1, [p1, k2] 4 times, p4, k2, [p1, k2] 4 times, p6, k1, p5, using D p3, k1, p6, k2.

15th row: Using D p2, k6, p1, k4, using C k4, p1, k6, p2, [k1, p2] 4 times, C4F, [p2, k1] 4 times, p1, using A p1, k1, p2, k6, p1, k6, *p2, [k1, p2] 5 times, C4F; rep from * once more, [p2, k1] 6 times, p1, using C [p1, k6]

twice, p2, [k1, p2] 4 times, C4F, [p2, k1] 3 times, p1, using D k4, p1, k6, p2.

16th row: Using D k2, p6, k1, p5, using C [p1, k2] 3 times, p4, k2, [p1, k2] 4 times, [p6, k1] twice, using A k1, [p1, k2] 6 times, *p4, k2, [p1, k2] 5 times; rep from * once more, p6, k1, p6, k2, p1, k1, using C k1, [p1, k2] 4 times, p4, k2, [p1, k2] 4 times, p6, k1, p3, using D p5, k1, p6, k2.

17th row: Using D p2, k6, p1, k6, using C k2, p1, k6, p2, [k1, p2] 4 times, k4, [p2, k1] 4 times, p1, using A p1, k1, p2, k6, p1, k6, *p2, [k1, p2] 5 times, k4; rep from * once more, [p2, k1] 6 times, p1, using C [p1, k6] twice, p2, [k1, p2] 4 times, k4, [p2, k1] twice, p2, using D k6, p1, k6, p2.

18th row: Using D k2, [p6, k1] twice, using C k1, [p1, k2] twice, p4, k2, [p1, k2] 4 times, [p6, k1] twice, using A k1, [p1, k2] 6 times, *p4, k2, [p1, k2] 5 times; rep from * once more, p6, k1, p6, k2, p1, k1, using C k1, [p1, k2] 4 times, p4, k2, [p1, k2] 4 times, p6, k1, p1, using D [k1, p6] twice, k2.

19th row: Using D p2, T13F, p2, using C p1, k6, p2, [k1, p2] 4 times, C4F, [p2, k1] 4 times, p1, using A p1, k1, p2, k6, p1, k6, *p2, [k1, p2] 5 times, C4F; rep from * once more, [p2, k1] 6 times, p1, using C [p1, k6] twice, p2, [k1, p2] 4 times, C4F, [p2, k1] twice, using D p2, T13F, p2.

20th row: Using D k2, p6, k1, p6, k2, p1, using C k2, p1, k2, p4, k2, [p1, k2] 4 times, [p6, k1] twice, using A k1, [p1, k2] 6 times, *p4, k2, [p1, k2] 5 times; rep from * once more, p6, k1, p6, k2, p1, k1, using C k1, [p1,

k2] 4 times, p4, k2, [p1, k2] 4 times, p6, using D p1, k2, p6, k1, p6, k2.

21st row: Using D p2, k6, p1, k6, p2, k1, p1, using C k5, p2, [k1, p2] 4 times, k4, [p2, k1] 4 times, p1, using A p1, k1, p2, k6, p1, k6, *p2, [k1, p2] 5 times, k4; rep from * once more, [p2, k1] 6 times, p1, using C [p1, k6] twice, p2, [k1, p2] 4 times, k4, p2, k1, p1, using D p1, k1, p2, k6, p1, k6, p2.

22nd row: Using D k2, p6, k1, p6, k2, p1, k2, using C p1, k2, p4, k2, [p1, k2] 4 times, [p6, k1] twice, using A k1, [p1, k2] 6 times, *p4, k2, [p1, k2] 5 times; rep from * once more, p6, k1, p6, k2, p1, k1, using C k1, [p1, k2] 4 times, p4, k2, [p1, k2] 4 times, p4, using D k2, p1, k2, p6, k1, p6, k2.

23rd row: Using D p2, k6, p1, k6, [p2, k1] twice, using C k3, p2, [k1, p2] 4 times, C4F, [p2, k1] 4 times, p1, using A p1, k1, p2, k6, p1, k6, *p2, [k1, p2] 5 times, C4F; rep from * once more, [p2, k1] 6 times, p1, using C [p1, k6] twice, p2, [k1, p2] 4 times, C4F, p2, using D [k1, p2] twice, k6, p1, k6, p2.

Continuing to work 1 st more in D and rib pattern at either side work 5 more rows, **at the same time** working T13F in C and A as before on 4th of these rows.

29th row: Using D p2, k6, p1, k6, [p2, k1] 4 times, using C p2, [k1, p2] 3 times, k4, [p2, k1] 4 times, p1, using A p1, k1, p2, k6, p1, k6, *p2, [k1, p2] 5 times, k4; rep from * once more, [p2, k1] 6 times, p1, using C [p1, k6] twice, p2, [k1, p2] 4 times, using D [k1, p2] 4 times, k6, p1, k6, p2.

30th row: Using D k2, p6, k1, p6, [k2, p1]

Geometric Pattern Sweater

3 times, k2, p2, using C k1, [p1, k2] 4 times, [p6, k1] twice, using A k1, [p1, k2] 6 times, *p4, k2, [p1, k2] 5 times; rep from * once more, p6, k1, p6, k2, p1, k1, using C k1, [p1, k2] 4 times, p4, [k2, p1] 3 times, k1, using D p2, k2, [p1, k2] 3 times, p6, k1, p6, k2.

31st row: Using D p2, k6, p1, k6, p2, [k1, p2] 3 times, k3, using C [k1, p2] 3 times, C4F, [p2, k1] 4 times, p1, using A p1, k1, p2, k6, p1, k6, *p2, [k1, p2] 5 times, C4F; rep from * once more, [p2, k1] 6 times, p1, using C [p1, k6] twice, [p2, k1] 4 times, using D k3, p2, [k1, p2] 3 times, k6, p1, k6, p2.

32nd row: Using D k2, p6, k1, p6, [k2, p1] 3 times, k2, p4, using C k2, [p1, k2] 3 times, [p6, k1] twice, using A k1, [p1, k2] 6 times, *p4, k2, [p1, k2] 5 times; rep from * once more, p6, k1, p6, k2, p1, k1, using C k1, [p1, k2] 4 times, p4, [k2, p1] twice, k2, using D p4, k2, [p1, k2] 3 times, p6, k1, p6, k2.

33rd row: Using D p2, T13F, [p2, k1] 3 times, p2, k4, p1, using C p1, [k1, p2] twice, k4, [p2, k1] 4 times, p1, using A p1, k1, p2, k6, p1, k6, *p2, [k1, p2] 5 times, k4; rep from * once more, [p2, k1] 6 times, p1, using C [p1, k6] twice, [p2, k1] 3 times, p1, using D p1, k4, p2, [k1, p2] 3 times, T13F, p2.

34th row: Using D k2, p6, k1, p6, k2, [p1, k2] 3 times, p4, k2, using C [p1, k2] 3 times, [p6, k1] twice, using A k1, [p1, k2] 6 times, *p4, k2, [p1, k2] 5 times; rep from * once more, p6, k1, p6, k2, p1, k1, using C k1, [p1, k2] 4 times, p4, [k2, p1] twice, using D k2, p4, [k2, p1] 3 times, k2, p6, k1, p6, k2.

35th row: Using D p2, k6, p1, k6, p2, [k1, p2] 3 times, C4F, p2, k1, using C p2, k1, p2,

C4F, [p2, k1] 4 times, p1, using A p1, k1, p2, k6, p1, k6, *p2, [k1, p2] 5 times, C4F; rep from * once more, [p2, k1] 6 times, p1, using C [p1, k6] twice, p2, [k1, p2] twice, using D k1, p2, C4F, [p2, k1] 3 times, p2, k6, p1, k6, p2.

36th row: Using D k2, p6, k1, p6, k2, [p1, k2] 3 times, p4, k2, p1, k1, using C k1, [p1, k2] twice, [p6, k1] twice, using A k1, [p1, k2] 6 times, *p4, k2, [p1, k2] 5 times; rep from * once more, p6, k1, p6, k2, p1, k1, using C k1, [p1, k2] 4 times, p4, k2, p1, k1, using D k1, p1, k2, p4, [k2, p1] 3 times, k2, p6, k1, p6, k2.

Continuing to work 1 st more in D and rib pattern at either side and working T13F on every 14th row throughout, work straight until back measures 60 cms [23½ ins] ending with a wrong side row. **Note:** when all sts in C have gone, continue in A and D only.

Next row: Keeping pattern correct cast off 48 sts, work until there are 92 sts on right-hand needle, cast off remaining 48 sts.

Slip remaining sts onto a holder.

FRONT

Work as given for Back until front is 21 rows shorter than back to shoulder, thus ending with a right side row.

Shape Neck

Next row: Work 65 sts in pattern, turn and complete this side first.

★ Cast off 6 sts at beg of next row, then 4 sts at beg of following alt row (work 1 extra row straight here for 2nd side). Dec 1 st at neck edge

on next 7 rows. 48 sts remain. Work 10 rows straight. Cast off.

Slip next 58 sts at centre onto a holder. With wrong side facing rejoin yarn to remaining 65 sts and complete as given for first side from ★ to end reversing shaping where indicated.

LEFT SLEEVE

Using smaller needles and A cast on 79 sts and work 4 cms [1½ ins] in k1, p1 rib ending with a right side row.

Next row (increase): Rib 3, *inc in next st, p1; rep from * to last 4 sts, inc in next st, rib 3. 116 sts ★★.

★★★ Change to larger needles and commence pattern:

1st row: Using D k9, [p2, k1] 4 times, p2, k4, p2, [k1, p2] 4 times, k6, p1, k4, using C k2, p2, k1, p1, using A p1, k1, p2, k2, using B k4, p1, k6, p2, [k1, p2] 4 times, k4, p2, [k1, p2] 4 times, k9.

2nd row: Using B p9, [k2, p1] 4 times, k2, p4, k2, [p1, k2] 4 times, p6, k1, p3, using A p3, k2, p1, k1, using C k1, p1, k2, p3, using D p3, k1, p6, k2, [p1, k2] 4 times, p4, k2, [p1, k2] 4 times, p9.

3rd row: Using D k9, [p2, k1] 4 times, p2, C4F, p2, [k1, p2] 4 times, k6, p1, k2, using C k4, p2, k1, p1, using A p1, k1, p2, k4, using B k2, p1, k6, p2, [k1, p2] 4 times, C4F, p2, [k1, p2] 4 times, k9.

4th row: Using B p9, [k2, p1] 4 times, k2, p4, k2, [p1, k2] 4 times, p6, k1, p1, using A p5, k2, p1, k1, using C k1, p1, k2, p5, using D p1, k1, p6, k2, [p1, k2] 4 times, p4, k2, [p1,

k2] 4 times, p9.

Continuing to work 1 st less in D and B and 1 st more in A and C at either side on every row as set, rep the last 4 rows twice more **at the same time** increasing 1 st at each end of 1st and 7th of these rows. 120 sts.

13th row: Using D k11, [p2, k1] 4 times, p2, k4, [p2, k1] 4 times, p1, using C p1, T13F, p2, k1, p1, using A p1, k1, p2, T13F, p1, using B p1, [k1, p2] 4 times, k4, p2, [k1, p2] 4 times, k11.

14th row: Using B p11, [k2, p1] 4 times, k2, p4, [k2, p1] 4 times, using A k2, p6, k1, p6, k2, p1, k1, using C k1, p1, k2, p6, k1, p6, k2, using D [p1, k2] 4 times, p4, k2, [p1, k2] 4 times, p11.

Continuing to work 1 st more in A and C as set and working T13F on every 14th row throughout, inc 1 st at each end of 3rd and every following 6th row until there are 132 sts.

48th row: Using B p14, using A p3, [k2, p1] 4 times, k2, p4, k2, [p1, k2] 4 times, p6, k1, p6, k2, p1, k1, using C k1, p1, k2, p6, k1, p6, k2, [p1, k2] 4 times, p4, k2, [p1, k2] 4 times, p3, using D p14.

49th row: Using D k13, using C k4, [p2, k1] 4 times, p2, k4, p2, [k1, p2] 4 times, k6, p1, k6, p2, k1, p1, using A p1, k1, p2, k6, p1, k6, p2, [k1, p2] 4 times, k4, p2, [k1, p2] 4 times, k4, using B k13.

50th row: Using B p13, using A p4, [k2, p1] 4 times, k2, p4, k2, [p1, k2] 4 times, p6, k1, p6, k2, p1, k1, using C k1, p1, k2, p6, k1, p6, k2, [p1, k2] 4 times, p4, k2, [p1, k2] 4 times, p4, using D p13.

51st row: Using D k12, using C k5, [p2, k1] 4 times, p2, C4F, p2, [k1, p2] 4 times, k6, p1, k6, p2, k1, p1, using A p1, k1, p2, k6, p1, k6, p2, [k1, p2] 4 times, C4F, p2, [k1, p2] 4 times, k5, using B k12.

52nd row: Using B p12, using A p5, [k2, p1] 4 times, k2, p4, k2, [p1, k2] 4 times, p6, k1, p6, k2, p1, k1, using C k1, p1, k2, p6, k1, p6, k2, [p1, k2] 4 times, p4, k2, [p1, k2] 4 times, p5, using D p12.

Continuing to work 1 st more in A and C on every **alt** row, inc 1 st at each end of next and every following 6th row until there are 142 sts. Work 7 rows straight. Cast off.

RIGHT SLEEVE

Work as given for Left Sleeve to ★★. Complete as given for Left Sleeve from ★★★ to end **but** using B in place of D, A in place of C, C in place of A and D in place of B.

TO MAKE UP

Press pieces according to instructions on ball band. Join left shoulder seam.

Neckband: Using smaller needles and A and with right side facing work across sts on at back neck decreasing 13 sts evenly, pick up and k25 sts down left front slope, knit across sts at front neck decreasing 8 sts evenly, then pick up and k25 sts up right front slope. 179 sts.

Work 8 rows in k1, p1 rib starting with the 2nd row. Cast off in rib.

Join right shoulder seam and ends of neckband. Sew sleeve to side edge placing centre at shoulder seam. Join side and sleeve seams.

Cotton Sweater

MEASUREMENTS

To fit bust sizes 75/80(85/90-95/100) cms [30/32(34/36-38/40) ins]. Width from wrist to wrist (approximately) 145(150-155) cms [58(60-62) ins]. Length to back of neck 67(68-69) cms [26¾(27¼-27½) ins].

MATERIALS

Coats 'Anchor' Knitting and Crochet Cotton No. 6 (50g) used double: 14(16-19) balls. Pair needles each size 4mm (No. 8) and 3¼mm (No. 10). Cable needle.

Coats Maxi 'Pellicano' Knitting and Crochet Cotton No. 5 (200g) used double: 4(4-5) balls. Pair needles each size 4½mm (No. 7) and 3¾mm (No. 9). Cable needle.

Note: You may find it easier to use a circular needle when knitting the sleeves in order to accommodate the large number of sts.

TENSION

With yarn used double: 22 sts and 30 rows = 10 cms [4 ins] square measured over st st using larger needles.

SPECIAL ABBREVIATIONS

Slip marker = make a slip knot in a short length of contrasting yarn and place on needle where indicated. On the following rows slip the marker from one needle to the other until the pattern is established and the marker is no longer required.

T2B (Twist 2 Back) = slip next st onto cable needle and hold at back of work, knit next st from left-hand needle, then purl st from cable needle.

T2F (Twist 2 Front) = slip next st onto cable needle and hold at front of work, purl next st from left-hand needle, then knit st from cable needle.

T2L (Twist 2 Left) = slip next st onto cable needle and hold at front of work, purl next st from left-hand needle, then knit st from cable needle.

T2R (Twist 2 Right) = slip next st onto cable needle and hold at back of work, knit next st from left-hand needle, then purl st from cable needle.

C3B (Cross 3 Back) = slip next st onto cable needle and hold at back of work, knit next 2 sts from left-hand needle, then knit st from cable needle.

C3F (Cross 3 Front) = slip next 2 sts onto cable needle and hold at front of work, knit next st from left-hand needle, then knit sts from cable needle.

C3L (Cross 3 Left) = slip next st onto cable needle and hold at front of work, purl next 2 sts from left-hand needle, then purl st from cable needle.

C3R (Cross 3 Right) = slip next 2 sts onto cable needle and hold at back of work, purl next st from left-hand needle, then purl sts from cable needle.

T3B (Twist 3 Back) = slip next st onto cable needle and hold at back of work, knit next 2 sts from left-hand needle, then purl st from cable needle.

T3F (Twist 3 Front) = slip next 2 sts onto cable needle and hold at front of work, purl next st from left-hand needle, then knit sts from cable needle.

T3L (Twist 3 Left) = slip next st onto cable needle and hold at front of work, purl next 2 sts from left-hand needle, then knit st from cable needle.

T3R (Twist 3 Right) = slip next 2 sts onto cable needle and hold at back of work, knit next st from left-hand needle, then purl sts from cable needle.

C4F (Cable 4 Front) = slip next 2 sts onto cable needle and hold at front of work, knit next 2 sts from left-hand needle, then knit sts from cable needle.

Cotton Sweater

CABLE PANEL (Worked across 32 sts between markers)

1st row: C3F, k26, T3B.

2nd row: K1, T3R, p24, C3L, p1.

3rd row: K2, T3F, k22, T3B, p2.

4th row: K3, T3R, p20, T3L, p3.

5th row: K2, p1, k1, T3F, k18, T3B, p4.

6th row: K5, T3R, p16, T3L, p1, k1, p3.

7th row: K2, [p1, k1] twice, T3F, k14, T3B, p6.

8th row: K7, T3R, p12, T3L, [p1, k1] twice, p3.

9th row: K2, [p1, k1] 3 times, T3F, k10, T3B, p8.

10th row: K9, T3R, p8, T3L, [p1, k1] 3 times, p3.

11th row: K2, [p1, k1] 4 times, T3F, k6, T3B, p10.

12th row: K11, T3R, p4, T3L, [p1, k1] 4 times, p3.

13th row: K2, [p1, k1] 5 times, T3F, k2, T3B, p12.

14th row: K13, T3R, T3L, [p1, k1] 5 times, p3.

15th row: K2, [p1, k1] 6 times, T3F, k1, p14.

16th row: K14, T3L, [p1, k1] 6 times, p3.

17th row: K2, [p1, k1] 7 times, T3F, p13.

18th row: K12, T3L, [p1, k1] 7 times, p3.

19th row: K2, [p1, k1] 8 times, T3F, p11.

20th row: K10, T3L, [p1, k1] 8 times, p3.

21st row: K2, [p1, k1] 9 times, T3F, p9.

22nd row: K8, T3L, [p1, k1] 9 times, p3.

23rd row: K2, [p1, k1] 10 times, T3F, p7.

24th row: K6, T3L, [p1, k1] 10 times, p3.

25th row: K2, [p1, k1] 11 times, T3F, p5.

26th row: K4, T3L, [p1, k1] 11 times, p3.

27th row: K2, [p1, k1] 12 times, T3F, p3.

28th row: K2, T3L, [p1, k1] 12 times, p3.

29th row: K2, [p1, k1] 13 times, T3F, p1.

30th row: T3L, [p1, k1] 13 times, p3.

31st row: T3F, [k1, p1] 13 times, C3B.

32nd row: P1, C3R, [k1, p1] 12 times, T3L, k1.

33rd row: P2, T3F, [k1, p1] 11 times, C3B, k2.

34th row: P3, C3R, [k1, p1] 10 times, T3L, k3.

35th row: P4, T3F, [k1, p1] 9 times, C3B, k4.

36th row: P5, C3R, [k1, p1] 8 times, T3L, k5.

37th row: P6, T3F, [k1, p1] 7 times, C3B, k6.

38th row: P7, C3R, [k1, p1] 6 times, T3L, k7.

39th row: P8, T3F, [k1, p1] 5 times, C3B, k8.

40th row: P9, C3R, [k1, p1] 4 times, T3L, k9.

41st row: P10, T3F, [k1, p1] 3 times, C3B, k10.

42nd row: P11, C3R, [k1, p1] twice, T3L, k11.

43rd row: P12, T3F, k1, p1, C3B, k12.

44th row: P13, C3R, T3L, k13.

45th row: P14, k1, C3B, k14.

46th row: P15, C3R, k14.

47th row: P13, C3B, k16.

48th row: P17, C3R, k12.

49th row: P11, C3B, k18.

50th row: P19, C3R, k10.

51st row: P9, C3B, k20.

52nd row: P21, C3R, k8.

53rd row: P7, C3B, k22.

54th row: P23, C3R, k6.

55th row: P5, C3B, k24.

56th row: P25, C3R, k4.

57th row: P3, C3B, k26.

58th row: P27, C3R, k2.

59th row: P1, C3B, k28.

60th row: P29, C3R.

These 60 rows form the Cable Panel.

SPECIAL NOTES

Yarn is used double throughout.

To keep edges of garment neat and easy to sew, work increases as follows:

To increase at the **beg** of a row, purl into front and back of first st.

To increase at the **end** of a row, purl into front and back of last but one st.

BACK AND FRONT ALIKE

Using smaller needles cast on 98(106-118) sts.

1st row (right side): K2, *p2, k2; rep from * to end.

2nd row: P2, *k2, p2; rep from * to end.

Rep the last 2 rows until rib measures 5 cms [2 ins] ending with a right side row.

Next row (increase): Rib 3(1-7), *inc in next st, rib 5; rep from * to last 5(3-9) sts, inc in next st, rib to end. 114(124-136) sts.

Change to larger needles and commence pattern:

1st row: P26, C4F, p11(16-22), slip marker, work 1st row of Cable Panel across next 32 sts, slip marker, p11(16-22), C4F, p26.

2nd row: K26, p4, k11(16-22), work 2nd row of Cable Panel, k11(16-22), p4, k26.

Keeping continuity of cable panel correct on sts between markers, rep the last 2 rows 3 times more. Bringing extra sts into reverse st st, inc 1 st at each end of next row (see Special Notes). Work 3 rows straight.

13th row: P24, T2B, p1, C4F, p11(16-22), work 13th row of Cable Panel, p11(16-22), C4F, p1, T2F, p24.

14th row: K23, T2L, k2, p4, k11(16-22), work 14th row of Cable Panel, k11(16-22), p4, k2, T2R, k23.

15th row: P22, [T2B] twice, p1, C4F, p11(16-22), work 15th row of Cable Panel, p11(16-22), C4F, p1, [T2F] twice, p22.

16th row: K21, [T2L] twice, k2, p4, k11(16-22), work 16th row of Cable Panel, k11(16-22), p4, k2, [T2R] twice, k21.

17th row: Inc in first st, p19, [T2B] 3 times, p1, C4F, p11(16-22), work 17th row of Cable Panel, p11(16-22), C4F, p1, [T2F] 3 times, p18, inc in next st, p1.

18th row: K20, [T2L] 3 times, k2, p4, k11(16-22), work 18th row of Cable Panel, k11(16-22), p4, k2, [T2R] 3 times, k20.

19th row: P19, [T2B] 3 times, p3, C4F, p11(16-22), work 19th row of Cable Panel, p11(16-22), C4F, p3, [T2F] 3 times, p19.

20th row: K18, [T2L] 3 times, k4, p4, k11(16-22), work 20th row of Cable Panel, k11(16-22), p4, k4, [T2R] 3 times, k18.

Keeping cable panel and diagonal stripe correct as set work 10 more rows, **at the same time** increasing 1 st at each end of 5th of these rows.

31st row: P8, [T2B] 3 times, p12, T2B, p1, C4F, p11(16-22), work 31st row of Cable Panel, p11(16-22), C4F, p1, T2F, p12, [T2F] 3 times, p8.

32nd row: K7, [T2L] 3 times, k12, T2L, k2, p4, k11(16-22), work 32nd row of Cable Panel, k11(16-22), p4, k2, T2R, k12, [T2R] 3 times, k7.

33rd row: Inc in first st, p5, [T2B] 3 times, p12, [T2B] twice, p1, C4F, p11(16-22), work 33rd row of Cable Panel, p11(16-22), C4F, p1, [T2F] twice, p12, [T2F] 3 times, p4, inc in next st, p1.

34th row: K6, [T2L] 3 times, k12, [T2L] twice, k2, p4, k11(16-22), work 34th row of Cable Panel, k11(16-22), p4, k2, [T2R] twice, k12, [T2R] 3 times, k6.

35th row: P5, [T2B] 3 times, p12, [T2B] 3 times, p1, C4F, p11(16-22), work 35th row of Cable Panel, p11(16-22), C4F, p1, [T2F] 3 times, p12, [T2F] 3 times, p5.

36th row: K4, [T2L] 3 times, k12, [T2L] 3 times, k2, p4, k11(16-22), work 36th row of Cable Panel, k11(16-22), p4, k2, [T2R] 3 times, k12, [T2R] 3 times, k4.

37th row: P3, [T2B] 3 times, p12, [T2B] 3 times, p3, C4F, p11(16-22), work 37th row of Cable Panel, p11(16-22), C4F, p3, [T2F] 3 times, p12, [T2F] 3 times, p3.

38th row: K2, [T2L] 3 times, k12, [T2L] 3 times, k4, p4, k11(16-22), work 38th row of Cable Panel, k11(16-22), p4, k4, [T2R] 3 times, k12, [T2R] 3 times, k2.

Keeping cable panel and diagonal stripes correct as set and carrying stripes to edge of work, work 10 more rows, **at the same time** increasing 1 st at each end of 3rd of these rows.

49th row: Inc in first st, p9, [T2B] 3 times, p12, T2B, p1, C4F, p11(16-22), work 49th row of Cable Panel, p11(16-22), C4F, p1, T2F, p12, [T2F] 3 times, p8, inc in next st, p1.

50th row: K10, [T2L] 3 times, k12, T2L, k2, p4, k11(16-22), work 50th row of Cable Panel, k11(16-22), p4, k2, T2R, k12, [T2R] 3 times, k10.

51st row: P9, [T2B] 3 times, p12, [T2B] twice, p1, C4F, p11(16-22), work 51st row of Cable Panel, p11(16-22), C4F, p1, [T2F] twice, p12, [T2F] 3 times, p9.

52nd row: K8, [T2L] 3 times, k12, [T2L] twice, k2, p4, k11(16-22), work 52nd row of Cable Panel, k11(16-22), p4, k2, [T2R] twice, k12, [T2R] 3 times, k8.

53rd row: P7, [T2B] 3 times, p12, [T2B] 3 times, p1, C4F, p11(16-22), work 53rd row of Cable Panel, p11(16-22), C4F, p1, [T2F] 3 times, p12, [T2F] 3 times, p7.

54th row: K6, [T2L] 3 times, k12, [T2L] 3 times, k2, p4, k11(16-22), work 54th row of Cable Panel, k11(16-22), p4, k2, [T2R] 3 times, k12, [T2R] 3 times, k6.

55th row: P5, [T2B] 3 times, p12, [T2B] 3 times, p3, C4F, p11(16-22), work 55th row of Cable Panel, p11(16-22), C4F, p3, [T2F] 3

times, p12, [T2F] 3 times, p5.

56th row: K4, [T2L] 3 times, k12, [T2L] 3 times, k4, p4, k11(16-22), work 56th row of Cable Panel, k11(16-22), p4, k4, [T2R] 3 times, k12, [T2R] 3 times, k4.

Keeping cable panel and diagonal stripes correct as set and bringing sts into diagonal stripes as before throughout, inc 1 st at each end of next and every following 8th row 3 times in all, 132(142-154) sts, then every alt row until there are 188(198-210) sts ending with the wrong side row.

Keeping pattern correct and bringing extra sts into diagonal stripe pattern, cast on 7 sts at beg of next 8 rows, 244(254-266) sts, then cast on 54 sts at beg of next 2 rows. 352(362-374) sts. Work 38(42-44) rows straight, thus ending with a wrong side row.

Neckband

Next row: Work 150 sts in pattern, k1(2-2), [p2, k2] 12(14-17) times, p2, k1(2-2), work 150 sts.

Next row: Work 150 sts, p1(2-2), [k2, p2] 12(14-17) times, k2, p1(2-2), work 150 sts.

Rep the last 2 rows once more. Cast off in pattern.

TO MAKE UP

Press pieces according to instructions on ball band. Join shoulder seams leaving ribbed neckband open at centre.

Cuffs: Using smaller needles and with right side of work facing, pick up and k64(70-76) sts evenly around lower edge of one sleeve.

Next row (decrease): P5, *p2tog, p1; rep from * to last 8 sts, p2tog, p6. 46(50-54) sts remain.

Work 5 cms [2 ins] in k2, p2 rib as given for Back. Cast off in rib.

Work other cuff in the same way.

Join side and underarm seams and ends of cuffs.

Panelled Sweater with Cables

MEASUREMENTS

To fit bust sizes 80(85-90-95-100-105) cms [32(34-36-38-40-42) ins]. Length to shoulder (approximately) 59 cms [23½ ins] all sizes. Width from cuff to cuff (approximately) 127(127-127-140-140-140) cms [50¾(50¾-50¾-56-56-56) ins].

MATERIALS

Patons Beehive Double Knitting 50g balls: 6(7-7-8-8-9) balls Colour A, 4(5-5-5-5-5) balls each in Colours B and C. Pair needles each size 4mm (No 8) and 3¼mm (No 10). Circular needle size 4mm (No 8) if required. Cable needle. Row counter if required.

TENSION

22 sts and 30 rows = 10 cms [4 ins] square measured over st st using larger needles.

SPECIAL ABBREVIATIONS

C4B (Cable 4 Back) = slip next 2 sts onto cable needle and hold at back of work, knit next 2 sts from left-hand needle then knit sts from cable needle.

MB (Make Bobble) = knit into front, back and front of next st, turn and p3, turn and k3, turn and p1, p2tog, turn and k2tog.

T3B (Twist 3 Back) = slip next st onto cable needle and hold at back of work, knit next 2 sts from left-hand needle then purl st from cable needle.

T3F (Twist 3 Front) = slip next 2 sts onto cable needle and hold at front of work, purl next st from left-hand needle then knit sts from cable needle.

CABLE PANEL (Worked across 16 sts)

1st row: P6, k2, p1, k2, p5.
2nd row: K5, p2, k1, p2, k6.
3rd row: P6, k2, MB, k2, p5.
4th row: As 2nd row.
5th row: P5, T3B, k1, T3F, p4.
6th row: K4, p2, k1, p1, k1, p2, k5.
7th row: P4, T3B, k1, p1, k1, T3F, p3.
8th row: K3, p2, k1, [p1, k1] twice, p2, k4.
9th row: P3, T3B, k1, [p1, k1] twice, T3F, p2.
10th row: K2, p2, k1, [p1, k1] 3 times, p2, k3.
11th row: P2, T3B, k1, [p1, k1] 3 times, T3F, p1.
12th row: K1, p2, k1, [p1, k1] 4 times, p2, k2.
13th row: P2, T3F, p1, [k1, p1] 3 times, T3B, p1.
14th row: As 10th row.
15th row: P3, T3F, p1, [k1, p1] twice, T3B, p2.
16th row: As 8th row.
17th row: P4, T3F, p1, k1, p1, T3B, p3.
18th row: As 6th row.
19th row: P5, T3F, MB, T3B, p4.
20th row: As 2nd row.
21st row: P5, MB, k2, p1, k2, MB, p4.
Rows 2 — 21 inclusive form the Cable Panel.

SPECIAL NOTE

To make shaped edges of garment neat and easy to sew, work increases as follows: increase at end of row in last but one st; increase at beg of row in first st.

BACK (Starting at right sleeve)

Note: Use separate lengths of yarn for each colour change, twisting yarns together on wrong side of work when changing colour to avoid making a hole.

Using larger needles and B cast on 2 sts, then using A cast on a further 4 sts, using C cast on 12 sts, using A cast on 4 sts and using B cast on 12 sts. 34 sts.

Commence pattern:

1st row (right side): Knit 12B, 4A, 12C, 4A, 2B.

2nd row: Purl 2B, 4A, 12C, 4A, 12B.

3rd row: K12B, using A C4B, k12C, using A C4B, k2B.

4th row: As 2nd row.

These 4 rows form the 4 st cables between panels of st st. Keeping the 4 rows of each cable correct and bringing extra sts into B, inc 1 st at **end** (underarm edge) of next and every following 4th row 3 times in all (see Special Note). Work 3 rows straight.

17th row: Using A knit to last 2 sts, inc in next st, k1. 38 sts.

18th row: Using A k6, [p4, k12] twice.

19th row: Using A [k12, C4B] twice, k6.

20th row: As 18th row.

21st row: Knit 12C, 4A, 12B, 4A, using C k5, inc in next st, k1. 39 sts.

22nd row: Purl 7C, 4A, 12B, 4A, 12C.

Panelled Sweater with Cables

23rd row: K12C, using A C4B, k12B, using A C4B, k7C.

24th row: As 22nd row.

Keeping pattern correct and bringing extra sts into C, inc 1 st at end of next and every following 4th row 3 times in all. 42 sts. Work 3 rows straight.

37th row: Using A knit to last 2 sts, inc in next st, k1. 43 sts.

38th row: Using A k11, [p4, k12] twice.

39th row: Using A [k12, C4B] twice, k11.

40th row: As 38th row.

These 40 rows establish the check pattern. Starting next row with 12 sts in B and bringing extra sts into check pattern, inc 1 st at underarm edge on next and every alt row until there are 68(64-60-76-72-68) sts, then on every row until there are 95 sts, thus ending with the 36th(32nd-28th-4th-40th-36th) row of pattern.

★ Shape Body

1st(6th) sizes only

1st row: Work to end, then turn and cast on 29 sts in A.

2nd row: Using A [k12, p4] twice, work in pattern to end.

(2nd-3rd) sizes only

1st row: Work to end, then turn and cast on 1 st in A, 12 sts in C, 4 sts in A then 12 sts in B.

2nd row: Purl 12B, 4A, 12C, 4A, work in pattern to end.

(4th-5th) sizes only

1st row: Work to end, then turn and cast on 1 st in A, 12 sts in B, 4 sts in A, then 12 sts in C.

2nd row: Purl 12C, 4A, 12B, 4A, work in pattern to end.

All sizes ★

124 sts. Keeping pattern correct work 32(36-40-44-48-52) rows straight thus ending with the 30th(30th-30th-10th-10th-10th) row of pattern.

Shape Back Neck

Keeping pattern correct dec 1 st at beg (neck edge) of next row and same edge of following 2 rows, then every alt row 3 times. 118 sts remain. Work 59 rows straight thus ending at neck edge. Inc 1 st at neck edge on next and every alt row 3 times in all, then following 3 rows. 124 sts.

Work 33(37-41-45-49-53) rows straight thus ending with the 19th(23rd-27th-11th-15th-19th) row of pattern.

Shape Left Sleeve

Keeping pattern correct cast off 29 sts at beg of next row. 95 sts remain. Dec 1 st at end (underarm edge) of next row and at same edge of every row until 68(64-60-76-72-68) sts remain, then every alt row until 43 sts remain. Dec 1 st at underarm edge on every following 4th row until 34 sts remain. Work 3 rows straight thus ending with the 16th row of pattern. Cast off in pattern.

FRONT (Starting at left sleeve)

Using larger needles and B cast on 2 sts, using A cast on a further 4 sts, using C cast on 12 sts, using A cast on 4 sts, using B cast on 12 sts and using A cast on 16 sts. 50 sts.

Commence pattern:

1st row (right side): Using A work 1st row of Cable Panel across first 16 sts, knit 12B, 4A, 12C, 4A, 2B.

2nd row: Purl 2B, 4A, 12C, 4A, 12B, using A work 2nd row of Cable Panel across remaining 16 sts.

3rd row: Using A work 3rd row of Cable Panel, k12B, using A C4B, k12C, using A C4B, k2B.

4th row: As 2nd row but working 4th row of Cable Panel.

Keeping the 20 rows of cable panel and the 40 rows of check pattern correct to match back, and bringing extra sts into check pattern, inc 1 st at **end** (underarm edge) of next and every following 4th row until there are 60 sts, then every alt row until there are 84(80-76-92-88-84) sts, then every row until there are 111 sts, thus ending with the 36th(32nd-28th-4th-40th-36th) row of check pattern and the 16th(12th-8th-4th-20th-16th) row of cable panel.

Work as given for Back from ★ to ★. 140 sts.
Keeping pattern correct work 32(36-40-44-48-52) rows straight, thus ending with the 30th(30th-30th-10th-10th-10th) row of check pattern and 10th row of cable panel.

Shape Front Neck

Keeping pattern correct cast off 16 sts at beg (neck edge) of next row. Dec 1 st at neck edge on next 4 rows, then every alt row twice. 118 sts remain. Work 59 rows straight thus ending at neck edge. Inc 1 st at neck edge on next and every alt row 3 times in all then following 3 rows. 124 sts.

Next row: Using A cast on 16 sts, work 11th row of Cable Panel across these sts, work in pattern to end. 140 sts.

Keeping cable panel and check pattern correct work 32(36-40-44-48-52) rows straight thus ending with the 19th(23rd-27th-11th-15th-19th) row of check pattern and 3rd(7th-11th-15th-19th-3rd) row of cable panel.

Shape Right Sleeve

Cast off 29 sts at beg of next row. 111 sts remain. Dec 1 st at end (underarm edge) of next row and same edge of every row until 84(80-76-92-88-84) sts remain, then every alt row until 59 sts remain. Dec 1 st at underarm edge on every 4th row until 50 sts remain. Work 3 rows straight thus ending with the 16th row of check pattern and 20th row of cable panel. Cast off in pattern.

FINISHING AND EDGINGS

Press according to instructions on ball band.

Welts: Using smaller needles and A and with right side of work facing pick up and k89(93-99-105-111-115) sts evenly along lower edge of one piece.

1st row: P1, *k1, p1; rep from * to end.

2nd row: K1, *p1, k1; rep from * to end.

Rep the last 2 rows until rib measures 7 cms [2¾ ins]. Cast off in rib.

Work 2nd welt in the same way.

Join left shoulder and sleeve seam.

Neckband: Using smaller needles and A and with right side of work facing, pick up and k6 sts down right back slope, 40 sts across back neck, 6 sts up left back slope to seam, 12 sts across cable panel, 6 sts down left front slope, 41 sts across front neck, 6 sts up right front slope and 12 sts across cable panel. 129 sts.

Work 7 rows in k1, p1 rib as given for Welts. Cast off in rib.

Join right shoulder and sleeve seam and ends of neckband.

Cuffs: Using smaller needles and A and with right side of work facing, pick up and k76 sts around one sleeve edge as follows: 1 st in each of next 2 sts, [3 sts in cable, 1 st in each of next 12 sts] twice, 12 sts across cable panel, [1 st in each of next 12 sts, 3 sts in cable] twice, 1 st in each of remaining 2 sts.

Next row (decrease): P2, *[p2tog] twice, p1; rep from * to last 4 sts, p2tog, p2. 47 sts remain.

Work 5 cms [2 ins] in k1, p1 rib as given for Welts, starting with the 2nd row. Cast off in rib.

Join side and underarm seams.

Relief Pattern Sweater

MEASUREMENTS

To fit bust sizes 88/92 cms [34/36 ins]. Length 56 cms [22 ins].

MATERIALS

Patons Visions 10 50g balls. Pair needles each size 5½mm (No 5) and 6mm (No 4). 5½mm (No 5) circular needle, 50 cms [20 ins] long.

TENSION

1st Pattern: 14 sts and 19 rows = 10 cms [4 ins] over pattern using 6mm needles.

2nd Pattern: 13 sts and 24 rows = 10 cms [4 ins] over pattern using 6mm needles.

SPECIAL ABBREVIATION

Sl 2P = slip 2 sts purlwise.

NOTE

Sweater is worked in one piece, starting at right cuff edge.

Using 5½mm needles cast on 26 sts.

1st row: *P2, k2; rep from * to last 2 sts, p2.

2nd row: *K2, p2; rep from * to last 2 sts, k2.

Rep 1st and 2nd rows for 6 cms [2¼ ins] ending with a 1st row.

Next row: Purl into front and back of each st to end. 52 sts.

Change to 6mm needles and continue in 1st pattern:

1st row: *K3, p1; rep from * to end.

2nd row: *K2, p1, k1; rep from * to end.

These 2 rows form the pattern. Work 12 more rows. Bringing extra sts into pattern, inc 1 st at each end of next row, then every 6th row until there are 66 sts, then every alt row until there are 76 sts.

Cast on at beg of next and following rows, 2 sts 10 times, 3 sts 4 times, 5 sts twice and 12 sts twice. 142 sts. Work 9 rows straight. Work 3 rows in st st.

Next row: P7, p2tog, *p16, p2tog; rep from * to last 7 sts, p7. 134 sts.

Continue in 2nd pattern:

1st row: *K6, sl 2P with yarn at back; rep from * to last 6 sts, k6.

2nd row: *K6, sl 2P with yarn at front; rep from * to last 6 sts, k6.

3rd row: As 1st row.

4th row: As 2nd row.

5th and 6th rows: Work in st st.

7th row: K2, *sl 2P with yarn at back, k6; rep from * to last 4 sts, sl 2P, k2.

8th row: K2, sl 2P with yarn at front, k6; rep from * to last 4 sts, sl 2P, k2.

9th row: As 7th row.

10th row: As 8th row.

11th and 12th rows: Work in st st.

These 12 rows form the pattern. Work 7 more rows.

Divide for Neck

Next row: Pattern 67 sts, turn leaving remaining sts on a spare needle.

Continue on these sts. Work 56 rows (the 4th row of 7th pattern should be completed). Break yarn.

Rejoin yarn to remaining sts at neck edge. Work until the 4th row of the 7th pattern has been completed.

Next row: Pattern to end, then work across sts on spare needle.

Work 18 rows in pattern, ending with 10th pattern row.

Next row: K7, inc in next st, *k16, inc in next st; rep from * to last 7 sts, k7. 142 sts.

Work 3 rows in st st.

Continue in 1st pattern. Work 9 rows. Cast off at beg of next and following rows, 12 sts twice, 5 sts twice, 3 sts 4 times and 2 sts 10 times. 76 sts.

Now dec 1 st at each end of next row, then every alt row until 64 sts remain, then every 6th row until 52 sts remain. Work 13 rows.

Next row: P2tog to end of row. 26 sts.

Change to 5½mm needles and work 6 cms [2¼

ins] in rib as other cuff. Cast off in rib.

Front Welt

Using 5½mm needles knit up 60 sts evenly along lower edge of front (approximately 1 st for each 2 rows).

1st row: K1, p2, *k2, p2; rep from * to last st, k1.

2nd row: P1, k2, *p2, k2; rep from * to last st, p1.

Rep 1st and 2nd rows for 6 cms [2¼ ins]. Cast off in rib.

Work Back Welt the same.

Collar

Using 5½mm circular needle and starting at left shoulder, knit up 96 sts evenly along neck edge. Work 20 cms [8 ins] in 1st pattern, turning at end of each row. Cast off.

MAKING UP

Press pieces according to instructions on ball band. Join side and undersleeve seams.

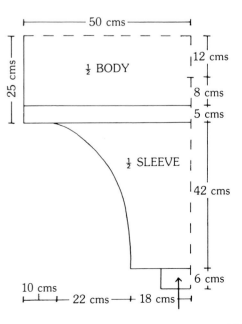

Cable Sweater with Roll Collar

MEASUREMENTS
To fit bust sizes 89/94 cms [35/37 ins]. Length 60 cms [24 ins].

MATERIALS
Patons Visions 10 50g balls. Pair needles each size 5½mm (No 5) and 6mm No 4). 5½mm (No 5) circular knitting needle, 50 cms [20 ins] long.

TENSION
15 sts and 18 rows = 10 cms [4 ins] over pattern using 6mm needles.

SPECIAL ABBREVIATION
C8F (Cable 8 Front) = slip next 4 sts onto cable needle and hold at front, k4, then k4 from cable needle.

NOTE
Sweater is worked in one piece, starting at front.

Using 5½mm needles cast on 74 sts.

1st row: *P2, k2; rep from * to last 2 sts, p2.

2nd row: *K2, p2; rep from * to last 2 sts, k2.

Rep 1st and 2nd rows for 6 cms [2½ ins] ending with a 2nd row and increasing 4 sts evenly spaced in last row. 78 sts.

Change to 6mm needles and commence pattern:

1st row: P2, k8, *p3, k8; rep from * to last 2 sts, p2.

2nd row: K2, p8, *k3, p8; rep from * to last 2 sts, k2.

3rd to 8th rows: Rep 1st and 2nd rows 3 times.

9th row: P2, C8F, *p3, k8, p3, C8F; rep from * to last 2 sts, p2.

10th row: As 2nd row.

11th row: As 1st row.

12th row: As 2nd row.

These 12 rows form the pattern. Work until the 9th row of the 3rd pattern has been completed. Inc 1 st at each end of next row, then every alt row until there are 88 sts.

Commence Undersleeve Shaping
Cast on at beg of next and following rows, 2 sts 6 times, 3 sts 6 times, 5 sts 6 times, 8 sts 4 times and 15 sts twice. 210 sts.

Work until the 8th row of the 6th pattern from beg has been completed.

Next row: P2, [C8F, p3] 3 times, *k8, p3, C8F, p3; rep from * to last 21 sts, C8F, p3, C8F, p2.

Continue in pattern as set. Work until the 4th row of the 8th pattern from beg has been completed.

Shape Neck
Next row: Pattern 97 sts, cast off 16 sts, pattern to end.

Continue on last set of sts leaving remainder on a spare needle.

Dec 1 st at neck edge on next 9 rows. Work 2 rows. Inc 1 st at neck edge on next row. Work 1 row, ending at neck edge. Break yarn.

Rejoin yarn to remaining sts at neck edge. Dec 1 st at neck edge on next 9 rows. Work 2 rows. Inc 1 st at neck edge on next row. Work 1 row.

Next row: Pattern to end, cast on 32 sts, then work in pattern across sts of other side.

Work until the 12th row of the 11th pattern from commencement has been completed.

Commence Undersleeve Shaping
Cast off at beg of next and following rows, 15 sts twice, 8 sts 4 times, 5 sts 6 times, 3 sts 6 times and 2 sts 6 times. Now dec 1 st at each end of next row, then every alt row until 78 sts remain. Work until the 3rd row of the 17th pattern from commencement has been completed.

Next row: Pattern to end decreasing 4 sts evenly spaced.

Change to 5½mm needles and work 6 cms [2½ ins] in rib as front welt. Cast off in rib.

Cuffs
With 5½mm needles knit up 28 sts evenly along sleeve edge. Work 6 cms [2½ ins] in k2, p2 rib. Cast off in rib.

Collar
Using circular needle knit up 80 sts evenly along neck edge. Work 20 cms [8 ins] in rounds of k1, p1 rib. Cast off in rib.

MAKING UP
Press pieces according to instructions on ball band. Join side and undersleeve seams. Fold collar in half to outside.

2 = rev st st
3 = Cable 8 Front
4 = 8 st in st st

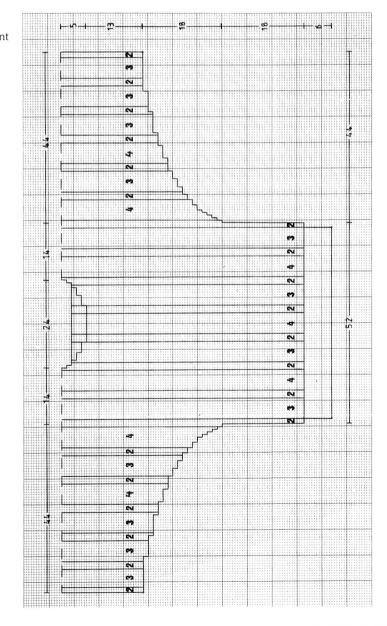

Dolman Sweater with Cables

MEASUREMENTS

To fit bust sizes 88/92 cms [34/36 ins]. Length (approximately) 57 cms [22½ ins].

MATERIALS

Patons Siberia 50g balls: 7 balls Main colour (M), Patons Visions 50g balls: 2 balls each in Contrast colours A, B and C. Pair needles size 5½mm (No 5). 7mm (No 2) circular needle, 80 cms [32 ins] long. Cable needle. 5mm crochet hook.

TENSION

12 sts and 17 rows = 10 cms [4 ins] over reverse st st using 7mm needles.

CABLE PANEL 1

1st row: Using A k6, p2, using B p2, k6.

2nd row: Using B p6, k2, using A k2, p6.

3rd and 4th rows: As 1st and 2nd rows.

5th row: Using A slip next 3 sts onto cable needle and hold at front, k3, then k3 from cable needle, p2, using B p2, slip next 3 sts onto cable needle and hold at front, k3, then k3 from cable needle.

6th row: As 2nd row.

7th and 8th rows: As 1st and 2nd rows.

These 8 rows form the pattern.

CABLE PANEL 2 (Using C)

1st row: Knit.

2nd row: Purl.

3rd to 10th rows: Rep 1st and 2nd rows 4 times.

11th row: Slip next 3 sts onto cable needle and hold at front, k3, then k3 from cable needle.

12th row: As 2nd row.

These 12 rows form the pattern.

CABLE PANEL 3 (Using B)

1st row: Knit.

2nd row: Purl.

3rd and 4th rows: As 1st and 2nd rows.

5th row: Slip next 3 sts onto cable needle and hold at front, k3, then k3 from cable needle.

6th row: As 2nd row.

7th and 8th rows: As 1st and 2nd rows.

These 8 rows form the pattern.

CABLE PANEL 4

As Cable Panel 3 **but** using A.

Use a separate ball of yarn for each part and ensure that yarns are twisted together when changing colour to avoid holes.

1 = Colour M, st st
2 = Cable Panel 1, Colour A/B
3 = Cable Panel 3, Colour B
4 = Cable Panel 3, Colour A
5 = Cable Panel 4, Colour C
Note: Figures at side of chart refer to cms.

Commence at left cuff edge

Using 5½mm needles and M cast on 34 sts.

1st row: K1, *p2, k4; rep from * to last 3 sts, p2, k1.

2nd row: K1, *k2, p4; rep from * to last 3 sts, k3.

3rd row: K1, *p2, slip next 2 sts onto cable needle and hold at front, k2, then k2 from cable needle; rep from * to last 3 sts, p2, k1.

4th row: As 2nd row.

Rep 1st to 4th rows twice more, then 1st row again.

Next row: Knit to end, increasing 6 sts evenly spaced. 40 sts.

Change to 7mm circular needle and continue in pattern working from chart.

1st row: P12M, work Cable Panel 1 over next 16 sts, p12M.

2nd row: K12M, Cable Panel 1 over next 16 sts, k12M.

Continue in reverse st st with cable panel in the centre. Work 4 more rows. Inc 1 st at each end of next row, then every 4th row until there are 66 sts, then every alt row until there are 74 sts, then every row until there are 88 sts.

Next row: Using M cast on 14 sts, work to end. Now with a separate strand of yarn cast on 14 sts and purl these sts on to end of last row.

Work 27 rows. In next row divide work in the centre for neck and continue over each piece for 38 rows. Now continue over all the sts, working Cable Panels 1 and 2 only. Work 28 rows.

Next row: Cast off 14 sts, work to last 14 sts, cast off these sts.

Break yarn. Turn and rejoin yarn to remaining sts. Dec 1 st at each end of every row until 72 sts remain, then every alt row until 64 sts remain, then every 4th row until 40 sts remain. Work 4 rows.

Change to 5½mm needles and continue in M over all sts.

Next row: Knit to end decreasing 6 sts evenly spaced.

Work 13 rows in pattern as first cuff. Cast off.

Front Welt

With 5½mm needles and M knit up 70 sts evenly along lower edge of front. Work 21 rows in pattern as given for Cuffs. Cast off.

Work Back Welt the same.

MAKING UP

Press pieces according to instructions on ball band. Join side and sleeve seams.

Neckband: Using 5mm crochet hook and working in matching colours, work 1 row of firm dc from right to left along neck edge. Join with a sl st but do not turn. Work a 2nd row of dc but working from left to right to form crab-st. Fasten off.

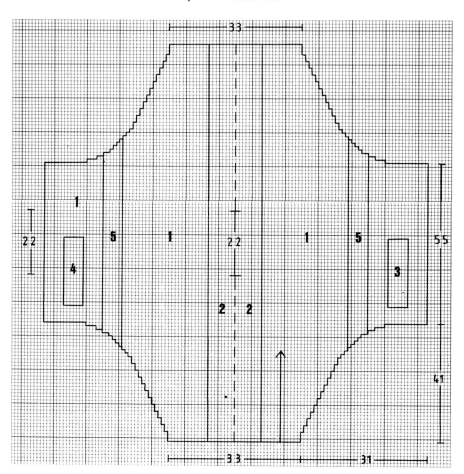

Snuggly Coverups

15 Fashionable Ways
to Look Elegant on Cold Days

Diamond Pattern Sweater

MEASUREMENTS

To fit bust sizes 80/85(90/95) cms [32/34(36/38) ins]. Finished measurement 93(102) cms [37(41) ins]. Length to shoulder (approximately) 59(61) cms [23½(24½) ins]. Sleeve seam (approximately) 46 cms [18½(18½) ins].

MATERIALS

Copley Cobweb 25g balls: 8(10) balls Main colour (M), 7(8) balls Contrast colour A, 4(6) balls Contrast colour B. Pair needles each size 5mm (No 6) and 4mm (No 8).

TENSION

17 sts and 22 rows = 10 cms [4 ins] square measured over st st using larger needles.

NOTE

Use a separate ball of M, A and B for each diamond. Twist yarns together when changing colour to avoid making a hole.

BACK

Using smaller needles and M cast on 79(87) sts.

1st row (right side): K1, *p1, k1; rep from * to end.

2nd row: P1, *k1, p1; rep from * to end.

Rep the last 2 rows until rib measures 6 cms [2½ ins], ending with a wrong side row.

Change to larger needles and commence pattern (see Note):

★ **1st row:** Knit 7(11)A, 1B, 31A, 1M, 31A, 1B, 7(11)A.

2nd and every alt row: Purl each st in same colour as previous row.

3rd row: Knit 6(10)A, 3B, 29A, 3M, 29A, 3B, 6(10)A.

5th row: Knit 5(9)A, 5B, 27A, 5M, 27A, 5B, 5(9)A.

Continue in this way until the row 'Knit 1A, 13(21)B, 19(11)A, 13(21)M, 19(11)A, 13(21)B, 1A' has been worked.

Next row: As 2nd row.

Next row: Knit 15(23)B, 17(9)A, 15(23)M, 17(9)A, 15(23)B.

Next row: As 2nd row.

Next row: Knit 16(24)B, 15(7)A, 17(25)M, 15(7)A, 16(24)B.

Continue in this way until the row 'Knit 23(27)B, 1A, 31M, 1A, 23(27)B' has been worked.

Next row: As 2nd row.

Next row: Knit 22(26)B, 3A, 29M, 3A, 22(26)B.

Next row: As 2nd row.

Next row: Knit 21(25)B, 5A, 27M, 5A, 21(25)B.

Continue in this way until the row 'Knit 15(23)B, 17(9)A, 15(23)M, 17(9)A, 15(23)B' has been worked.

Next row: As 2nd row.

Next row: Knit 1A, 13(21)B, 19(11)A, 13(21)M, 19(11)A, 13(21)B, 1A.

Next row: As 2nd row.

Next row: Knit 2A, 11(19)B, 21(13)A, 11(19)M, 21(13)A, 11(19)B, 2A ★.

Continue in this way until the row 'Knit 7(11)A, 1B, 31A, 1M, 31A, 1B, 7(11)A' has been worked.

Next row: As 2nd row.

Using A work 2 rows. 64 rows worked.

Now work as given from ★ to ★ once more using M instead of B, and B instead of M.

2nd size only: Continue in this way until the row 'Knit 8A, 7M, 25A, 7B, 25A, 7M, 8A' has been worked.

Both sizes

Next row: As 2nd row. 116(120) rows worked.

Shape Shoulders

Keeping pattern correct cast off 9(10) sts at beg of next 6 rows. Slip remaining 25(27) sts onto a holder for polo collar.

FRONT

Work as given for Back until the row 'Knit 23(27)M, 1A, 31B, 1A, 23(27)M' has been worked. 95 rows worked.

Keeping pattern correct work 6(8) more rows, thus ending with a knit row.

Shape Neck

1st row: Work 32(35) sts in pattern, turn and complete this side first.

★★ Keeping pattern correct dec 1 st at neck edge on next 3 rows, then every alt row until 27(30) sts remain. Work 8(10) rows straight (work 1 row less here for 2nd side), thus ending at side edge.

Shape Shoulder

Keeping pattern correct cast off 9(10) sts at beg of next and following alt row. Work 1 row. Cast

Diamond Pattern Sweater

off remaining 9(10) sts.

Slip next 15(17) sts at centre onto a holder for polo collar. With wrong side of work facing rejoin yarn to neck edge of remaining sts and keeping pattern correct purl to end.

Complete to match first side from ★★ to end reversing shaping.

SLEEVES

Using smaller needles and M cast on 35(39) sts and work 6 cms [2½ ins] in k1, p1 rib as given for Back ending with a right side row.

Next row (increase): Inc in each st to last 1(3) sts, rib to end. 69(75) sts.

Change to larger needles and commence pattern:

★★★ **1st row:** Knit 2(5)A, 1B, 31A, 1M, 31A, 1B, 2(5)A.

2nd and every alt row: Purl each st in same colour as previous row.

3rd row: Knit 1(4)A, 3B, 29A, 3M, 29A, 3B, 1(4)A.

2nd size only

5th row: Knit 3A, 5B, 27A, 5M, 27A, 5B, 3A.

Continue in this way until the row 'Knit 1A, 9B, 23A, 9M, 23A, 9B, 1A' has been worked.

Both sizes

Next row: As 2nd row.

Next row: Knit 5(11)B, 27(21)A, 5(11)M, 27(21)A, 5(11)B.

Next row: As 2nd row.

Next row: Knit 6(12)B, 25(19)A, 7(13)M, 25(19)A, 6(12)B.

Next row: As 2nd row.

Next row: Knit 7(13)B, 23(17)A, 9(15)M, 23(17)A, 7(13)B ★★★.

Continue in this way until the row 'Knit 18(21)B, 1A, 31M, 1A, 18(21)B' has been worked.

Next row: As 2nd row.

Next row: Knit 17(20)B, 3A, 29M, 3A, 17(20)B.

Next row: As 2nd row.

Next row: Knit 16(19)B, 5A, 27M, 5A, 16(19)B.

Continue in this way until the row 'Knit 5(11)B, 27(21)A, 5(11)M, 27(21)A, 5(11)B' has been worked.

Next row: As 2nd row.

Next row: Knit 1A, 3(9)B, 29(23)A, 3(9)M, 29(23)A, 3(9)B, 1A.

Next row: As 2nd row.

Next row: Knit 2A, 1(7)B, 31(25)A, 1(7)M, 31(25)A, 1(7)B, 2A.

Next row: As 2nd row.

2nd size only

Continue in this way until the row 'Knit 5A, 1B, 31A, 1M, 31A, 1B, 5A' has been worked.

Next row: As 2nd row.

Both sizes

Using A, work 2 rows. 64 rows worked.

Work as given from ★★★ to ★★★ once more using M instead of B and B instead of M.

Continue in this way until the row 'Knit 14(17)M, 9A, 23B, 9A, 14(17)M' has been worked.

Next row: As 2nd row. 88 rows worked.

Cast off.

FINISHING AND POLO COLLAR

Press pieces according to instructions on ball band. Join left shoulder seam.

Polo collar: Using larger needles and M and with right side of work facing, knit across sts on holder at back neck decreasing 1 st at centre, pick up and k17(19) sts evenly down left front slope, knit across sts on holder at centre front and pick up and k17(19) sts evenly up right front slope. 73(81) sts.

Work 8 rows in k1, p1 rib as given for Back.

Next row (increase): K1, *[p1, k1, p1] into next st, k1; rep from * to end. 145(161) sts.

Continue in k1, p1 rib as given for Back, starting with the 2nd row, until collar measures 20 cms [8 ins]. Cast off in rib.

Join right shoulder seam and ends of polo collar, reversing seam on collar. Fold sleeves in half lengthways and mark centre of cast off edge. Sew sleeve to side edge placing centre at shoulder seam. Join side and sleeve seams. Press seams. Turn back collar.

Mohair Sweater

MEASUREMENTS

To fit bust 88/96 cms [34½/37½ ins]. Length 59 cms [23¼ ins]. Sleeve length 48 cms [19 ins].

MATERIALS

5 50g balls Jaeger Mohair Gold (A), 5 50g balls Patons Beehive Chunky Twirl (B) and 2 25g balls Patons Visions (C). Pair needles each size 6mm (No 4) and 7mm (No 2). Cable needle.

TENSION

Mohair Gold: 11 sts and 16 rows = 10 cms [4 ins] over st st using 7mm needles.
Beehive Chunky Twirl: 15 sts and 20 rows = 10 cms [4 ins] over pattern using 7mm needles.

SPECIAL ABBREVIATION

Cable 4 = slip next 2 sts onto cable needle and hold at front, k2, then k2 from cable needle.

BACK

Using 6mm needles and B cast on 72 sts.
1st row: P1, k2, *p2, k2; rep from * to last st, p1.
2nd row: K1, p2, *k2, p2; rep from * to last st, k1.
Rep 1st and 2nd rows for 6 cms [2½ ins] ending with a 2nd row and increasing 10 sts evenly spaced in last row by picking up loop from between needles and working into the back of it. 82 sts.
Change to 7mm needles and commence pattern:
1st row: P3, k4, *p2, k4; rep from * to last 3 sts, p3.
2nd row: K3, p4, *k2, p4; rep from * to last 3 sts, k3.
3rd row: P3, Cable 4, *p2, Cable 4; rep from * to last 3 sts, p3.
4th row: As 2nd row.
These 4 rows form pattern.
Join in A. Ensure that yarns are twisted together on wrong side when changing colour to avoid holes ★.

Commence Diagonal Pattern

Note: Decreases are to offset differences in yarn thicknesses.
1st row: Using A k2, k2tog, using B pattern to end.
2nd row: Using B pattern to last 3 sts, using A p3.
3rd row: Using A k5, k2tog, using B pattern to end.
4th row: Using B pattern to last 6 sts, using A p6.
5th row: Using A k8, k2tog, using B pattern to end.
6th row: Using B pattern to last 9 sts, using A purl to end.

7th row: Using A k11, k2tog, using B pattern to end.
Continue to work 2 sts less in pattern on every row and dec 1 st on every alt row in this way until 62 sts remain.
Next row: Using B pattern 2, using A purl to end.
Continue with A in st st until back measures 59 cms [23¼ ins] from beg, ending with a purl row. Cast off.

FRONT

Work as given for Back to ★.
Continue as back but reverse pattern panel as follows:
1st row: Using B pattern to last 4 sts, using A k2tog, k2.
2nd row: Using A p3, using B pattern to end.
When decreases are completed, continue with A in st st until front measures 53 cms [20¾ ins] from beg, ending with a purl row.

Shape Neck
Next row: K25, cast off 12 sts, knit to end.
Continue on last set of sts. Dec 1 st at neck edge on next 7 rows. Work 2 rows. Cast off remaining 18 sts.
Rejoin yarn to remaining sts at neck edge and complete to match other side.

SLEEVES

Using 6mm needles and A cast on 38 sts.
1st row: *P2, k2; rep from * to last 2 sts, p2.
2nd row: *K2, p2; rep from * to last 2 sts, k2.
Rep 1st and 2nd rows for 8 cms [3 ins] ending with a 2nd row and increasing 4 sts evenly spaced in last row. 42 sts.
Change to 7mm needles. Continuing in st st and A work 4 rows. Inc 1 st at each end of next row then every 8th row until there are 54 sts, then every 4th row until there are 62 sts. Work 3 rows. Cast off loosely.

COLLAR

Using 6mm needles and B cast on 28 sts and work approximately 48 cms [19 ins] in cable pattern. Cast off in pattern.

MAKING UP

Press pieces according to instructions on ball band. Join shoulder seams. Place a marker 28 cms [11 ins] on each side of shoulder seams to mark depth of armholes. Join cast off edge of sleeves to armhole edges. Join side and sleeve seams. Join cast on and cast off edges of collar. Place seam at centre back and sew one edge of collar to neck edge. Fold collar in half to wrong side and slip st in position.
Using 6mm needles and C cast on 5 sts and work in st st until strip is of required length to fit across front along diagonal line. Cast off.
Work another piece the same for back. Sew strips to front and back with large looped sts as shown.

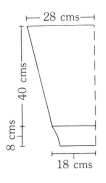

Mohair Cardigan

MEASUREMENTS

To fit bust sizes 88/92 cms [34/36 ins]. Length (approximately) 64 cms [25 ins]. Sleeve length (approximately) 51 cms [20 ins].

MATERIALS

4 50g balls Jaeger Mohair Gold (A), 7 50g balls Patons Beehive Chunky Twirl (B) and 2 50g balls Patons Visions (C). Pair needles each size 6mm (No 4) and 7mm (No 2). Cable needle. 6 buttons.

TENSION

Mohair Gold: 11 sts and 16 rows = 10 cms [4 ins] over st st using 7mm needles.

Beehive Chunky Twirl: 15 sts and 20 rows = 10 cms [4 ins] over pattern using 7mm needles.

SPECIAL ABBREVIATION

Cable 4 = slip next 2 sts onto cable needle and hold at front, k2, then k2 from cable needle.

BACK

Using 6mm needles and B cast on 80 sts.

1st row: *P2, k4; rep from * to last 2 sts, p2.

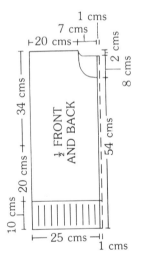

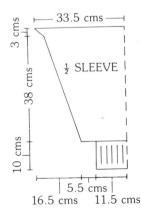

2nd row: *K2, p4; rep from * to last 2 sts, k2.

3rd row: *P2, Cable 4; rep from * to last 2 sts, p2.

4th row: As 2nd row.

These 4 rows form the cable pattern. Work until back measures approximately 10 cms [4 ins] from beg, ending with a right side row.

Next row: [P2tog] 3 times, *p2, p2tog; rep from * to last 2 sts, p2tog. 58 sts.

Break off B and join in A. Change to 7mm needles and work in st st until back measures 30 cms [12 ins] from beg, ending with a purl row.

Continue as follows:

1st row: Using B p2, k2, using A k50, using B k2, p2.

Ensure that yarns are twisted together on wrong side when changing colour to avoid holes.

2nd row: Using B k2, p2, using A p50, using B p2, k2.

3rd and 4th rows: As 1st and 2nd rows.

5th row: Using B p2, k3, using A k48, using B k3, p2.

6th row: Using B k2, p3, using A p48, using B p3, k2.

7th row: Using B p2, k3, inc 1 st by picking up loop from between needles and working into back of it, using A k48, using B inc 1 st, k3, p2.

8th row: Using B k2, p4, using A p48, using B p4, k2.

9th row: Using B p2, Cable 4, p1, using A k46, using B p1, Cable 4, p2.

10th row: Using B k2, p4, k1, using A p46, using B k1, p4, k2.

11th row: Using B p2, k4, p1, using A k46, using B p1, k4, p2.

12th row: As 10th row.

13th row: Using B p2, Cable 4, p2, inc 1 st, using A k44, using B inc 1 st, p2, Cable 4, p2.

Continue in this way working 1 st more towards the centre in B at each side on every 4th row and increasing 1 st more in B at each side on every 6th row (increased sts are to offset difference in yarn thicknesses).

Work until 26 sts are left in A in the centre, ending on an inc row. Work 1 row.

Shape Neck

Next row: Pattern 30 sts, cast off 14 sts, pattern to end.

Continue on last set of sts.

1st row: Work to last 2 sts, p2tog.

2nd row: Using A k4, using B pattern to end.

3rd row: As 1st row.

Cast off remaining 28 sts.

Rejoin yarn to remaining sts at neck edge and complete to match other side.

LEFT FRONT

Using 6mm needles cast on 38 sts and work 10 cms [4 ins] in cable rib as given for Back ending with a right side row.

Next row: *P2tog, p2; rep from * to last 2 sts, p2tog. 28 sts.

Break off B and join in A.

Change to 7mm needles and work in st st until front measures 30 cms [12 ins] from beg, ending with a purl row ★.

Continue to work cable panel as for back at side edge and inc on every 6th row until there are 34 sts. Work 1 row.

Shape Neck

Next row: Work to last 3 sts, cast off these sts.

Break yarn. Turn and rejoin yarn to remaining sts. Work 1 row.

Continue to work 1 st more towards the centre in B on next and following 4th rows and inc 1 st on 6th rows from previous increase, **at the same time** dec 1 st at neck edge on next row and following alt rows until 28 sts remain. Work 5 rows. Cast off.

RIGHT FRONT

Work as given for Left Front to ★. Continue to work cable panel as for back at side edge increasing on every 6th row until there are 34 sts. Work 1 row.

Shape Neck

Next row: Cast off 3 sts, work to end.

Complete to match Left Front.

SLEEVES

Using 6mm needles and B cast on 38 sts and work 10 cms [4 ins] in cable rib as given for Back. Break off B and join in A.

Change to 7mm needles and st st. Work 2 rows. Inc 1 st at each end of next row, then every 4th row until there are 66 sts, then every alt row until there are 74 sts. Work 1 row. Cast off loosely.

BUTTON BAND

Using 6mm needles and A cast on 7 sts.

1st row: K2, [p1, k1] twice, k1.

2nd row: [K1, p1] 3 times, k1.

Rep 1st and 2nd rows until band, when slightly stretched, fits along front edge. Leave sts on a safety pin.

Work Buttonhole Band as Button Band but making 5 buttonholes, the first 2.5 cms [1 inch] from lower edge, the rest equally spaced, allowing for the 6th in neckband, as follows: k2, p1, yrn, p2tog, k2. Leave sts on safety pin.

MAKING UP

Press pieces accorrding to instructions on ball band. Join shoulder seams. Sew cast off edge of sleeves to armhole edges. Join side and sleeve seams. Sew bands to fronts.

Neckband: Using 6mm needles and A rib across 7 sts at right neck edge, knit up 51 sts along neck edge then rib across sts at left neck edge. Work 5 cms [2 ins] in k1, p1 rib making 6th buttonhole to match other buttonholes when 2.5 cms [1 inch] has been worked. Cast off in rib.

Sew on buttons.

Using 6mm needles and C cast on 5 sts and work strips of st st to fit along diagonal lines and round armholes as shown. Sew strips in position with large looped sts.

2-Colour Cable Sweater

MEASUREMENTS

To fit bust sizes 88/92 cms [34/36 ins]. Length (approximately) 62 cms [24½ ins]. Sleeve length (approximately) 43 cms [17 ins].

MATERIALS

Jaeger Mohair Gold 3 50g balls each in Colours A and B. Pair needles each size 6mm (No 4) and 8mm (No 0) or circular needles each size 6mm (No 4) and 8mm (No 0), 70 cms [27½ ins] long. Cable needle.

TENSION

10 sts and 15 rows = 10 cms [4 ins] using 8mm needles.

SPECIAL ABBREVIATIONS

C8B (Cable 8 Back) = slip next 4 sts onto cable needle and hold at back, knit next 4 sts, then k4 sts from cable needle.

C8F (Cable 8 Front) = slip next 4 sts onto cable needle and hold at front, knit next 4 sts, then k4 sts from cable needle.

NOTE

Use a separate ball of yarn for each part and ensure that yarns are twisted together at back of work when changing colour to avoid holes.

Commence at left cuff edge

Using 6mm needles and A cast on 26 sts.

1st row: *P2, k2; rep from * to last 2 sts, p2.

2nd row: *K2, p2; rep from * to last 2 sts, k2.

Rep 1st and 2nd rows for 8 cms [3¼ ins] ending with a 1st row.

Next row: Purl to end increasing in 2nd then every st to last st, p1. 50 sts.

Change to 8mm needles and commence pattern:

1st row: P15A, k4A, 4B, p4B, k4B, 4A, p15A.

2nd row: K15, p8, k4, p8, k15, working in colours as set.

3rd and 4th rows: As 1st and 2nd rows.

5th row: P14A, C8B, p6B, C8F, p14A.

6th row: K14, p8, k6, p8, k14, working in colours as set.

7th row: P14, k8, p6, k8, p14, working in colours as set.

8th row: As 6th row.

These 8 rows form cable pattern.

Next row: P13, k8, p8, k8, p13.

Continue in pattern, working 1 st less at each side in A and 2 sts more in centre in B on every 4th row until the 1st row of the 7th pattern has been completed.

Continue in pattern as set. Work 3 rows.

Next row: Cast on 30 sts, work to end.

With separate strand of yarn cast on 30 sts and work over these sts at end of last row. 110 sts. Work 19 rows ending with a wrong side row.

Divide for Neck

Next row: Work 55 sts, cast off 1 st, work to end.

Continue on last set of sts, leaving remainder on spare needle.

Work 1 row. Dec 1 st at neck edge on next row, then the 2 following alt rows. Work 19 rows. Inc 1 st at neck edge on next row, then the 2 following alt rows.

Next row: Work to end, turn and cast on 1 st.

Break yarn. With wrong side facing rejoin yarn to remaining sts at neck edge. Work 31 rows.

Next row: Work to end, then work across sts on spare needle.

Work 19 rows.

Next row: Cast off 30 sts, work to last 30 sts, cast off these sts.

Break yarn. Turn and rejoin yarn to remaining sts. Work until the 8th row of the 22nd pattern from beg has been completed.

Change to 6mm needles.

Next row: Using A k1, now k2tog to last st, k1. 26 sts.

Work 8 cms [3¼ ins] in rib as first cuff. Cast off in rib.

SIDE INSERTS (Make 2)

Using 8mm needles and B cast on 3 sts. Work in reverse st st (purl 1 row, knit 1 row alternately). Work 6 rows. Inc 1 st at each end of next row, then every 6th row until there are 17 sts. Work 5 rows. Dec 1 st at each end of next row, then every 6th row until 3 sts remain. Work 5 rows. Cast off.

MAKING UP

Press pieces according to instructions on ball band.

Collar: Using 6mm needles and A cast on 8 sts and work 54 cms [21¼ ins] in st st. Cast off.

Work another piece in B in same way.

Twist the pieces round each other and join at ends. Sew collar in place round neck. Sew inserts to side and undersleeve edges on back and front, omitting cuffs. Join cuff seams.

Welts: Using 6mm needles and A knit up 46 sts evenly along lower edge of front. Work 7 cms [2¾ ins] in rib as cuffs, starting with a 2nd row. Cast off in rib.

Work back welt the same. Join welt seams.

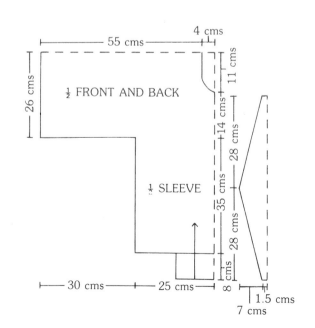

Cable Sweater

MEASUREMENTS

To fit bust sizes 92 cms [36 ins]. Length (approximately) 55 cms [21½ ins]. Sleeve length (approximately) 43 cms [16¾ ins].

MATERIALS

5 50g balls Jaeger Mohair Gold. Pair needles each size 6mm (No 4) and 8mm (No 0) or circular needles size 6mm (No 4) and 8mm (No 0), 80 cms [31½ ins] long. Cable needle. Beads as required.

TENSION

10 sts and 15 rows = 10 cms [4 ins] using 8mm needles.

SPECIAL ABBREVIATION

C8F (Cable 8 Front) = slip next 4 sts onto cable needle and hold at front, knit next 4 sts, then k4 sts from cable needle.

Commence at cuff edge

Using 6mm needles cast on 31 sts and work 4 cms [1½ ins] in k1, p1 rib.

Next row: Purl to end increasing in every alt st. 46 sts.

Change to 8mm needles and commence pattern:

1st row: K18, p1, k8, p1, k18.
2nd row: P18, k1, p8, k1, p18.
3rd and 4th rows: As 1st and 2nd rows.
5th row: K18, p1, C8F, p1, k18.
6th row: As 2nd row.

These 6 rows form the pattern. Bringing extra sts into st st, inc 1 st at each end of next row, then every 7th row until there are 58 sts, then every 3rd row until there are 66 sts. Work 2 rows.

Continue for back and front.

1st row: Cast on 22 sts, p3, k8, p1, k38, p1, k8, p1, k28, now with a separate strand of yarn cast on 22 sts and work in pattern over these sts at end of last row as follows: k10, p1, k8, p3.

2nd row: K3, p8, [k1, p38, k1, p8] twice, k3.

3rd row: P3, C8F, [p1, k38, p1, C8F] twice, p3.

Continue with 3 cable panels. Work until the 2nd row of the 14th pattern from beg has been completed.

Divide for Neck

Next row: P3, k8, p1, k38, p1, k4, turn leaving remaining sts on a spare needle.

Continue on these sts with 4 sts at neck edge in st st. Work 34 rows, ending with a 1st pattern row. Break yarn and leave sts on spare needle.

With right side facing rejoin yarn to remaining sts at neck edge. Work 35 rows ending with a 1st pattern row.

Next row: Pattern to end, then work in pattern over sts on spare needle.

Continue over all the sts in pattern. Work 23 rows.

Next row: Cast off 22 sts, work to last 22 sts, cast off these sts.

Break yarn. Turn and rejoin yarn to remaining sts. Work 2 rows. Dec 1 st at each end of next row, then every 3rd row until 56 sts remain, then every 7th row until 46 sts remain. Work 5 rows.

Change to 6mm needles.

Next row: *P1, p2tog; rep from * to last st, p1. 31 sts.

Work 4 cms [1½ ins] in rib as given for first cuff. Cast off in rib.

MAKING UP

Press pieces according to instructions on ball band. Join side and undersleeve seams. Sew on beads, spaced along neck edge and cables on sleeves.

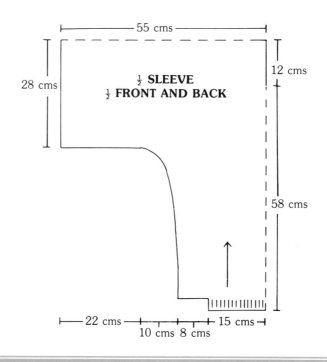

Long-Line Sweater with Shawl Collar

MEASUREMENTS

To fit bust sizes 81(86-91-96) cms [32(34-36-38) ins]. Finished bust measurement at underarm 103(108-114-120) cms [41(43½-45½-48) ins]. Length 80(81.5-81.5-82.5) cms [31½(32-32-32½) ins]. Sleeve width at upper arm 46.5(49-49-52) cms [18½(19¾-19¾-21).

MATERIALS

Jaeger Gypsy 12(13-13-14) 50g balls. Pair needles each size 4mm (No 8) and 5mm (No 6). Circular knitting needle size 4mm (No 8), 80 cms [29 ins] long. Pair needles size 6mm (No 4) for shoulder pads. Cable needle. Fabric lining for pockets.

TENSION

14 sts and 22 rows = 10 cms [4 ins] over reverse st st using 5mm needles.

18 sts and 28 rows = 10 cms [4 ins] over k1, p1 rib for collar using 4mm needles.

BACK

Using 4mm needles cast on 67(71-75-79) sts and work in k1, p1 rib for 6.5 cms [2½ ins], increasing 5 sts evenly spaced across last wrong side row. 72(76-80-84) sts.

Change to 5mm needles.

1st row (right side): Purl.

2nd row: Knit.

Rep 1st and 2nd rows for reverse st st until back measures 13 cms [5 ins] from beg, ending with a wrong side row.

Pocket Extensions

1st row (right side): Cast on 4 sts at beg of row, purl across cast-on sts, slip next st purlwise wyib, purl to end.

2nd row (wrong side): Cast on 4 sts, knit across cast on sts, p1, knit to last 5 sts, p1, k4. 80(84-88-92) sts.

3rd row: P4, slip next st purlwise wyib, purl to last 5 sts, slip next st purlwise wyib, p4.

4th row: K4, p1, knit to last 5 sts, p1, k4.

Rep 3rd and 4th rows until pocket extension measures 16.5 cms [6½ ins], ending with a wrong side row. Cast off 4 sts at beg of next 2 rows. 72(76-80-84) sts.

Work straight in reverse st st until back measures 56 cms [22 ins], ending with a wrong side row.

Shape Armhole

Cast off 2(3-3-2) sts at beg of next 2 rows, then cast off 2 sts at beg of next 4(4-4-6) rows. 60(62-66-68) sts.

Work straight in reverse st st until armhole measures 24(25.5-25.5-26.5) cms [9½(10-10-10½) ins], ending with a wrong side row.

Shape Shoulder

Cast off 8 sts at beg of next 4(2-0-0) rows, 9 sts at beg of next 0(2-4-2) rows, 10 sts at beg of next 0(0-0-2) rows. Cast off remaining 28(28-30-30) sts.

FRONT

Cast on and work rib as given for Back, increasing 11 sts evenly spaced across last wrong side

Designed by Deborah Newton
Photographed by Tony McGee

Long-Line Sweater with Shawl Collar

row. 78(82-86-90) sts.

Change to 5mm needles. Commence cable pattern:

1st row (right side): P33(35-37-39), place marker, k12, place marker, p33(35-37-39).

2nd, 4th, 6th and 8th rows (wrong side): Knit to marker, slip marker, p12, slip marker, knit to end.

3rd row: Purl to marker, slip marker, slip 4 sts to cable needle and hold at back of work, k4, k4 sts from cable needle, k4, slip marker, purl to end.

5th row: As 1st row.

7th row: Purl to marker, slip marker, k4, slip 4 sts to cable needle and hold at front of work, k4, k4 sts from cable needle, slip marker, purl to end.

Rep these 8 rows working reverse st st on 2 outer panels and cable pattern on centre 12 sts between markers until front measures 13 cms [5 ins] from beg, ending with a wrong side row.

Work pocket extensions as given for Back, then continue in reverse st st and cable pattern as set until front measures 48.5 cms [19 ins] from beg, or 7.5 cms [3 ins] less than back to arm-hole, ending with 2nd row of cable pattern.

Shape Neck

Next row (right side): P33(35-37-39), slip marker, [sl 1, k1, psso] 3 times, [k2tog] 3 times, slip marker, purl to end.

Next row (wrong side): K33(35-37-39), remove marker, join 2nd ball of yarn, cast off centre 6 sts purlwise, remove marker, knit to end.

Working both sides at same time with separate balls of yarn, dec 1 st at each neck edge every 6th row 11(11-12-12) times, and **at the same time,** when front measures same as back to armhole, work armhole and shoulder shapings as for Back.

SLEEVES

Using 4mm needles cast on 33(35-35-37) sts and work in k1, p1 rib for 6.5 cms [2½ ins], increasing 14 sts evenly spaced across last row. 47(49-49-51) sts.

Change to 5mm needles. Work straight in reverse st st for 2.5 cms [1 inch], ending with a knit row.

Inc 1 st each end of next row and rep inc every 6th row 8(9-9-10) times more. 65(69-69-73) sts.

Work straight in reverse st st until sleeve meas-

ures 43(44.5-44.5-46) cms [17(17½-17½-18) ins] from beg, or required length to underarm, ending with a wrong side row.

Shape Cap

Cast off 3(3-2-2) sts at beg of next 2 rows, 2 sts at beg of next 10(12-12-14) rows, 4(4-5-5) sts at beg of next 2 rows. Cast off remaining 31 sts on next row.

COLLAR

Using circular needle cast on 23(25-25-27) sts and work 1 row in k1, p1 rib. Continue in rib, casting on 3 sts at beg of next 42(44-44-46) rows. 149(157-157-165) sts.

Work straight in k1, p1 rib for 8.5 cms [3½ ins] (or 24 rows). Cast off 3 sts loosely at beg of next 42(44-44-46) rows. 23(25-25-27) sts. Cast off all sts loosely. Place marker at centre st of these cast-off sts.

FINISHING

Press pieces according to instructions on ball band. Sew shoulder seams. Sew side seams, joining pocket extensions at top and bottom and folding to inside along slip stitch line. Cut out and sew pockets from lining material. Attach pocket lining to pocket extensions inside sweater. Sew sleeve seams. Set in sleeves.

With right side of pieces facing, match marker on collar to centre back neck. Baste along edge of collar around back neck and left front neck edge, easing in any fullness. With seam at wrong side, sew this edge of collar in place. Fold collar in half lengthwise to inside and sew straight 8.5 cm [3½ inch] edge to top of cable. Baste and sew right side of collar in same way, overlapping straight edge of left collar at top of cable. With collar folded to inside, sew other long edge of collar along seamline.

Shoulder Pads (optional — make 2)

Using 6mm needles and 2 strands of yarn held tog, cast on 3 sts. Work in garter st (every row knit), increasing 1 st at each end of next row (right side), then on every alt row until there are 21 sts, ending with a right side row. Mark centre st.

Dec row (wrong side): Knit until 1 st before centre st, slip 1 st and centre st tog knitwise, k1, p2sso, knit to end.

Continue to increase each end of every alt row until there are 25 sts. Rep decrease row. 23 sts.

Continue to inc each end of every alt row until there are 29 sts. Rep decrease row. 27 sts. Cast off all sts loosely. Tack in shoulder pads.

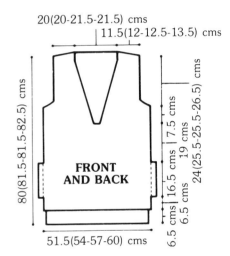

20(20-21.5-21.5) cms
11.5(12-12.5-13.5) cms
80(81.5-81.5-82.5) cms
24(25.5-25.5-26.5) cms
7.5 cms
19 cms
16.5 cms
6.5 cms
6.5 cms

FRONT AND BACK

51.5(54-57-60) cms

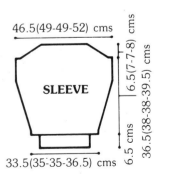

46.5(49-49-52) cms
6.5(7-7-8) cms
36.5(38-38-39.5) cms
6.5 cms

SLEEVE

33.5(35-35-36.5) cms

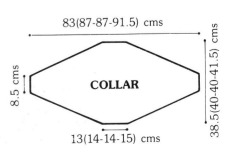

83(87-87-91.5) cms
38.5(40-40-41.5) cms
8.5 cms

COLLAR

13(14-14-15) cms

Sweater with Lace Panels

MEASUREMENTS

To fit bust sizes 80(85-90-95-100-105) cms [32(34-36-38-40-42) ins]. Finished measurement 90(94-101-105-110-114) cms [36(37½-40½-42-44-45½) ins]. Length to shoulder (approximately) 57 cms [22½ ins]. Sleeve length (approximately) 46 cms [18 ins].

MATERIALS

Patons Visions 9(10-10-10-11-11) 50g balls. Pair needles each size 5mm (No 6) and 4mm (No 8).

TENSION

18 sts and 24 rows = 10 cms [4 ins] square measured over st st using larger needles.

SPECIAL ABBREVIATION

Slip marker = make a slip knot in a short length of contrasting yarn and place on needle where indicated. On the following rows slip the marker from one needle to the other until the pattern is established and the marker is no longer required.

LACE PANEL (Worked across 27 sts between markers)

1st row: P2, k10, p3, k10, p2.

2nd and every alt row: K2, p10, k3, p10, k2.

3rd row: P2, k6, k3tog, yf, k1, yfrn, p3, yon, k1, yf, sl 1, k2tog, psso, k6, p2.

5th row: P2, k4, k3tog, k1, [yf, k1] twice, p3, k1, [yf, k1] twice, sl 1, k2tog, psso, k4, p2.

7th row: P2, k2, k3tog, k2, yf, k1, yf, k2, p3, k2, yf, k1, yf, k2, sl 1, k2tog, psso, k2, p2.

9th row: P2, k3tog, k3, yf, k1, yf, k3, p3, k3, yf, k1, yf, k3, sl 1, k2tog, psso, p2.

10th row: As 2nd row.

These 10 rows form the Lace Panel.

FRONT

Using smaller needles cast on 71(75-81-85-89-95) sts.

1st row (right side): K1, *p1, k1; rep from * to end.

2nd row: P1, *k1, p1; rep from * to end.

Rep the last 2 rows until rib measures 6 cms [2½ ins] ending with a right side row ★.

Next row (increase): Rib 5(7-4-6-8-7), *inc in next st, rib 4(4-5-5-5-7); rep from * to last 6(8-5-7-9-8) sts, inc in next st, rib to end. 84(88-94-98-102-106) sts.

Change to larger needles and commence pattern:

1st row: K2(2-4-4-6-6), slip marker, work 1st row of Lace Panel across next 27 sts, slip marker, knit to end.

2nd row: P55(59-63-67-69-73), work 2nd row of Lace Panel, purl to end.

These 2 rows form the st st at either side of Lace Panel. Rep these 2 rows, **at the same time** keeping the 10 rows of lace panel correct on sts between markers, until front measures approximately 52 cms [20½ ins] or 5 cms [2 ins] less than required length to shoulder ending with a 10th row of panel.

Next row (increase): K7(7-7-6-6-4), *inc in next st, k16(11-12-13-14-11); rep from * to last 9(9-9-8-6-6) sts, inc in next st, knit to end. 89(95-101-105-109-115) sts.

Change to smaller needles and work 5 cms [2 ins] in k1, p1 rib as given at beg starting with the 2nd row. Cast off firmly in rib.

BACK

Work as given for Front to ★.

Next row (increase): Rib 3(5-4-6-3-5), *inc in next st, rib 6(6-7-7-8-11); rep from * to last 5(7-5-7-5-6) sts, inc in next st, rib to end. 81(85-91-95-99-103) sts.

Change to larger needles and work in st st, starting knit, until back measures same as front to start of shoulder ribbing ending with a purl row.

Next row (increase): K8(6-9-6-8-7), *inc in next st, k8(7-7-8-8-7); rep from * to last 10(7-10-8-10-8) sts, inc in next st, knit to end. 89(95-101-105-109-115) sts.

Change to smaller needles and work 5 cms [2 ins] in k1, p1 rib as given for Front starting with the 2nd row. Cast off firmly in rib.

SLEEVES

Using smaller needles cast on 37(39-41-41-43-45) sts and work 8 cms [3 ins] in k1, p1 rib as given for Front, ending with a right side row.

Next row (increase): Rib 5(5-4-1-1-2), *inc in each of next 2 sts, work 1 st; rep from * to last 8(7-7-4-3-4) sts, inc in each of next 2 sts, rib to end. 55(59-63-67-71-73) sts.

Change to larger needles and commence pattern:

1st row: K14(16-18-20-22-23), slip marker, work 1st row of Lace Panel across next 27 sts, slip marker, k14(16-18-20-22-23).

2nd row: P14(16-18-20-22-23), work 2nd row of Lace Panel, p14(16-18-20-22-23).

Keeping the 10 rows of lace panel correct on sts between markers throughout, work 4 more rows. Bringing extra sts into st st, inc 1 st at each end of next and every following 5th row until there are 87(91-95-99-103-105) sts. Work straight until sleeve measures approximately 46 cms [18 ins], or required sleeve length ending with a 10th row of panel. Cast off.

TO FINISH

Press pieces according to instructions on ball band. Join shoulder seams leaving approximately 25 cms [10 ins] open at centre for neck. Fold sleeves in half lengthways and mark centre of cast off edge. Sew sleeve to side edge placing centre at shoulder seam. Note: armholes should measure approximately 23(24-25-26-28-28) cms [9(9½-9¾-10¼-11-11) ins]. Join side and sleeve seams. Press seams.

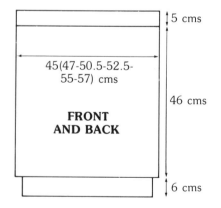

5 cms

45(47-50.5-52.5-55-57) cms

46 cms

FRONT AND BACK

6 cms

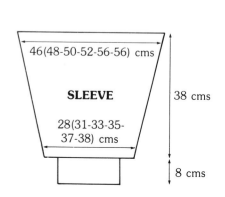

46(48-50-52-56-56) cms

SLEEVE

38 cms

28(31-33-35-37-38) cms

8 cms

Machine or Handknit Sweater

MEASUREMENTS

To fit bust sizes 81(86-91-96) cms [32(34-36-38) ins]. Finished bust measurement at under-arm 100(104-110-114) cms [40(42-44-46) ins]. Length 66(68.5-71-73.5) cms [26(27-28-29) ins]. Sleeve width at upper arm 62.5(65-65-67.5) cms [25(26-26-27) ins].

MATERIALS

Patons Solo 6(7-7-8) 50g balls. Knitting machine OR pair needles each size 4½mm (No 7) and 5½mm (No 5). 1m [1 yd] of 7.5 cm [3 inch] wide matching ribbon for bow.

TENSION

16 sts and 21 rows = 10 cms [4 ins] over st st using size 5½mm needles.

HANDKNIT INSTRUCTIONS

BACK

Using larger needles cast on 80(84-88-92) sts. Work in st st (1 row knit, 1 row purl) for 63.5(66-68.5-71) cms [25(26-27-28) ins], ending with a purl row.

Shape Neck

Next row (right side): K33(34-36-37), join 2nd ball of yarn and cast off centre 14(16-16-18) sts, knit to end.

Next row: Purl first 25(26-28-29) sts and slip to a holder for left shoulder (to be worked later), p8, with 2nd ball of yarn cast off 3 sts from neck edge, purl to end.

Next row: Knit sts of first side, cast off 3 sts from neck edge of 2nd side, knit to end.

Continue to shape neck edge by casting off 3 sts from each neck edge once more, then 2 sts once. Cast off remaining 25(26-28-29) sts for right shoulder.

FRONT

Cast on and work as given for Back for 56(58.5-61-63.5) cms [22(23-24-25) ins], ending with a purl row.

Shape Neck

Next row (right side): K37(38-40-41) sts, join

2nd ball of yarn and cast off centre 6(8-8-10) sts, knit to end.

Working both sides at same time with separate balls of yarn, dec 1 st each side of neck edge every row 12 times. 25(26-28-29) sts each side.

Work straight until front measures 63.5(66-68.5-71) cms [25(26-27-28) ins] from beg, ending with a purl row.

Next row (right side): K25(26-28-29) sts and slip to holder for left shoulder, knit remaining 25(26-28-29) sts.

Working on sts for right shoulder only, work 6 rows in st st. Cast off.

SLEEVES

Starting at upper (armhole) edge of sleeve and using larger needles cast on 100(104-104-108) sts. Working in st st, dec 1 st each end of every 4th row 3(4-4-4) times, then every 2nd row 26(26-26-27) times. 42(44-44-46) sts.

Work straight for 6 rows. Sleeve measures approximately 33.5(35-35-36) cms [13½(14-14-14½) ins] from beg. Cast off.

FINISHING

Press pieces according to instructions on ball band. Sew right shoulder seam.

Using smaller needles work across 25(26-28-29) sts from holder for back left shoulder. Inc 2(1-1-2) sts on first row and work in k1, p1 rib on 27(27-29-31) sts for 6 rows. Cast off loosely in rib. Sew edge of rib to side of back neck. Work across sts from holder for front left shoulder in same way.

Neckband

Starting at top of rib on front neck edge and using smaller needles pick up and k84(88-88-92) sts evenly around neck edge. Work in k1, p1 rib for 6 rows. Cast off loosely in rib.

Place markers on front and back at 32(33-33-34) cms [12½(13-13-13½) ins] down from shoulders. Sew top of sleeves to armholes between markers. Sew side and sleeve seams. Sew one length of ribbon at top inside edge of back and front ribbed shoulder edge. Tie as in photo.

Machine or Handknit Sweater

MACHINE KNITTED INSTRUCTIONS

Note: If you are using a fine tension knitting machine, you can adjust the tension by casting on sts on every alt needle.

BACK

Cast on 80(84-88-92) sts. Work in st st until 132(136-142-146) rows OR 63.5(66-68.5-71) cms [25(26-27-28) ins] have been worked from beg.

Shape Neck

Cast off centre 14(16-16-18) sts, place remaining left-hand sts on hold. Working right hand side only, shape neck by casting off 3 sts from neck edge twice, 2 sts once. Cast off remaining 25(26-28-29) sts for right shoulder.

Work across first 8 sts of left shoulder (neck edge) and leave remaining sts on hold. Shape neck by casting off 3 sts from neck edge twice, 2 sts once. Working on 25(26-28-29) sts for left shoulder, transfer every alt st to back bed of machine and work in 1 x 1 rib for 6 rows. Cast off.

Note: If using single bed machine, transfer sts to knitting needles and work as for left shoulder in handknit instructions.

FRONT

Cast on and work in st st as given for Back until 116(120-126-130) rows OR 56(58.5-61-63.5) cms [22(23-24-25) ins] have been worked from beg.

Shape Neck

Cast off centre 6(8-8-10) sts, place remaining left-hand sts on hold.

Working right-hand side only, shape neck by decreasing 1 st at neck edge every row 12 times. 25(26-28-29) sts. Work in st st until 132(136-142-146) rows OR 63.5(66-68.5-71) cms [25(26-27-28) ins] have been worked from beg. Work in 1 x 1 rib for 6 rows as for Back. Cast off.

Work left hand sts to correspond, reversing neck shaping and working last 6 rows in st st instead of 1 x 1 rib.

SLEEVES

Work as given for Sleeves in Handknit Instructions.

FINISHING

Work as for Finishing in Handknit Instructions, omitting shoulder ribbing and working neckband on machine if required.

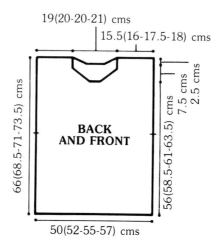

19(20-20-21) cms
15.5(16-17.5-18) cms
66(68.5-71-73.5) cms
7.5 cms
2.5 cms
56(58.5-61-63.5) cms

BACK AND FRONT

50(52-55-57) cms

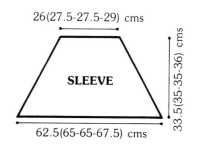

26(27.5-27.5-29) cms
33.5(35-35-36) cms

SLEEVE

62.5(65-65-67.5) cms

Aran-Style Sweater

MEASUREMENTS

To fit bust sizes 81/86(91/96) cms [32/34(36/38) ins]. Finished bust measurement at underarm 107(114) cms [42(45) ins]. Length 67 cms [26½ ins]. Sleeve width at upper arm 69 cms [27¼ ins].

MATERIALS

Patons Diana 17(18) 50g balls. Pair needles each size 4½mm (No 7) and 5½mm (No 5). Circular needles size 4½mm (No 7) and 5½mm (No 5), 40 cms [16 ins] long. Cable needle.

TENSION

17 sts and 22 rows = 10 cms [4 ins] over reverse st st (1 row purl, 1 row knit) using 5½mm needles.

Centre cable pattern of 68 sts measures approx 38 cms [15 ins] using size 5½mm needles.

FAN CABLES (multiple of 30 sts plus 8 extra)

1st row (wrong side): K3, *k5, p7, k8, p7, k3; rep from *, ending k5.

2nd row: P5, *in next st work [k1, p1, k1, p1, k1], pass 4th, 3rd, 2nd and first sts separately over last st made — called make bobble (MB), p2, slip next 4 sts to cable needle and hold at back of work, k3, k4 sts from cable needle (cable made over 7 sts — C7), p2, MB, p5, C7, p5; rep from *, ending p3.

3rd row: As 1st row.

4th row: P5, *p3, k7, p6, k3tog, yo, k1, yo, k2tog, [yo, k1] twice, yo, k3tog tbl, p3; rep from *, ending p3.

5th row: K3, *k3, p11, k6, p7, k3; rep from *, ending k5.

6th row: P5, *p3, k7, p5, [k2tog, yo] 3 times, k1 tbl, [yo, k2tog tbl] 3 times, p2; rep from *, ending p3.

7th row: K3, *k2, p13, k5, p7, k3; rep from *, ending k5.

8th row: P5, *p3, k7, p3, k3tog, [yo, k2tog] twice, yo, k1 tbl, yo, k1, yo, k1 tbl, [yo, k2tog tbl] twice, yo, k3tog tbl; rep from *, ending p3.

9th row: K3, *p17, k3, p7, k3; rep from *, ending k5.

10th row: P5, *p3, C7, p1, MB, p2, [k2tog, yo] 3 times, k1 tbl, k1, k1 tbl, [yo, k2tog tbl] 3 times, p1; rep from *, ending p1, MB, p1.

11th row: K3, *k1, p15, k4, p7, k3; rep from *, ending k5.

12th row: P5, *p3, k7, p2, MB, p2, [k2tog, yo] twice, k1 tbl, k3, k1 tbl, [yo, k2tog tbl] twice, p2; rep from *, ending MB, p2.

13th row: As 7th row.

14th row: P5, *p3, k7, p3, MB, p2, k2tog, yo, k1 tbl, k5, k1 tbl, yo, k2tog tbl, p2, MB; rep from *, ending p3.

15th row: As 5th row.

16th row: P5, *p3, k7, p4, MB, p3, k7, p3, MB, p1; rep from *, ending p3.

17th row: K5, *k3, p7, k8, p7, k5; rep from *, ending k3.

18th row: P3, *p5, C7, p5, MB, p2, C7, p2, MB; rep from *, ending p5.

19th row: As 17th row.

20th row: P3, *p3, k3tog, yo, k1, yo, k2tog, yo, [k1, yo] twice, k3tog tbl, p6, k7, p3; rep from *, ending p5.

21st row: K5, *k3, p7, k6, p11, k3; rep from *, ending k3.

22nd row: P3, *p2, [k2tog, yo] 3 times, k1 tbl, [yo, k2tog tbl] 3 times, p5, k7, p3; rep from *, ending p5.

23rd row: K5, *k3, p7, k5, p13, k2; rep from *, ending k3.

24th row: P3, *k3tog, [yo, k2tog] twice, yo, k1 tbl, yo, k1, yo, k1 tbl, [yo, k2tog tbl] twice, yo, k3tog tbl, p3, k7, p3; rep from *, ending p5.

25th row: K5, *k3, p7, k3, p17; rep from *, ending k3.

26th row: P1, MB, p1, *p1, [k2tog, yo] 3 times, k1 tbl, k1, k1 tbl, [yo, k2tog tbl] 3 times, p2, MB, p1, C7, p3; rep from *, ending p5.

27th row: K5, *k3, p7, k4, p15, k1; rep from *, ending K3.

28th row: P2, MB, *p2, [k2tog, yo] twice, k1 tbl, k3, k1 tbl, [yo, k2tog tbl] twice, p2, MB, p2, k7, p3; rep from *, ending p5.

29th row: As 23rd row.

30th row: P3, *MB, p2, k2tog, yo, k1 tbl, k5, k1 tbl, yo, k2tog tbl, p2, MB, p3, k7, p3; rep from *, ending p5.

31st row: As 21st row.

32nd row: P3, *p1, MB, p3, k7, p3, MB, p4, k7, p3; rep from *, ending p5.

Rep these 32 rows for Fan Cable Pattern.

BOBBLE CLUSTER (over 3 sts)

1st row (wrong side): Knit.

2nd row: MB, p1, MB.

3rd row: Knit.

4th row: P1, MB, p1.

5th row: Knit.

6th row: Purl.

7th row: Knit.

8th row: As 4th row.

Rep these 8 rows for Bobble Cluster.

Aran-Style Sweater

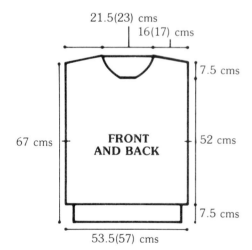

21.5(23) cms

16(17) cms

7.5 cms

67 cms

**FRONT
AND BACK**

52 cms

7.5 cms

53.5(57) cms

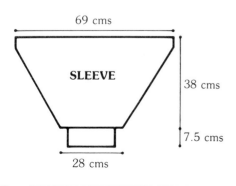

69 cms

SLEEVE

38 cms

7.5 cms

28 cms

BACK

Using smaller needles cast on 89(95) sts. Work in k1, p1 rib for 7.5 cms [3 ins], increasing 1 st at end of last (right side) row. 90(96) sts.

Change to larger needles and commence pattern:

1st row (wrong side): K4(7), place marker, work 1st row of bobble cluster over next 3 sts, place marker, k4, place marker, work 1st row of fan cables over next 68 sts, place marker, k4, place marker, work 1st row of bobble cluster over next 3 sts, place marker, k4(7).

Continue to work patterns as set, slipping markers every row and working reverse st st between cable and bobbles, until back measures 67 cms [26½ ins] from beg.

Shape Shoulder

Cast off 13(14) sts at beg of next 4 rows. Cast off remaining 38(40) sts.

FRONT

Cast on and work as given for Back until front measures 59.5 cms [23½ ins] from beg, ending with a right side row.

Shape Neck

Next row (wrong side): Continuing in patterns, work 40(42) sts, join 2nd ball of yarn and cast off centre 10(12) sts, work to end.

Working both sides at the same time with separate balls of yarn, cast off from each neck edge 3 sts once, 2 sts 5 times, 1 st once. Work straight on remaining 26(28) sts each side until same length as Back to shoulder. Shape shoulder as for Back.

SLEEVES

Using smaller needles cast on 35 sts. Work in

k1, p1 rib for 7.5 cms [3 ins], ending with a wrong side row. Change to larger needles.

Next row (right side): Purl, increasing 13 sts evenly spaced. 48 sts.

Commence pattern:

1st row (wrong side): K5 (reverse st st), work 1st row of fan cables over next 38 sts, k5, (reverse st st).

Continue to work patterns as set, increasing 1 st each end every alt row 36 times (working inc sts into reverse st st), and **at the same time,** when there are 9 sts each side of fan cables work a bobble cluster on each side of fan cables as given for Back.

After all increases have been worked, work straight in patterns on 120 sts until sleeve measures 45.5 cms [18 ins] from beg, or required sleeve length. Cast off.

FINISHING

Press pieces according to instructions on ball band. Sew shoulder seams.

Neckband: With right facing and smaller circular needle, pick up and k96(100) sts around entire neck edge. Join and work in rounds of k1, p1 rib for 2 cms [¾ inch]. Cast off in rib.

Collar: With wrong side facing and smaller circular needle, pick up and k96(100) sts around first round of neckband. Join and work in rounds of k1, p1 rib for 12.5 cms [5 ins].

Change to larger circular needle and work in rib until collar measures 25 cms [10 ins] from beg. Cast off loosely in rib.

Place markers on front and back 34.5 cms [13½ ins] down from shoulder seams. Insert sleeves between markers. Sew side and sleeve seams.

Designed by Susan Prince and Barbara Nudelman
Photographed by Tony McGee

Wide Collar Sweater

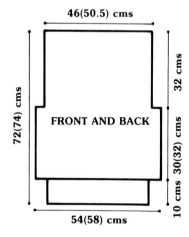

46(50.5) cms

72(74) cms

FRONT AND BACK

32 cms

30(32) cms

10 cms

54(58) cms

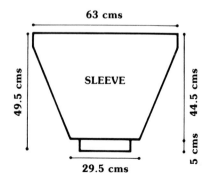

63 cms

49.5 cms

SLEEVE

44.5 cms

5 cms

29.5 cms

MEASUREMENTS

To fit bust sizes 81/86(91/96) cms [32/34(36/38) ins]. Finished bust measurement at underarm 108(116) cms [43(46) ins]. Length 72(74) cms [28½(29) ins]. Sleeve width at upper arm 63 cms [25 ins].

MATERIALS

10(11) 50g balls of Berger du Nord Kid Mohair in colour 7427 light green (M). 2 balls of colour 6109 beige (C). Pair needles each size 3¾mm (No 9) and 4½mm (No 7).

TENSION

19 sts and 26 rows = 10 cms [4 ins] over st st using 4½mm needles.

BACK

Using smaller needles and M cast on 83(91) sts. Work in k1, p1 rib for 10 cms [4 ins], increasing 19 sts evenly spaced across last row. 102(110) sts.

Change to larger needles and work in st st (1 row knit, 1 row purl) until back measures 40(42) cms [16(16½) ins] from beg, or required length to underarm, ending with a wrong side row.

Shape Armhole

Cast off 7 sts at beg of next 2 rows. 88(96) sts. Work straight until armhole measures 32 cms [12½ ins]. Cast off.

FRONT

Work as given for Back.

SLEEVES

Using smaller needles and M cast on 38 sts. Work in k1, p1 rib for 5 cms [2 ins], increasing 18 sts evenly spaced across last row. 56 sts.

Change to larger needles and st st, inc 1 st each end alternately every 2nd and 4th row (therefore 4 sts are increased every 6 rows) until there are 120 sts. Work straight until sleeve measures 49.5 cms [19½ ins] from beg, or required sleeve length. Cast off.

COLLAR (make 2 — 1 in M and 1 in C)

Using larger needles cast on 190(202) sts. Work in k1, p1 rib for 16 cms [6½ ins]. Cast off loosely in rib.

FINISHING

DO NOT PRESS. Sew first and last 2 sts of front and back tog for shoulder seam. Sew top of sleeve to straight edge of armhole, then sew last 10 rows of sleeves to cast-off sts of front and back. Sew side and sleeve seams. Sew together short sides of each collar forming tubes. Place C collar inside M collar and sew tubes together along cast-on edges. With M collar facing, sew both collars to neck edge from right side.

Designed by Stephane Carn
Photographed by Patrick Demarchelier

Patterned Cardigan

MEASUREMENTS

To fit bust sizes 81/86(91/96-101) cms [32/34(36/38-40) ins]. Finished measurement at underarm 102(113.5-124) cms [40¾(44¾-49¼) ins]. Length 57.5(58.5-60) cms [22¾(23-24) ins]. Sleeve width at upper arm 50(53-55.5) cms [20(21-22) ins].

MATERIALS

9(9-10) 20g balls of Berger du Nord Angora 70% in colour 8425 Light Yellow (A). 7(7-8) 50g balls of Berger du Nord Coton Mercerisé in colour 8197 tan (B). Pair needles each size 2¼mm (No 13) and 4mm (No 8). 6 10mm buttons.

TENSION

22 sts and 38 rows = 10 cms [4 ins] over pattern st using size 4mm needles.

PATTERN STITCH (multiple of 6 sts plus 2 extra)

1st row (right side): Using B knit.
2nd row: Using B p1, *sl next 3 sts wyib, yarn to front, p3; rep from * ending p4 instead of p3.
3rd row: Using A knit.
4th row: Using A p4, *sl next 3 sts wyib, yarn to front, p3; rep from * ending p1 instead of p3.
5th row: Using B *k5, insert right-hand needle from front to back into next horizontal B strand 3 rows below and k this strand tog with next A st on left-hand needle; rep from * ending k2.
6th row: Using B as 2nd row.
7th row: Using A k2, *insert right-hand needle into next horizontal A strand 3 rows below and k this strand tog with next B st on left-hand needle, k5; rep from * to end.
Rep 4th to 7th rows for pattern stitch.

BACK

Using smaller needles and A cast on 74(86-98) sts. Work in k1, p1 rib for 7.5 cms [3 ins].
Change to larger needles. Work in pattern st for 10 rows. Continuing in pattern stitch, inc 1 st each end of next row and rep inc every 4th row 17 times more (being sure to work inc sts into pattern st). 110(122-134) sts. Work straight in pattern until piece measures 30.5 cms [12 ins] from beg, ending with a wrong side row.

Shape Raglan Armhole

Cast off 5 sts at beg of next 2 rows. Dec 1 st at each end of every 4th row 16(14-13) times, every alt row 18(24-29) times. Cast off remaining 32(36-40) sts for back of neck.

LEFT FRONT

Using smaller needles and A cast on 37(43-49) sts. Work in k1, p1 rib for 7.5 cms [3 ins]. Change to larger needles.

Commence Pattern St

1st row (right side): Using B knit.

2nd row: Using B rep from * of 2nd pattern row ending p4.
Continue in pattern st as set until 10 rows of pattern have been worked above rib.
Next row (right side): Inc 1 st (underarm edge), work in pattern to end.
Continue to inc 1 st at underarm edge only every 4th row 17 times more. 55(61-67) sts. Work straight in pattern until piece measures same as back to armhole, ending with a wrong side row.

Shape Raglan Armhole

Next row (right side): Cast off 5 sts, work in pattern to end.
Continue to dec 1 st at underarm edge only every 4th row 22(20-19) times, then every alt row 6(12-17) times, and **at the same time** when 80(84-90) rows have been worked above armhole cast off, cast off from neck edge (beg of wrong side rows) 5(6-7) sts once, 3 sts 3 times, 2 sts 2(3-4) times and 1 st 4(3-2) times.

RIGHT FRONT

Work to match Left Front, reversing all shaping.

SLEEVES

Using smaller needles and A cast on 50(56-62) sts. Work in k1, p1 rib for 8 cms [3¼ ins].
Change to larger needles. Work in pattern st, inc 1 st each end every 4th row 20 times, every 6th row 10 times (working inc sts into pattern). 110(116-122) sts. Work straight in pattern st until piece measures 45.5 cms [18 ins] from beg, or required length to underarm.

Shape Raglan Cap

Cast off 5 sts at beg of next 2 rows. Dec 1 st at each end of every alt row 49(51-54) times. Cast off remaining 2(4-4) sts.

FINISHING

DO NOT PRESS. Sew raglan caps to front and back armholes. Sew side and sleeve seams.
(**Note.** Sweater is buttoned as for man's style. If required, reverse bands).
Button Band: With right side facing, smaller needles and A pick up and k123(127-131) sts along straight edge of right front. Work in k1, p1 rib for 2 cms [¾ inch]. Cast off loosely in rib.
Place markers on band for 5 buttons, the first marker 1.5 cms [½ inch] from lower edge, and the last marker 8 cms [3¼ ins] from top edge.
Buttonhole Band: Work as given for Button Band along left front edge, working 5 buttonholes after 2 rows of rib have been worked, opposite markers as follows:
Next row: Rib, casting off 3 sts for each buttonhole.
Next row: Rib, casting on 3 sts over each set of cast off st.
Work straight in rib until band measures same as button band. Cast off loosely in rib.

Neckband: With right side facing, smaller needles and A beg at right front neck edge, pick up and k6 sts along front band, 99(105-113) sts along right front, back and left front neck edges, 6 sts along front band. 111(117-125) sts. Work in k1, p1 rib for 2 rows.
Next row (wrong side): Rib 2 sts, cast off next 3 sts (buttonhole), rib to end.
Next row: Rib, casting on 3 sts over cast off sts.
Work straight in rib until band measures 2 cms [¾ inch]. Cast off loosely in rib.
Sew on buttons.

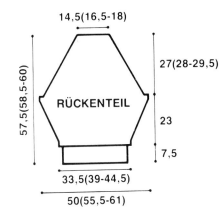

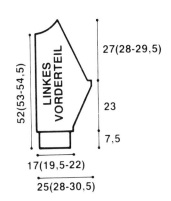

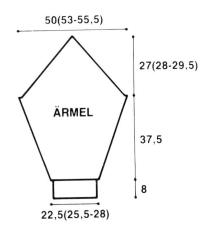

Sweater with Raglan Sleeves

MEASUREMENTS

To fit bust sizes 92/96 cms [36/38 ins]. Length 62 cms [24½ ins]. Sleeve seam 45 cms [17¾ ins].

MATERIALS

5 50g balls Jaeger Mohair Gold (A), 3 50g balls Patons Cotton top (B) and 3 50g balls Jaeger Cotton Flammé (C). Pair needles each size 7mm (No 2) and 8mm (No 0). 7mm (No 2) circular needle, 50 cms [20 ins] long.

TENSION

10 sts and 14 rows = 10 cms [4 ins] over st st using A.

BACK

Using 7mm needles and using 1 strand of B and 1 strand of C together cast on 58 sts.

Continue with double yarn.

1st row: *P2, k2; rep from * to last 2 sts, p2.

2nd row: *K2, p2; rep from * to last 2 sts, k2.

Rep 1st and 2nd rows 9 times more.

Change to 8mm needles and 1 strand of A. Continue in st st. Work 34 rows (24 cms) ending with a purl row. Mark each end of last row to indicate start of armholes.

Shape Raglan Armholes

Dec 1 st at each end of every row until 40 sts remain, then every alt row until 18 sts remain. Work 1 row. Cast off.

FRONT

Work as given for Back.

SLEEVES

Using 7mm needles and 1 strand of B and 1 strand of C together, cast on 26 sts.

Continue with double yarn.

Work 12 rows in rib as given for Back. Change to 8mm needles and 1 strand of A.

Next row: Knit to end increasing 8 sts evenly spaced by picking up loop from between needles and knitting into back of it. 34 sts.

Continue in st st, starting with a purl row. Work 5 rows. Inc 1 st at each end of next row, then every 10th row until there are 44 sts. Work until sleeve measures 45 cms [17¾ ins] from beg, ending with a purl row. Mark each end of last row to indicate start of sleeve top.

Shape Top

Dec 1 st at each end of every row until 34 sts remain, then every alt row until 22 sts remain, then every 4th row until 14 sts remain. Work 2 rows. Cast off.

MAKING UP

Press pieces according to instructions on ball band. Join raglan seams. Join side and sleeve seams.

Collar: Using circular needle and 1 strand of B and C together, knit up 72 sts evenly round neck edge and work 22 cms [8¾ ins] in rounds of st st (every round knit). Cast off.

Using 1 strand of B and C together make twisted cords and thread along raglan seams as shown. Now make a twisted cord 40 cms [16 ins] long and thread through knitting on front in a cross shape as shown. Knot ends.

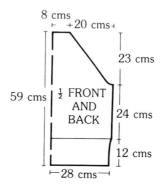

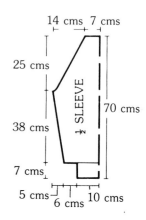

Roll Neck Sweater

MEASUREMENTS

To fit bust 88/92 cms [34/36 ins]. Length (approximately) 58 cms [22¾ ins]. Sleeve seam 48 cms [19 ins].

MATERIALS

8 50g balls Patons Cotton Top (B) and 2 50g balls Jaeger Cotton Flammé (C). Pair needles each size 3¼mm (No 10) and 4mm (No 8).

TENSION

16 sts and 26 rows = 10 cms [4 ins] over reverse st st using 4mm needles.

NOTE

When changing from B to C twist yarns together on wrong side of work to avoid holes.

FRONT

Using 3¼mm needles and B cast on 78 sts.

1st row: *P2, k2; rep from * to last 2 sts, p2.

2nd row: *K2, p2; rep from * to last 2 sts, k2.

Rep 1st and 2nd rows for 8 cms [3¼ ins] ending with a 2nd row and increasing 4 sts evenly spaced in last row. 82 sts.

Change to 4mm needles and continue in pattern:

1st row: Using B p5, [k8, p8] twice, using C k8, using B p8, k8, p8, using C k8, using B p5.

2nd row: Working in same colours as previous row, k5, p8, *k8, p8; rep from * to last 5 sts, k5 ★.

Rep 1st and 2nd rows 21 times more.

Next row: Using B p5, k8, *p8, k8; rep from * to last 5 sts, p5.

Next row: Using B k5, p8, *k8, p8; rep from * to last 5 sts, k5.

Rep last 2 rows 18 times more. Continue as follows:

1st row: Using B p5, k8, p8, using C k40, using B p8, k8, p5.

2nd row: Using B k5, p8, k8, using C p40, using B k8, p8, k5.

3rd and 4th rows: As 1st and 2nd rows.

5th row: Using B p5, using C k8, using B p8, k40, p8, k8, p5.

6th row: Using B k5, p8, k56, using C p8, using B k5.

7th and 8th rows: As 5th and 6th rows.

Rep 1st to 8th rows 4 times more, then 1st to 7th rows again.

Next row: Cast off 21 sts, k40 including st on needle and leave on a holder, cast off remaining sts.

BACK

Work as given for Front to ★. Rep last 2 rows until back measures same as front to shoulder ending with a right side row.

Next row: Cast off 21 sts, pattern 40 sts including st on needle and leave on a holder, cast off remaining sts.

SLEEVES

Using 3¼mm needles and B cast on 46 sts and work 6 cms [2½ ins] in rib as given for Front increasing 6 sts evenly spaced in last row. 52 sts.

Change to 4mm needles and reverse st st (purl 1 row, knit 1 row alternately) and work 4 rows. Inc 1 st at each end of next row, then every 6th row until there are 82 sts, then every 4th row until there are 90 sts. Work until sleeve measures 48 cms [19 ins] from beg. Cast off loosely.

MAKING UP

Press pieces according to instructions on ball band. Join right shoulder seam.

Collar: Slip the 80 sts from holder onto a 4mm needle. Work in stripes of 4 rows in C in st st and 4 rows in B in garter st for approximately 10 cms [4 ins]. Cast off.

Join left shoulder seam. Fold collar in half to wrong side and slip stitch. Place a marker 27 cms [10¾ ins] on each side of shoulder seams to mark depth of armholes. Join cast off edge of sleeves to armhole edges. Join side and sleeve seams.

1 = Colour B, st st
2 = Colour B, reverse st st
3 = Colour C, st st
4 = Colour C, stripe pattern

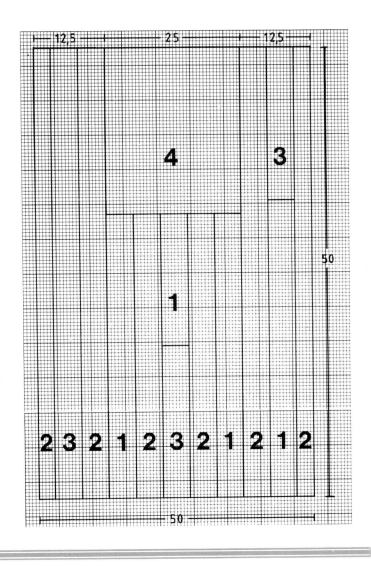

Waistcoat with Asymmetrical Fastening

MEASUREMENTS

To fit bust 88/92 cms [34/36 ins]. Length 52 cms [20½ ins].

MATERIALS

3 50g balls Jaeger Mohair Gold (A), oddments of Patons Cotton Top (B) and Jaeger Cotton Flammé (C). 30 cms [12 ins] of feather ribbon. Pair needles size 8mm (No 0). Crochet hook. 2 buttons.

TENSION

10 sts and 15 rows = 10 cms [4 ins] over st st using 8mm needles.

BACK

Using 8mm needles and A cast on 54 sts. Work in st st, starting with a purl row, until back measures 49 cms [19¼ ins] from beg, ending with a purl row.

Shape Back of Neck

Next row: K18, cast off 18 sts, knit to end.

Continue on last set of sts. Dec 1 st at neck edge on next 2 rows. Work 1 row. Cast off remaining sts.

Rejoin yarn to remaining sts at neck edge and complete to match other side.

LEFT FRONT

Using 8mm needles and A cast on 34 sts. Work in st st, starting with a purl row. Work 3 rows.

Shape Front Slope

Dec 1 st at end of next row, then every 4th row until 16 sts remain, at the same time when front measures 33 cms [13 ins] from beg, work over

the centre 12 sts on right side of work using A and Feather ribbon together.

When work measures 38 cms [15 ins] work over centre 8 sts in same way. Work until front measures same as back. Cast off.

RIGHT FRONT

Using 8mm needles and A cast on 4 sts.

1st row: Knit.

2nd row: Cast on 8 sts, purl to end.

3rd row: K2tog, knit to end.

Rep 2nd and 3rd rows 3 times more.

10th row: Purl.

11th row (buttonhole): K2tog, k2, yf, k2tog, knit to end.

12th row: Purl.

Now dec 1 st at centre front edge on next row and following alt rows until 31 sts remain. Work 3 rows.

Next row: K2tog, k2, yf, k2tog, knit to end. Now continue to dec at centre front edge on every 4th row until 16 sts remain. Work until front measures same as back. Cast off.

MAKING UP

Press pieces according to instructions on ball band. Join shoulder seams. Join side seams leaving 27 cms [10¾ ins] open for armholes.

Using crochet hook and A work 1 row of firm double crochet along centre front edges. Fasten off.

Twist 2 strands each of B and C into cords and use these for oversewing along all edges.

Sew on buttons.

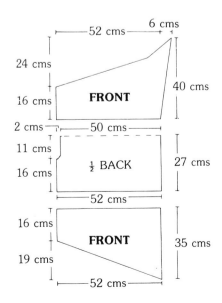

2-Colour Mohair Sweater

MEASUREMENTS

To fit bust sizes 86/92 cms [34/36 ins]. Length (approximately) 56 cms [22¼ ins].

MATERIALS

Jaeger Mohair Gold 3 50g balls each in Colours A and B. Pair needles each size 6mm (No 4) and 8mm (No 0). Circular needles each size 6mm (No 4) and 8mm (No 0), 50 cms [20 ins] long.

TENSION

10 sts and 15 rows = 10 cms [4 ins] over st st using 8mm needles.

NOTE

Garment is worked in one piece, starting at front. Use a separate ball of yarn for each part, and ensure that yarns are twisted together on wrong side when changing colour to avoid holes.

Using 6mm needles and A cast on 42 sts and work 8 cms [3¼ ins] in k1, p1 rib.

Next row: Rib to end increasing in 3rd then every 5th st. 50 sts.

Change to 8mm needles and continue in st st, working in colour pattern from chart.

1st row: Knit 10B, 38A, 2B.

Work until the 30th row has been completed.

Inc 1 st at each end of next row, then every alt row until there are 60 sts.

Commence Sleeves

Next row: Cast on 31 sts, k29A, 17B, 17A, 28B, now with a separate strand of B cast on 31 sts and knit these sts onto end of last row.

Work until the 66th row has been completed.

Shape Neck

Next row: K57, cast off 8 sts, knit to end.

Continue on last set of sts leaving remainder on a spare needle. Work 1 row. Cast off 3 sts at beg of next and following alt row. Work 1 row. Break yarn and leave sts on a spare needle.

With wrong side facing rejoin yarn to remaining sts at neck edge. Cast off 3 sts at beg of next and following alt row. Work 2 rows.

Continue for back:

1st row: Knit 44A, 2B, 2A, 3B, using B cast on 20 sts, knit to end.

2nd row: Purl 74B, 2A, 2B, 44A.

3rd row: Knit 43A, 3B, 3A, 73B.

Work 1 more st in A and B in centre and 1 st less at each side until there are 17 sts in A and B in centre, ending with a purl row. Continue colour pattern to match front.

Next row: Cast off 31 sts, knit to last 31 sts, cast off these sts.

Break yarn. Turn and rejoin yarn to remaining sts. Work 1 row. Dec 1 st at each end of next row, then every alt row until 50 sts remain. Work 29 rows.

Change to 6mm needles and continue with A.

Next row: K1, p1, *k2tog, [p1, k1] twice, p2tog, [k1, p1] twice; rep from * to end. 42 sts.

Work 8 cms [3¼ ins] in k1, p1 rib. Cast off in rib.

Left Cuff

Using 6mm needles and A knit up 26 sts evenly along sleeve edge. Work 10 cms [4 ins] in k1, p1 rib. Cast off in rib.

Work Right Cuff the same **but** using B.

Neckband

Using 6mm circular needle and B knit up 58 sts round neck edge. Work 10 rounds in k1, p1 rib. Cast off in rib.

Collar

Using 8mm circular needle and B cast on 44 sts. Work 16 cms [6¼ ins] in rounds of k1, p1 rib. Cast off in rib.

MAKING UP

Press according to instructions on ball band. Fold neckband in half to wrong side and slip stitch to picked up edge. Sew cast on edge of collar to neck edge inside border. Join side and undersleeve seams. Press seams.

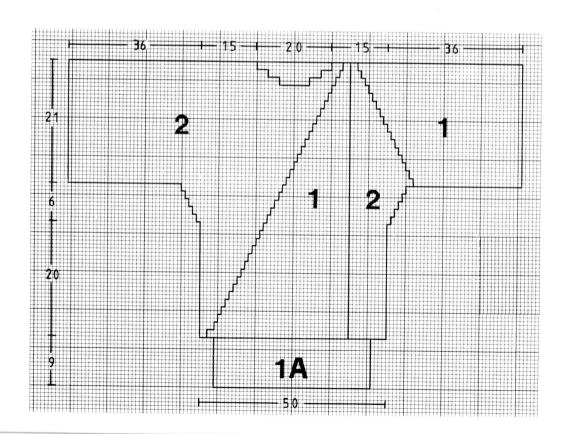

1A = Colour A, st st
1A = Colour A, rib
2A = Colour B, st st
Note: Figures at side of chart refer to cms.

Holiday Classics

19 Classic Styles for all Seasons

Square Neck Top

MEASUREMENTS

To fit bust sizes 80(85-90/95-100-105) cms [32(34-36/38-40-42) ins]. Finished measurement 91(97-103-109-115) cms [36½(39-41-43½-46) ins]. Length to shoulder 56(57-59-60-61) cms [22(22½-23¼-23½-24) ins].

MATERIALS

Patons Promise Double Knitting 4(4-5-5-6) 40g balls. Pair needles each size 4mm (No 8) and 3¼mm (No 10).

TENSION

20 sts and 30 rows = 10 cms [4 ins] square measured over pattern using larger needles.

BACK

Using smaller needles cast on 91(97-103-109-115) sts.

1st row (right side): K1, *p1, k1; rep from * to end.

2nd row: P1, *k1, p1; rep from * to end.

Rep the last 2 rows until rib measures 7 cms [2¾ ins] ending with a wrong side row.

Change to larger needles and commence pattern:

1st row: K1, *yf, sl 1, k1, psso, k1, k2tog, yf, k1; rep from * to end.

2nd row: Purl.

3rd row: K2, *yf, sl 1, k2tog, psso, yf, k3; rep from * to last 5 sts, yf, sl 1, k2tog, psso, yf, k2.

4th row: Purl.

These 4 rows form the pattern. Continue in pattern until back measures approximately 37 cms [14½ ins] or required length to sleeves ending with a 4th row of pattern.

Shape Sleeves

1st row: Cast on 9 sts, k3, work 1st row of pattern to end.

2nd row: Cast on 9 sts, k3, purl to last 3 sts, k3. 109(115-121-127-133) sts.

3rd row: K3, work 3rd row of pattern to last 3 sts, k3 ★.

Keeping the 3 sts at each end in garter st (every row knit) and remainder in pattern as set, work straight until sleeves measure 19(20-22-23-24) cms [7½-8-8¾-9-9½) ins] ending with a wrong side row.

Shape Shoulders

Cast off 33(36-39-42-45) sts **loosely** at beg of next 2 rows.

Work 5 rows in garter st on remaining 43 sts. Cast off knitwise.

FRONT

Work as given for Back to ★.

Keeping the 3 sts at each end in garter st and remainder in pattern as set, work straight until sleeves measure approximately 9(9-11-11-12) cms [3½(3½-4¼-4¼-4¾) ins] ending with a 4th row of pattern.

Shape Neck

1st(3rd-5th) sizes only

1st row: K4, *[yf, sl 1, k1, psso, k1, k2tog, yf, k1] 4(5-6) times, yf, sl 1, k1, psso, k1, k2tog, yf*, k43, rep from * to * once more, k4.

2nd row: K3, p30(36-42), k43, p30(36-42), k3.

2nd(4th) sizes only

1st row: K4, *[yf, sl 1, k1, psso, k1, k2tog, yf, k1] 5(6) times*, yf, sl 1, k1, psso, k43, k2tog, yf, k1, rep from * to * once more, k3.

2nd row: K3, p33(39), k43, p33(39), k3.

All sizes

3rd row: K5, *[yf, sl 1, k2tog, psso, yf, k3] 4(4-5-5-6) times, yf, sl 1, k2tog, psso, yf*, k45(51-45-51-45), rep from * to * once more, k5.

4th row: As 2nd row.

5th row: As 1st row.

6th row: Work 36(39-42-45-48) sts in pattern, cast off next 37 sts knitwise, work to end.

Work on these 36(39-42-45-48) sts first. Keeping the 3 sts at each end in garter st and remainder in pattern as set, work straight until front measures same as back to shoulder ending with a wrong side row. Cast off **loosely**.

With right side of work facing rejoin yarn to neck edge of remaining sts and work to end. 36(39-42-45-48) sts. Keeping the 3 sts at each end in garter st and remainder in pattern as set, work straight until front measures same as back to shoulder ending with a right side row. Cast off **loosely**.

TO FINISH

Press pieces according to instructions on ball band. Join shoulder, side and sleeve seams.

V-Back Crochet Sweater

MEASUREMENTS

To fit bust sizes 76/81(86/91-91/96) cms [30/32(34/36-36/38) ins]. Width from cuff to cuff 121(126-128) cms [49(51-52) ins]. Length 65(66-66) cms [26(26½-26½) ins]. Sleeve width at upper arm 90 cms [36 ins].

MATERIALS

15(16-17) 50g balls of Georges Picaud/Merino Zig in colour 37 light sea green (M), 1 ball of colour 1 white (C). Crochet hook size 4.00mm. 4 25mm [1 inch] buttons.

TENSION

20 sts and 32 rows = 10 cms [4 ins] over pattern st using 4.00mm hook.

NOTE

Top is worked in one piece from cuff to cuff.

PATTERN ST (any no. of ch)

1st row: 1 dc in 2nd ch from hook, *1 dc in next ch; rep from * to end, turn.

2nd row: 1 ch, working into back loop only of top of each dc, work 1 dc in each dc to end, turn.

Rep 2nd row for pattern.

BODY

Right Sleeve

Using M make 41 ch for cuff edge of sleeve.

1st row: Work 1st row of pattern st. 40 dc.

2nd row: Work 2nd row of pattern st.

3rd row: 1 ch, working in pattern work 2 dc in first dc and 2 dc in last dc (2 increases made), turn. 42 dc.

Continue in pattern increasing 1 st at each end of every 4th row 16 times more. 74 dc. Now keeping to pattern, inc 1 st at each end of every alt row 15 times then at each end of every row 38 times. 180 dc. Sleeve measures approx 42 cms [17 ins] from beg.

Front and Back

Inc for front and back as foll:

Next row: 41(43-43) ch, 1 dc in 2nd ch from hook, 1 dc into each of next 39(41-41) ch, work in pattern across 180 dc, then with a separate length of yarn make 40(42-42) ch, then continue row across these ch working 1 dc into each ch, turn. 260(264-264) dc.

Work straight in pattern for 16(24-28) rows.

Shape Back Neck

Next row: Work in pattern across first 128(130-130) dc, leave remaining dc unworked (for front), turn.

Next row: (Mark this side of work as right side) Sl st into each of first 2 dc, work in pattern across remaining dc, turn.

Next row: Work in pattern to last 2 dc, leave last 2 dc unworked, turn.

Rep last 2 rows (decreasing 2 sts at neck edge on every row) until 40(42-42) dc remain. Fasten off.

Work left side of back as follows:

With M make 41(43-43) ch.

1st row: Work as for 1st row of pattern st. 40(42-42) dc.

2nd row (right side): 3 ch, 1 dc in 2nd ch from hook, 1 dc in next ch, work in pattern across dc, turn.

3rd row: 1 ch, work in pattern to last 2 sts, 2 dc in each of next 2 dc, turn. 44(46-46) dc.

Rep last 2 rows until there are 130(132-132) dc, thus ending with a right side row. Set aside left side of back until front is complete.

Front

With wrong side facing miss 3 sts at neck edge and work in pattern across remaining 129(131-131) dc, turn.

Next row (right side): Work in pattern to end, turn.

Next row: 1 ch, miss first dc, work in pattern across remaining 128(130-130) dc, turn.

Rep last 2 rows until 115(117-117) dc remain thus ending with a wrong side row.

Work 30 rows straight in pattern, thus ending with a wrong side row.

Next row (right side): Work in pattern to last dc, 2 dc in last dc, turn.

Next row: Work in pattern to end, turn.

Rep last 2 rows until there are 130(132-132) dc, thus ending with a right side row.

Left Sleeve

Join front and back as follows:

With wrong side of left back facing, work in pattern across all 130(132-132) dc, then with wrong side of front facing continue in pattern across 130(132-132) dc of front, turn. 260(264-264) dc.

Work straight in pattern for 16(24-28) rows. Now commence shaping for left sleeve.

Next row: 1 ch, sl st in first 40(42-42) dc, 1 ch, and work pattern in next 180 dc, leave remaining 40(42-42) dc unworked, turn.

Dec 1 st at each end of every row 38 times, at each end of every alt row 15 times, then at each end of every 4th row 17 times. 40 dc. Work 1 row straight. Fasten off.

BACK INSERT

Using C make 23 ch.

1st row: 1 dc in 2nd ch from hook, *1 dc in next ch; rep from * to end, turn. 22 dc.

2nd row: 1 Ch, 1 dc in each dc to end (working through both loops of top of st), turn.

3rd row: 1 ch, 2 dc in first dc, 1 dc in each dc to last dc, 2 dc in last dc, turn.

Continue to inc 1 st at each end of every 3rd row 8 times more, working in stripe pattern of 4 rows C, 4 rows M alternately, until 28 rows have been worked from beg (4 C stripes and 3 M stripes). 40 dc. Fasten off.

FINISHING

Press according to instructions on ball band. Sew side and sleeve seams. Work reversed dc evenly along back and neck edges, working tightly along front neck. Overlap backs and sew together. Sew on 4 buttons evenly spaced down lower back. Pin striped insert to backs so that it will cover bra strap and hold backs together. Sew insert in place.

Striped Batwing Sweater

MEASUREMENTS

To fit bust sizes 81/96 cms [32/38 ins]. Finished measurement at underarm 100 cms [40 ins]. Length 55.5 cms [22 ins].

MATERIALS

Copley Chorus 4 Ply 100g balls: 4 balls Main colour (M), 2 balls Contrast colour (C). Circular knitting needle size 3¾mm (No 9), 80 cms [29 ins] long. Pair needles size 2¾mm (No 12). Set of 4 double pointed needles size 2¾mm (No 12).

TENSION

25 sts and 33 rows = 10 cms [4 ins] over st st using size 3¾mm needles.

NOTES

Pullover is made in 2 pieces in M only with all stripes and ribbed edgings worked later.

Yarn markers are placed throughout work as a guideline for placement of applied stripes.

BACK

Using circular needle, M and starting at lower edge above band, cast on 113 sts.

Working back and forth in rows, work in st st increasing 1 st at each end of every 8th row 6 times. 125 sts.

Work straight until back measures 15 cms [6 ins] from beg.

Shape Dolman Sleeve

Inc 1 st at each end of every alt row 10 times, place yarn markers at each end of last row. Inc 1 st at each end of every row 21 times. 187 sts.

Cast on 7 sts at beg of next 4 rows, place yarn markers at each end of last row, cast on 7 sts at beg of next 14 rows. 313 sts.

Work straight on all these sts (for sleeve cuff) for 7 cms [2¾ ins], taking measurement from last cast on. Place yarn markers at each end of last row.

Work straight for 7 cms [2¾ ins] more from last yarn markers ending with a wrong side row.

Shape Shoulder and Neck

To begin shaping top of sleeve cast off 11 sts at beg of next 18 rows. 115 sts.

Continue top of sleeve shaping and begin neck shaping as follows:

Next row (right side): Cast off 8 sts, knit until there are 31 sts on right hand needle, join a 2nd ball of yarn and cast off centre 37 sts, knit to end.

Continuing to work each side with separate balls of yarn, cast off 8 sts at beg of next row and cast off 3 sts at each neck edge twice, 4 sts at each neck edge once, and **at the same time** as shaping neck, continue to shape shoulders on sleeve by casting off 7 sts 3 times at each shoulder edge.

FRONT

Work as given for Back including dolman sleeve shaping placement of markers until sleeve edge measures 14 cms [5½ ins], ending with a wrong side row. 313 sts.

Shape Neck and Shoulder

To begin shaping top of sleeve cast off 11 sts at beg of next 4 rows. Front should measure approximately 48 cms [19 ins] from beg measured at centre.

Continue top of sleeve shaping and begin neck shaping as follows:

Next row: Cast off 11 sts, knit until there are 107 sts on right-hand needle, join 2nd ball of yarn and cast off centre 33 sts, knit to end.

Working both sides at same time with separate balls of yarn, cast off 11 sts at shoulder edge on next row and cast off 4 sts at each neck edge once, cast off 3 sts at each neck edge once, dec 1 st at each neck edge on every alt row 5 times, and **at the same time** as shaping neck, continue to shape shoulders on sleeve (as for back) by casting off 11 sts at each shoulder (sleeve) edge 6 times more (a total of nine 11 st cast offs at each shoulder edge), then cast off 8 sts at each shoulder edge once, cast off 7 sts 3 times.

APPLIED STRIPES

Work applied stripes for back as follows:

Stripe A (Make 4): 53 cms [21 ins] long.

Using larger needles and C cast on 128 sts leaving a long end for sewing. Work in short rows as follows:

1st row (wrong side): Knit.

2nd row: Knit to last 16 sts, leave these sts unworked, turn.

3rd row: Sl 1, knit to end.

4th row: Knit to last 32 sts, leave these sts unworked, turn.

5th row: As 3rd row.

6th row: Knit to last 48 sts, leave these sts unworked, turn.

7th row: As 3rd row.

8th row: Knit to last 64 sts, leave these sts unworked, turn.

9th row: As 3rd row.

10th row: Knit all sts closing holes made by short rows as follows:

Insert tip of left-hand needle from front to back into centre of st 2 rows below last st on right-hand needle, sl st onto left hand needle and k2 sts tog. Cast off leaving a long end for sewing.

Stripe B (Make 2): 38 cms [15 ins] long. Using larger needles and C cast on 92 sts. Work as given for Stripe A.

Stripe C (Make 2): 48 cms [19 ins] long. Using larger needles and C cast on 116 sts. Work as given for Stripe A.

Stripe D (Make 2): 53 cms [21 ins] long. Using larger needles and C cast on 128 sts. Work as given for Stripe A.

Work applied stripes for front as follows:

Stripe A (Make 4): 48 cms [19 ins] long. Using larger needles and C cast on 116 sts. Work as given for Stripe A of Back.

Stripe B (Make 2): 33 cms [13 ins] long. Using larger needles and C cast on 80 sts. Work as given for Stripe A.

Stripe C (Make 2): 35.5 cms [14 ins] long. Using larger needles and C cast on 86 sts. Work as given for Stripe A.

Stripe D (Make 2): 53 cms [21 ins] long. Using larger needles and C cast on 128 sts. Work as given for Stripe A.

FINISHING

Press pieces according to instructions on ball band. Lay back piece flat and pin to measurements. Place yarn markers at lower edge at each side seam and at 15 cm [6 inch] and 30 cm [12 inch] intervals. Place 10 yarn markers around neck edge at 2.5 cm [1 inch] intervals. Using contrast yarn baste stripes from markers at outside edge of pullover to corresponding markers at neck. With 2 C ends at lower edge, sew stripes in place. Placing markers at intervals of 3 cms [1¼ ins] around front neck edge, baste and sew on stripes to front as for back. If required, reinforce stripes with thread. Sew sleeve seams at top (shoulder) edge.

With smaller needles and M pick up and k112 sts evenly across lower back edge, working through both thicknesses at stripes. Work in k2, p2 rib for 10 cms [4 ins]. Cast off in rib.

Work front lower bands as for back lower bands.

Using smaller needles and M pick up and k68 sts evenly across cuff edge of sleeves, working through both thicknesses at stripes. Work in k2, p2 rib for 12.5 cms [5 ins]. Cast off in rib.

Using set of double pointed needles and M, pick up and k156 sts around neck edge as follows: 1 st in each C stripe, 5 sts between each stripe at back neck, 7 sts between each stripe at front neck and 14 sts between stripes at each shoulder. Join and work in rounds. Purl 1 round, knit 1 round. Work in k2, p2 rib for 11 rounds. Knit 1 round, purl 1 round. Cast off knitwise tightly. Sew sleeve and side seams.

Lacy Sweater

MEASUREMENTS

To fit bust sizes 81/86(91-96) cms [32/34(36-38) ins]. Finished measurement at underarm 94(102-110) cms [38(41-44) ins]. Length 53.5(56.5-59.5) cms [21(22¼-23½) ins]. Sleeve width at upper arm 40(44-47) cms [16(17½-19) ins].

MATERIALS

Patons Cotton Perlé 10(11-12) 50g balls. Pair needles each size 3¾mm (No 9) and 4mm (No 8). 3 buttons.

TENSION

22 sts and 28 rows = 10 cms [4 ins] over pattern st using 2 strands of yarn and size 4mm needles.

NOTE

Use 2 strands of yarn held tog throughout.

PATTERN STITCH (multiple of 8 sts)

1st and all wrong side rows: Purl.

2nd row: Knit.

4th row: K3, *yo, ssk, k6; rep from * ending k3 instead of k6.

6th row: K1, *k2tog, yo, k1, yo, ssk, k3; rep from * ending k2 instead of k3.

8th row: As 4th row.

10th row: Knit.

12th row: K7; rep from * of 4th row, ending k1.

14th row: K5; rep from * of 6th row, ending k3.

16th row: As 12th row.

Rep these 16 rows for pattern st.

BACK

Using smaller needles cast on 104(112-120) sts and work in k1, p1 rib for 5 cms [2 ins]. Change to larger needles.

Work in pattern st until piece measures 53.5(56.5-59.5) cms [21(22¼-23½) ins] from beg, or required length to shoulder.

Shape Shoulders

Continuing in st st only (1 row k, 1 row p), cast off 10(11-12) sts at beg of next 4 rows, 11(12-13) sts at beg of next 2 rows. Cast off remaining 42(44-46) sts for back of neck.

FRONT

Work as given for Back until piece measures 33.5(36.5-39.5) cms [13(14¼-15½) ins] from beg, ending with a right side row.

Next row (wrong side): P49(53-57) sts, place centre 6 sts on holder for beg of placket opening, join 2nd ball of yarn, p to end.

Working both sides at same time with separate balls of yarn, work straight in pattern st until placket measures 15 cms [6 ins].

Shape Neck

Cast off from each neck edge 8(9-10) sts once, 3 sts twice, 2 sts twice. 31(34-37) sts each side.

Work straight in pattern until same length as back to shoulder.

Shape Shoulders

Cast off from each armhole edge 10(11-12) sts twice, 11(12-13) sts once.

SLEEVES

Using smaller needles cast on 38(40-44) sts and work in k1, p1 rib for 5 cms [2 ins].

Change to larger needles and k next row on right side increasing 10(16-20) sts evenly across row. 48(56-64) sts. **(Note:** When working inc sts into pattern st, only work an eyelet pattern when there are sufficient sts each end of row so that eyelet does not fall on first and 2nd sts from ends).

Working in pattern st, inc 1 st each end alternately every 4th and 6th row (therefore 4 sts are inc every 10 rows) until there are 88(96-104) sts. Work straight in pattern until piece measures 44.5 cms [17½ ins] from beg, or required sleeve length. Cast off.

MAKING UP

Press pieces according to instructions on ball band.

Right Front Placket

Using smaller needles knit across 6 sts on holder, increasing 2 sts evenly across row. Work in k1, p1 rib on 8 sts for 4 cms [1½ ins].

1st buttonhole row: Rib 3 sts, cast off next 2 sts, rib to end.

2nd buttonhole row: Rib casting on 2 sts over cast-off sts.

Work until band measures 15 cms [6 ins], making 2 more buttonholes at 15 cm [2 inch] intervals. Slip sts onto a holder.

Left Front Placket

Using smaller needles cast on 8 sts and work in k1, p1 rib for 15 cms [6 ins]. Slip sts onto a holder.

Collar

Sew shoulder seams.

With right side facing, smaller needles and starting at right front placket, rib across 8 sts on holder, pick up and k89(93-97) sts around entire neck edge, rib across 8 sts of left front placket. 105(109-113) sts. Work in k1, pl rib for 6.5 cms [2½ ins].

Change to larger needles and rib until piece measures 8 cms [3¼ ins] from beg. Cast off sts in rib.

Place markers on front and back 20(22-23.5) cms [8(8¾-9½) ins] down from shoulder seam for armhole.

Sew top of sleeve to front and back between markers. Sew side and sleeve seams. Sew inside edges of placket to fronts. Sew lower edge of left front placket under right front placket. Sew on buttons.

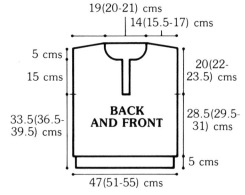

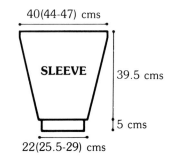

Sleeveless Top

MEASUREMENTS

To fit bust sizes 81(86-91-96) cms [32(34-36-38) ins]. Finished measurement at underarm 81(85-89-95) cms [32(34-36-38) ins]. Length 52(54-54.5-56) cms [20¾(21¼-21½-22) ins].

MATERIALS

Jaeger Monte Cristo 9 50g balls. Pair needles each size 2¼mm (No 13) and 4mm (No 8).

TENSION

20 sts and 28 rows = 10 cms [4 ins] over st st using size 4mm needles.

FRONT

Using smaller needles cast on 81(85-89-95) sts and work in k1, p1 rib for 6 cms [2¼ ins]. Change to larger needles.

Work in st st (1 row k, 1 row p) until piece measures 28 cms [11 ins] from beg, or required length to underarm, ending with a wrong side row.

Shape Armholes

Cast off 3(3-4-5) sts at beg of next 2 rows. Dec 1 st at each end of every alt row 6(8-9-11) times. 63 sts.

Note 1: All rows of chart are written for right side rows only. Purl all wrong side rows. **Note 2:** Work armhole decreases in st st only and not in chart pattern.

Commence Chart Pattern

1st row (right side): K2tog (armhole dec), k27, k2tog, yo, k1, yo, sl 1, k1, psso (skp), k27, k2tog (armhole dec). 61 sts.

Continue in this way to follow chart for front, decreasing 1 st each end of every alt row as before for armholes, until 28 rows have been worked in pattern.

All armhole decreases have been worked and there are 35 sts on needle.

Continue to follow chart only and on 37th row cast off centre 11 sts for neck and working both sides at same time with separate balls of yarn follow chart to 53rd row.

Place remaining 15 sts each side on holders for shoulders.

BACK

Work as given for Front to armholes.

Shape Armholes

Cast off 2(3-3-4) sts at beg of next 2 rows. Dec 1 st each end alternately every 2nd and 4th row (therefore 4 sts are dec every 6 rows) until there are 69(69-71-73) sts. Mark centre 5 sts of row.

Continue armhole decreases as before, working 1st row of chart pattern for back over centre 5 sts and remaining sts in st st and continue in chart pattern over centre sts until st st area joins lace pattern (all armhole decreases have been worked). Continue to follow chart only and on 47th row cast off centre 13 sts and working both

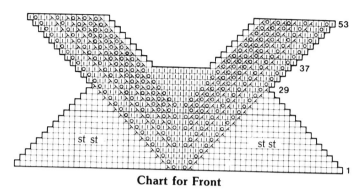

Chart for Front

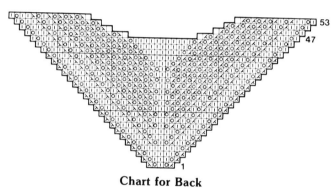

Chart for Back

☐ = knit
☐(o) = yo
☒ = K2tog
☒ = sl 1, k1, psso (skp)

sides at same time with separate balls of yarn, cast off from each neck edge 2 sts once, 1 st twice. Place remaining 15 sts each side on holders for shoulders.

FINISHING

Press pieces according to instructions on ball band. Weave together right shoulder seam.

Neckband: With right side facing and smaller needles, pick up and k118 sts evenly around entire neck edge. Work in k1, p1 rib for 5 rows. Cast off in rib. Weave tog left shoulder seam, including neckband.

Shoulder Bands: With right side facing and smaller needles, pick up and k38 sts along openwork pattern at sides of front and back shoulder. Work in k1, p1 rib for 5 rows. Cast off in rib. Sew side seams.

Armhole Bands (Make 2): Using smaller needles cast on 9 sts. Work in k1, p1 rib until band measures around one armhole edge of back and front below shoulder bands. Cast off in rib.

Sew one long edge of band to armhole. Sew ends of armhole band to sides of shoulder band.

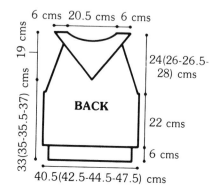

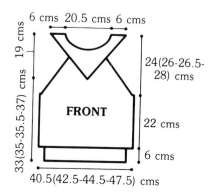

Textured Sweater

MEASUREMENTS

To fit bust sizes 81/86(91/96) cms [32/34(36/38) ins]. Finished length from sleeve edge to sleeve edge (without cuffs) 108(110) cms [43(45) ins]. Length (including lower band) 59(64) cms [23(25) ins].

MATERIALS

Jaeger Monte Cristo 10(12) 50g balls. Pair needles each size 2¾mm (No 12), 3¼mm (No 10 and 3¾mm (No 9). Stitch markers. Cable needle.

TENSION

19 sts = 9 cms [3½ ins] and 27 rows = 10 cms [4 ins] over double moss st and cable patterns using size 3¾mm needles. (Note: To work tension swatch, cast on 19 sts and work a panel of 9 sts in double moss st and a cable pattern over 10 sts).

NOTES

Work all inc sts in 2nd st from edge.

For easier working, keep count of inc sts and dec sts at **both** shoulder and underarm edges.

DOUBLE MOSS ST (any odd number of sts)

1st and 4th rows: K1, *p1, k1; rep from * to end.

2nd and 3rd rows: P1, *k1, p1; rep from * to end.

Rep 1st to 4th rows for double moss st.

CABLE PATTERN (panel of 10 sts)

1st and 5th rows (right side): Ssk, yo, k6, yo, k2tog.

2nd and all wrong side rows: Purl.

3rd row: Ssk, yo, sl 2 sts to cable needle and hold to **back** of work, k2, k2 sts from cable needle, k2, yo, k2tog.

7th row: Ssk, yo, k2, sl 2 sts to cable needle and hold to **front** of work, k2, k2 sts from cable needle, yo, k2tog.

8th row: Purl.

Rep these 8 rows for cable pattern.

BACK

Using size 3¾mm needles and beginning at right sleeve edge, cast on 35(37) sts. Knit 1 row.

Commence cable and double moss st patterns:

1st row (right side): K1, p1, k1, place marker, work 10 sts in 1st row of cable pattern, place marker, work 9 sts in 1st row of double moss st, place marker, work 10 sts in 1st row of cable pattern, place marker, [k1, p1] once(twice), k1.

2nd row (wrong side): P1, [k1, p1] once(twice), slip marker, work 2nd row of cable pattern, slip marker, work 9 sts in 2nd row of double moss st, slip marker, work 2nd row of cable pattern, slip marker, p1, k1, p1.

Shape Shoulder and Underarm Edge

Continuing in patterns as set (working inc sts into patterns by alternating 10-st cable and 9 sts in double moss st), inc at shoulder edge (beg of right side rows) 1 st every 4th row 14 times, then 1 st every alt row 4 times and **at the same time** inc at underarm edge (end of right side rows) 1 st every 6th row 10 times, 1 st every 4th row twice, 2 sts every alt row twice, cast on 4 sts 10(12) times. 109(119) sts. When shoulder edge measures 11.5(12.5) cms [4½(5½) ins] from last shoulder inc, end with a wrong side row and beg neck shaping.

Shape Neck

Next row (right side): Cast off 3 sts (neck edge), work in pattern to end.

Continue to cast off from neck edge 3 sts 3 times more, 2 sts 10 times, and 1 st 9 times. 68(78) sts. Work 2 rows even.

At neck edge cast on 1 st 9 times, 2 sts 10 times, 3 sts 4 times. 109(119) sts. When lower edge measures 36.5 cms [14½ ins] from last underarm inc, cast off at underarm edge 4 sts 10(12) times, 2 sts twice, dec 1 st every 4th row twice, every 6th row 10 times and **at the same time** work straight at shoulder edge until shoulder measures 11.5(12.5) cms [4½(5½) ins] from end of neck edge, then dec 1 st at shoulder edge every alt row 4 times, every 4th row 14 times. Cast off.

FRONT

Beg at left sleeve edge, work as given for Back until same length as back to neck shaping.

Shape Neck

Cast off from neck edge, 2 sts 6 times, 1 st 9 times, 2 sts 5 times, 1 st 3 times. Work 2 rows straight. Cast on 1 st at neck edge 3 times, 2 sts 5 times, 1 st 9 times, 2 sts 6 times.

Continue in pattern working decreases as for Back. Cast off.

FINISHING

Press pieces according to instructions on ball band. Sew upper sleeve and shoulder seams, taking care to match patterns.

Sleeve Cuffs: With right side facing and size 3¼mm needles, pick up and k66(70) sts along sleeve edge. Work in k1, p1 rib for 8 cms [3 ins]. Cast off loosely in rib.

Lower Bands: With right side facing and size 3¼mm needles, pick up and k94(100) sts along

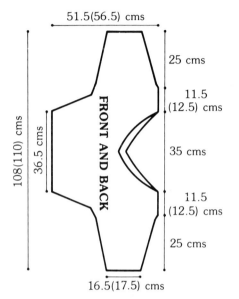

51.5(56.5) cms

25 cms

11.5 (12.5) cms

35 cms

11.5 (12.5) cms

25 cms

16.5(17.5) cms

108(110) cms

36.5 cms

FRONT AND BACK

lower back edge. Work in k1, p1 rib for 8 cms [3 ins]. Cast off loosely in rib.

Work front bands as for back band.

Sew side and sleeve seams including lower bands. Fold band in half to inside and sew in place.

Right Neckband: With right side facing and size 2¾mm needles and beg at front neck, pick up 10 sts along left neck edge beg 3 cms [1¼ ins] above centre point of neck. Knit 1 row.

Commence Short Rows and K1, P1 Rib

1st row (right side): Rib 3 sts, turn.

2nd row: Rib to end.

3rd row: Rib 5 sts, turn.

4th row: Rib to end.

5th row: Rib 7 sts, turn.

6th row: Rib to end.

Continue in rib on all 10 sts for approximately 22 cms [8½ ins] until neckband fits along right neck edge to shoulder, ending with a right side row.

Short Rows For Shoulder Shaping

1st row (wrong side): Rib 7 sts, turn.

2nd row: Rib 5 sts, turn.

3rd row: Rib 3 sts, turn.

4th row: Rib 4 sts, turn.

5th row: Rib 7 sts, turn.

6th row: Rib 8 sts, turn.

Continue in rib on 10 sts for approximately 25 cms [10 ins] or until neckband fits right back edge to centre point.

Commence Short Rows

1st row (wrong side): Rib 7 sts, turn.

2nd row: Rib to end.

3rd row: Rib 5 sts, turn.

4th row: Rib to end.

5th row: Rib 3 sts, turn.

6th row: Rib to end.

Next row: Rib across all 10 sts.

Cast off.

Sew cast off edge to left back 3 cms [1¼ ins] above back centre point.

Left Neckband: With right side facing and size 2¾ mm needles and beginning at 3 cms [1¼ ins] above centre point of neck on right neck edge

(overlapping right band), pick up 10 sts.

Commence Short Rows

1st row (wrong side): Rib 7 sts, turn.

2nd row: Rib to end.

3rd row: Rib 5 sts, turn.

4th row: Rib to end.

5th row: Rib 3 sts, turn.

6th row: Rib to end.

Continue in rib on 10 sts to shoulder as for right band.

Commence Short Rows for Shoulder Shaping

1st row (right side): Rib 7 sts, turn.

2nd row: Rib 5 sts, turn.

3rd row: Rib 3 sts, turn.

4th row: Rib 4 sts, turn.

5th row: Rib 7 sts, turn.

6th row: Rib 8 sts, turn.

Rib straight as for Right Band.

Commence Short Rows

1st row (right side): Rib 7 sts, turn.

2nd row: Rib to end.

3rd row: Rib 5 sts, turn.

4th row: Rib to end.

5th row: Rib 3 sts, turn.

6th row: Rib to end.

Cast off in rib. Sew band along side as for right band overlapping right band with cast off sts.

Designed by Margaret Bruzelius
Photographed by Patrick Demarchelier

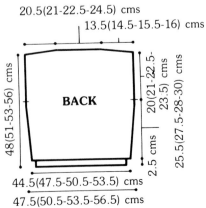

20.5(21-22.5-24.5) cms

13.5(14.5-15.5-16) cms

48(51-53-56) cms

BACK

20(21-22.5-23.5) cms

25.5(27.5-28-30) cms

2.5 cms

44.5(47.5-50.5-53.5) cms

47.5(50.5-53.5-56.5) cms

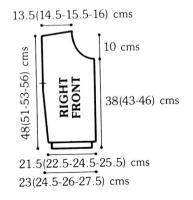

13.5(14.5-15.5-16) cms

10 cms

48(51-53-56) cms

RIGHT FRONT

38(43-46) cms

21.5(22.5-24.5-25.5) cms

23(24.5-26-27.5) cms

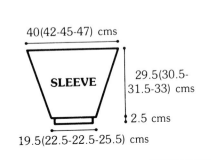

40(42-45-47) cms

SLEEVE

29.5(30.5-31.5-33) cms

2.5 cms

19.5(22.5-22.5-25.5) cms

Short Cardigan

MEASUREMENTS

To fit bust sizes 76/81(86-91-96-101) cms [30/32(34-36-38-40) ins]. Finished measurement at underarm (buttoned) 95(101-107-113) cms [38(39½-43-45) ins]. Length 48(51-53-56) cms [19(20-21-22) ins]. Sleeve width at upper arm 40(42-45-47) cms [16(17-18-19) ins].

MATERIALS

Patons Beehive Knits as 4 Ply 50g balls: 5(5-6-6) balls Colour A, 2 balls each in Colours B and C. Pair needles each size 2¾mm (No 12) and 3¼mm (No 10)½ Circular knitting needle size 2¾mm (No 12). 60 cms [24 ins] long. 8(8-9-9) buttons. Shoulder pads (optional).

TENSION

26 sts and 36 rows = 10 cms [4 ins] over pattern st using size 3¼mm needles.

NOTES

Use separate bobbins of colours B and C for easier working.

To avoid pulling in, work pattern st rows with contrasting colours loosely.

Substitute a single st dot for a rosette when making an inc which falls close to side edge.

Knit the first and last st of every row to form a selvage st. This aids in seaming and picking up sts later. To avoid long strands at side of work, carry colours not in use along selvage by twisting every right side row.

ROSETTE PATTERN ST (multiple of 8 sts plus 3 extra)

1st row (right side): Using A knit.

2nd row: Using A purl.

3rd row: Using B *sl 3 purlwise, k1, sl 3, [k1, yo, k1, yo, k1, yo, k1] in next st; rep from * to last 3 sts, sl 3.

4th row: Using B sl all A sts wyif and k all B sts.

5th row: Using A k1, *k5, k2tog, k5, ssk; rep from * to last 2 sts, k2.

6th row: Using A p2, *p2tog, p1, sl 1, p1, p2tog, p5; rep from * to last st, p1.

7th row: Using A k1, *k5, k2tog, sl 1, ssk; rep from * to last 2 sts, k2.

8th and 10th row: Using A purl.

9th row: Using A knit.

11th row: Using C *sl 3, [k1, yo, k1, yo, k1, yo, k1] in next st, sl 3, k1; rep from * to last 3 sts, sl 3.

12th row: Using C sl all A sts wyif and k all C sts.

13th row: Using A k2, *k2tog, k5, ssk, k5; rep from * to last st, k1.

14th row: Using A p1, *p5, p2tog, p1, sl 1, p1, p2tog; rep from * to last 2 sts, p2.

15th row: Using A k2, *k2tog, sl 1, ssk, k5; rep from * to last st, k1.

16th row: Using A purl.

Rep these 16 rows for rosette pattern st.

BACK

Using smaller needles and A cast on 117(125-133-141) sts. Work in k1, p1 rib for 2.5 cms [1 inch]. Change to larger needles.

Commence Pattern St

1st row (right side): K1 (selvage st), work 1st row of pattern st, ending k1 (selvage st).

2nd row (wrong side): K1 (selvage st), work 2nd row of pattern st, ending k1 (selvage st).

Continuing in pattern st, k first and last st of every row, until one pattern rep (16 rows) has been completed.

Next row (increase — right side): K1, make one **(m1)**, work 1st row of pattern st to last st, ending m1, k1.

Continue in pattern st, working inc row on each 1st row of pattern st (working inc sts into pattern st) 3 times more. 125(133-141-149) sts. Work straight in pattern until piece measures 48(51-53-56) cms [19(20-21-22) ins] from beg.

Shape Shoulder

Cast off 12(13-14-15) sts at beg of next 4 rows, then 12(13-13-13) sts at beg of next 2 rows. Slip remaining 53(55-59-63) sts onto a holder.

RIGHT FRONT

Using smaller needles and A cast on 58(61-66-69) sts and work in k1, p1 rib for 2.5 cms [1 inch]. Change to larger needles.

Commence Pattern St

1st row (right side): K1 (selvage st), work 1st row of pattern st, ending k1 (selvage st).

2nd row (wrong side): K1 (selvage st), work 2nd row of pattern st, ending k1 (selvage st).

3rd row: K1, work from * of 3rd row of pattern st, ending k1 instead of [k1, yo, k1, yo, k1, yo, k1] on 1st and 3rd sizes only.

Continue working selvage and pattern sts as set (working single st dot in place of rosette at underarm edge for 1st and 3rd sizes only), for a total of 16 rows.

Next row (increase — right side): K1, work 1st row of pattern to last st, ending m1, k1.

Continue in pattern st working inc row on each 1st row of pattern st (working inc sts into pattern st) 3 times more. 62(65-70-73) sts.

Work straight until piece measures 38(41-43-46) cms [15(16-17-18) ins] from beg, ending with a wrong side row.

Shape Neck

Next row (right side): Sl first 9(9-13-13) sts onto a holder, work in pattern to end.

Continue in pattern dec 1 st at neck edge every alt row 17(17-16-17) times. 36(39-41-43) sts. Work until piece measures same as back to shoulder, ending with a right side row.

Shape Shoulders

Cast off 12(13-14-15) sts at armhole edge only twice. Cast off remaining 12(13-13-13) sts.

LEFT FRONT

Work as given for Right Front, reversing all shaping and pattern st placement.

SLEEVES

Using smaller needles and A cast on 53(61-61-69) sts and work in k1, p1 rib for 2.5 cms [1 inch].

Change to larger needles. Working 1 selvage st at beg and end of rows, work in pattern st as given for back and working increases into pattern, inc 1 st at each end every 4th row 26(26-26-28) times, then every alt row 0(0-3-0) times. 105(113-119-125) sts. If necessary, work straight until piece measures 32(33-34-35.5) cms [12½(13-13½-14) ins] from beg or required sleeve length. Cast off.

FINISHING AND NECKBAND

Press pieces according to instructions on ball band. Sew shoulder seams.

Neckband: With right side facing, circular needle and A and starting at right front, slip 9(9-13-13) sts from holder to needle, pick up and k30 sts along right front neck edge, slip 53(55-59-63) sts from holder for back neck, pick up and k30 sts along left front neck edge and slip 9(9-13-13) sts from left front holder. 131(133-145-149) sts. Do not join. Work back and forth in k1, p1 rib for 2.5 cms [1 inch]. Cast off knitwise.

Left Front Band: With right side facing, smaller needles and A pick up and k90(96-102-108) sts along left front edge including neckband. Work 6 rows in k1, p1 rib. Cast off knitwise.

Right Front Band: Work as given for Left Front Band for 2 rows.

1st buttonhole row: Rib 5 sts, cast off next 2 sts, *rib until there are 9(10-9-10) sts from last cast off, cast off next 2 sts; rep from * 6(6-7-7) times more, rib to end.

2nd buttonhole row: Rib, casting on 2 sts over each set of cast-off sts.

Work 2 more rows in rib. Cast off knitwise.

Place markers 20(21-22.5-23.5) cms [8(8½-9-9½) ins] down from shoulder seams on front and back for armhole. Sew top of sleeve between markers. Sew side and sleeve seams. Sew on buttons.

Ribbed Pattern Sweater

MEASUREMENTS

To fit bust sizes 81/86(91/96) cms [32/34(36/38) ins]. Finished measurement from sleeve edge to sleeve edge 118(123.5) cms [47(49½) ins]. Length including ribbing 53(58) cms [21(23½) ins].

MATERIALS

10(12) 50g balls of Berger du Nord Tissé in colour 8827 Blue. Pair needles each size 3mm (No 11) and 5mm (No 6). 3mm (No 11) circular knitting needle, 40 cms [16 ins] long. Stitch markers. Cable needle.

TENSION

17 sts and 24 rows = 10 cms [4 ins] over k3, p2 rib using size 5mm needles. (**Note:** Block piece by pressing lightly before measuring).

NOTES

Sweater is worked in one piece beg with right sleeve edge.

For easier knitting, keep careful count of incs and decs.

CABLE PATTERN ST (worked over 14 sts)

1st row (right side): [P2, k4] twice, p2.

2nd and 4th rows: [K2, p4] twice, k2.

3rd row: P2, sl next 2 sts to cable needle and hold to **back** of work, knit next 2 sts, knit sts from cable needle, p2, sl 2 sts to cable needle and hold to **front** of work, knit next 2 sts, knit sts from cable needle, p2.

Rep these 4 rows for cable pattern.

BODY

Starting at right sleeve edge and using smaller needles cast on 42(46) sts.

1st rib row (right side): K2, *p2, k2; rep from * to end.

2nd rib row: P2, *k2, p2; rep from * to end. Rep last 2 rows for k2, p2 rib for 5 cms [2 ins], ending with a wrong side row.

Change to larger needles.

Commence Cable and Rib Patterns

1st row (right side): K1(3), [p2, k3] twice, p2, k1, place marker, work cable pattern st over next 14 sts, place marker, k1, p2, [k3, p2] twice, k1(3).

2nd and all wrong side rows: Knit the k sts and purl the p sts.

3rd and 5th rows: As 1st row.

7th row (increase): Work in rib pattern to 1 st before marker, inc 1 st in next st, slip marker, work cable pattern over next 14 sts, slip marker, inc 1 st in next st, work to end.

Continuing to work in rib and cable patterns, inc 1 st each side of marker (working inc sts into rib pattern) every 4th (cable twist) row 8 times more. 60(64) sts. Work 3 rows straight. Piece measures approx 23 cms [9 ins] from beg.

Commence Underarm Shaping

Continue to inc 1 st each side of markers as

before every 4th row 9(10) times more, **at the same time** inc 1 st at beg and end every alt row 15(17) times. Piece measures approx 38(39.5) cms [15(15½) ins] from beg. 108(118) sts.

Cast on 6(7) sts at beg of next 10 rows. 168(188) sts. Place markers each end of last row for shoulder. Work straight in patterns until there are 25(26) sets of cable twist — approx 46.5(48.5) cms [18½(19½) ins] from beg, ending with 4th row of cable. Place markers each end of last row for shoulder.

Divide for Neck

Next row (right side): Work in rib pattern st to first marker, p2, k4, inc 1 st in next purl st (1 selvage st for neck edge). Place remaining sts on holder for back to be worked later.

Working on front only, continue to work straight in pattern sts until 15(16) cable twists have been worked from dividing point, ending with a 3rd row of cable twist. Place front sts on holder.

Back Section

Slip sts from holder onto needle, inc 1 st in first purl st for neck selvage, k4, p2, slip marker, work in rib st to end. Continue to work straight in patterns until 17(18) cable twists have been worked from dividing point, ending with a 3rd row of cable twist.

Rejoin Back and Front

Next row (wrong side): Work across back sts to marker in rib st, k2, p4, k2tog, work sts from front holder as follows: k2tog, p4, k2, sl mar-

ker, work in rib pattern to end.

Work straight in pattern until same number of rows have been worked as on first half of body between shoulder markers.

Commence Underarm Shaping

Cast off 6(7) sts at beg of next 10 rows. Dec l st each side of marker (working dec sts into rib pattern) every 4th row 9(10) times.

Note: For neater decs, k2tog at first marker and sl 1 st, k1 st and pass sl st over k st — (SKP) at 2nd marker) and **at the same time,** after 1(2) cable decs have been made, beg dec 1 st each side edge every alt row 15(17) times. 60(64) sts. Dec 1 st each side of marker every 4th row 9 times. 42(46) sts.

Change to smaller needles and work in k2, p2 rib for 5 cms [2 ins]. Cast off loosely in rib.

FINISHING

Press pieces according to instructions on ball band.

Lower Edge Ribs: Starting at lower edge of front, with right side facing and smaller needles, pick up and k82(86) sts along lower front edge. Work in k2, p2 rib for 3 cms [1¼ ins]. Cast off loosely in rib.

Rep band along lower back edge. Sew side and sleeve seams.

Neckband: With right side facing and circular needle, pick up and k128(132) sts evenly around neck edge. Join and work in k2, p2 rib for 6 rounds.

Cast off loosely in rib.

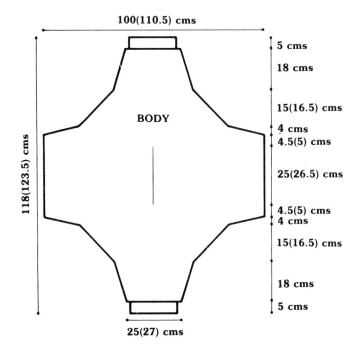

Fairisle Waistcoat

MEASUREMENTS

To fit bust/chest sizes 86(91-96-101-106-112) cms [34(36-38-40-42-44) ins]. Finished measurement at underarm (buttoned) 97(102-107-111-117-122) cms [38½(40½-42½-44½-46½-48½) ins]. Length 65(66-67.5-69.5-72.5-73.5) cms [25½(26-26½-27½-28½-29) ins].

MATERIALS

Patons Diploma Double Knitting 50g balls: 5(5-6-6-6-6) balls Colour A, 2(2-2-3-3-3) balls each in Colours B, C, D, E,F, G, H, I and J. Pair needles each size 3¼mm (No 10) and 4mm (No 8). 6 buttons.

TENSION

24 sts and 28 rows = 10 cms [4 ins] over colour work pattern using size 4mm needles.

NOTE

When working with more than one colour, carry yarn not in use loosely across back of work.

BACK

Using smaller needles and A cast on 109(115-121-127-133-139) sts.

Work in k1, p1 rib for 6 cms [2¼ ins] ending with a wrong side row.

Change to larger needles and knit next row increasing 7 sts evenly across row. 116(122-128-134-140-146) sts. Purl 1 row.

1st Colour pattern row (right side): Following chart from right to left, *k24 sts of 1st row of chart; rep from * 3(4-4-4-4-5) times, ending knit first 20(2-8-14-20-2) sts of chart.

2nd Colour pattern row: Beg at same point on chart where last knit row ended, purl across following 2nd row of chart from left to right.

Working straight in st st rep 1st to 84th rows of chart until back measures 42(42-42-43-44.5-44.5) cms [16½(16½-16½-17-17½-17½) ins]

from beg, ending with a wrong side row.

Shape Armhole

Continuing to follow chart cast off 10(10-11-11-11-12) sts at beg of next 2 rows. Dec 1 st at each end of every row 4(5-5-7-8-8) times, then dec 1 st at each end of every alt row 4(5-5-5-5-5) times. 80(82-86-88-92-96) sts.

Work straight in pattern until armhole measures 23(24-25.5-26.5-28-29) cms [9(9½-10-10½-11-11½) ins], ending with a wrong side row. Keeping to pattern cast off 22(22-22-22-23-24) sts at beg of next 2 rows for shoulders. Cast off remaining 36(38-42-44-46-48) sts for back of neck.

POCKETS (Make 2)

Using larger needles and A cast on 28(28-28-30-32-32) sts. Work straight in st st until pocket measures 21.5 cms [8½ ins], ending with a purl row. Slip all sts onto a holder.

LEFT FRONT

Using smaller needles and A cast on 59(62-65-68-71-74) sts and work in k1, p1 rib for 2 cms [¾ inch] ending with a right side row.

Man's Cardigan Only

1st Buttonhole row (wrong side): Work first 3 sts in rib, cast off next 3 sts, rib to end.

2nd Buttonhole row: Work in rib casting on 3 sts over cast off sts on previous row.

Man's and Woman's Cardigan

Continue in rib until rib measures 6 cms [2¼ ins] from beg, ending with a right side row.

Next row (wrong side): Slip first 8(8-8-10-10-10) sts onto a holder for centre front band, rib to end.

Change to larger needles and knit next row increasing 3(3-3-5-5-5) sts evenly across row. 54(57-60-63-66-69) sts. Purl 1 row.

Following chart as given for back and starting with 1st row of chart, work straight in st st to 28th row, ending with a wrong side row.

FINISHING

Press pieces according to instructions on ball band. Sew side and sleeve seams. Sew shoulder seams.

Hem: With right side facing, longer 4mm circular needle and double knitting yarn and beginning at lower left front edge, pick up 1 st in back loop of every cast on st along lower edge. Starting with a purl row, work in st st for 2 cms [¾ inch]. Do **not** cast off. Fold hem to wrong side and sew st by st in place. Press hem flat with damp cloth and warm iron.

Outer Ribbed Sleeve: Using shorter size 4½mm circular needle and M pick up and k124(130) sts along sleeve edge. Join and place marker to indicate beg of round.

Work in rounds of k1, p1 rib for 23 cms [9 ins]. Change to size 4mm circular needle and continue in rib until ribbed sleeve measures 28 cms [11 ins] from beg, or required length. Cast off in rib.

Inner Ribbed Sleeve: Using double pointed needle and M cast on 40 sts for lower edge of inner sleeve and divide sts evenly over 3 needles. Place marker to indicate beg of rounds and join, taking care not to twist sts on needles. Work in rounds of k1, p1 rib for 7.5 cms [3 ins].

Next round: [K1, p1] 1(0) times, *knit into front and back of next st, make one (m1), knit into front and back of next st; rep from * to last 2(0) sts, [k1, p1] 1(0) times. 94(100) sts.

Continue to work in rounds of k1, p1 rib until

all sts will fit on smaller size 4½mm circular needle (approx 1.5 cms [½ inch] more).

Continue in rib on circular needle until piece measures 25 cms [10 ins] from beg. Now work in st st (every round knit) until piece measures 30.5 cms [12 ins] from beg. Cast off loosely.

Sew cast off edge underneath outer ribbed sleeve along ridge formed by picked up sts for outer sleeve.

Front Band: With right side facing, longer 4½mm circular needle and M and beginning at lower right front edge, pick up and k193(196) sts along right front edge to shoulder, 37(39) sts along back of neck and 193(196) sts along left front edge. 423(431) sts. Do not join, Work back and forth in k1, p1 rib for 18 cms [7 ins]. Cast off loosely in rib.

Short-Sleeved Crochet Top

MEASUREMENTS

To fit bust sizes 80(85-90-95-100-105) cms [32(34-36-38-40-42) ins]. Width from cuff to cuff (approximately) 88(90-92-96-98-100) cms [35¼(36-36¾-38½-39¼-40) ins]. Length to shoulder (approximately) 53(54-55-56-57-58) cms [21¼(21½-22-22½-22¾-23¼) ins].

MATERIALS

Coats Maxi 'Pellicano' Knitting and Crochet Cotton No. 8 (200 g) 2(2-2-2-2-3) balls. Crochet hook size 1.25mm. 1 reel metallic thread for neckband and cuffs.

TENSION

38 sts and 20 rows = 10 cms [4 ins] square measured over pattern.

SPECIAL ABBREVIATION

Tr2tog = work 1 tr into next st until 2 loops remain on hook, work 1 tr into next st until 3 loops remain on hook, yo and through the 3 loops.

SPECIAL NOTE

Count each ch, tr and dtr as 1 stitch.

BACK AND FRONT (Alike)

Make 49(51-55-57-59-61) ch, work 1 tr into 4th ch from hook, 1 tr into each ch to end. 46(48-52-54-56-58) tr plus 3 ch at beg of row.

Commence Pattern: 1st row (wrong side): 3 ch (count as 1 tr), **working into back loop only** work 1 tr into each tr to end, 1 tr into 3rd of 3 ch at beg of previous row. **2nd row:** 4 ch (count as 1 tr, 1 ch), *miss 1 tr, 1 tr into next tr, 1 ch; rep from * to last 2 sts, miss 1 tr, 1 tr into 3rd of 3 ch at beg of previous row. **3rd row:** 3 ch, work 1 tr into each tr and each ch to end. **4th row:** 3 ch, **working into back loop only** work 1 tr into each tr to end.

These 4 rows form the pattern. Keeping pattern correct throughout, continue as follows:

5th row: Work in pattern to last 2 tr, 2 tr into next tr, 1 tr into 3rd of 3 ch at beg of previous row (1 st increased at end of row — underarm edge). **6th row:** 3 ch, 1 tr into next tr, 1 ch, *miss 1 tr, 1 tr into next tr, 1 ch; rep from * to last 2 sts, miss 1 tr, 1 tr into 3rd of 3 ch at beg of previous row. Work 1 row. **8th row:** 3 ch, work 2 tr into next st, work in pattern to end (1 st increased at beg of row — underarm edge). Work 2 rows straight. Inc 1 st at underarm edge as before on next row. Work 2 rows straight.

14th row: 4 ch (count as 1 tr, 1 ch), 1 tr into next tr, work in pattern to end (1 st increased at underarm edge). **15th row:** Work in pattern to last 2 sts, 2 tr into 4th and 1 tr into 3rd of 4 ch at beg of previous row (1 st increased at underarm edge).

Continue to inc 1 st at underarm edge as before on next 9 rows thus ending with a 4th row of pattern. 61(63-67-69-71-73) sts.

25th row: Work in pattern to last 3 sts, 2 tr into each of next 2 tr, 1 dtr into last tr (2 sts increased at underarm edge). **26th row:** 4 ch (count as 1 tr, 1 ch), 1 tr into dtr of previous row, 1 ch, miss next tr, work in pattern to end (2 sts increased at underarm edge). **27th row:** Work in pattern to last 3 sts, 2 tr into next tr, 2 tr into 4th and 1 dtr into 3rd of 4 ch at beg of previous row. **28th row:** 4 ch, 1 tr into 4th ch from hook (count as 2 tr), 1 tr into next dtr, work in pattern to end.

Rep the last 4 rows 4 times more, then work 25th, 26th and 27th rows again. 107(109-113-115-117-119) sts.

48th row: 90(90-90-92-94-96) ch, work 1 tr into 4th ch from hook, 1 tr into each ch, then working into back loop only, work 1 tr into each tr to end. 195(197-201-205-209-213) sts.

Keeping pattern correct work 19(21-23-25-27-29) rows straight, thus ending at lower edge with a 3rd(1st-3rd-1st-3rd-1st) row of pattern.

Shape Neck

1st(3rd-5th) sizes only, 1st row: Work in pattern to last 25(27-29) sts, [tr2tog] twice, 1 dtr into next st, turn. **2nd row:** 3 ch, [tr2tog] twice, work to end. **3rd row:** Work to last 3 sts, 1 tr into next tr, miss next tr, 1 tr into last tr. **4th row:** 3 ch, tr2tog, work to end. **5th row:** Work to last 3 sts, tr2tog, 1 tr into last tr. **6th row:** 3 ch, tr2tog, work to end.

Dec 1 st at neck edge in this way on next 2 rows. 165(169-175) sts remain. Work 25(25-29) rows straight, thus ending at neck edge with a 4th row of pattern.

Next row: 3 ch, 2 tr into next tr, work in pattern to end. **Next row:** Work in pattern to last 2 sts, 1 ch, 1 tr into last tr. **Next row:** 3 ch, 2 tr into next st, work in pattern to end. **Next row:** Work in pattern to last 2 sts, 2 tr into next tr, 1 tr into last tr.

Inc 1 st at neck edge in this way on next 2 rows.

Next row: 4 ch, 1 tr into 4th ch from hook (count as 2 tr), 1 tr into next tr, work to end. **Next row:** Work to last 3 sts, 2 tr into each of next 2 tr, 1 dtr into last tr.

2nd(4th-6th) sizes only, 1st row: Work in pattern to last 24(26-28) sts, miss next tr, 1 tr into next tr, miss next tr, 1 dtr into next tr, turn. **2nd row:** 3 ch, [tr2tog] twice, work to end. **3rd row:** Work to last 3 sts, tr2tog, 1 tr into last tr. **4th row:** 3 ch, tr2tog, work to end. **5th row:** Work to last 3 sts, 1 tr into next tr, miss 1 tr, 1 tr into last tr. **6th row:** 3 ch, tr2tog, work to end.

Dec 1 st at neck edge in this way on next 2 rows. 167(173-179) sts remain. Work 25(29-29) rows straight, thus ending at neck edge with a 2nd row of pattern.

Next row: 3 ch, 2 tr into next st, work to end. **Next row:** Work to last 2 tr, 2 tr into next tr, 1 tr into last tr. **Next row:** 3 ch, 2 tr into next tr, work to end. **Next row:** Work to last 2 sts, 1 tr into next tr, 1 ch, 1 tr into last tr.

Inc 1 st at neck edge in this way on next 2 rows.

Next row: 4 ch, 1 tr into 4th ch from hook (count as 2 tr), 1 tr into next tr, work to end. **Next row:** Work to last 3 sts, [1 tr into next tr, 1 ch] twice, 1 dtr into last tr.

All sizes, Next row: 22(22-24-24-26-26) ch, work 1 tr into 4th ch from hook, 1 tr into each of next 18(18-20-20-22-22) ch, 1 tr into each st to end. 195(197-201-205-209-213) sts. Work 19(21-23-25-27-29) rows straight, thus ending at shoulder edge with a 4th row of pattern.

2nd Sleeve, 1st row: 3 ch, work 1 tr into each of next 101(103-107-109-111-113) tr, [tr2tog] twice, 1 dtr into next tr, turn. 105(107-111-113-115-117) sts remain. **2nd row:** 3 ch, [miss next tr, 1 tr into next tr] twice, *1 ch, miss next tr, 1 tr into next tr; rep from * to end (2 sts decreased at underarm edge). **3rd row:** Work to last 5 sts, [tr2tog] twice, 1 dtr into last tr (2 sts decreased at underarm edge). **4th row:** 3 ch, [tr2tog] twice, work to end (2 sts decreased at underarm edge). **5th row:** As 3rd row.

Rep the last 4 rows 4 times more, then work 2nd and 3rd rows once more. 61(63-67-69-71-73) sts remain.

Next row: 3 ch, tr2tog, work to end. **Next row:** Work to last 3 sts, 1 tr into next tr, miss 1 tr, 1 tr into last tr. **Next row:** 3 ch, tr2tog, work to end. **Next row:** Work to last 3 sts, tr2tog, 1 tr into last tr.

Dec 1 st at underarm edge on next 7 rows, 50(52-56-58-60-62) sts remain, then every following 3rd row 3 times. 47(49-53-55-57-59) sts remain. Work 5 rows straight, thus ending with a 4th row of pattern. Fasten off.

TO MAKE UP

Press pieces according to instructions on ball band.

Lower Edging: With right side of one piece facing work 1 row of dc along lower edge, working 2 dc into every row.

1st row: 1 ch, **working into back loop only** work 1 dc into each dc to end. Rep the last row 5 times more. Fasten off.

Join shoulder, side and sleeve seams.

Neckband: Make 34 ch, work 1 dc into 2nd ch from hook, 1 dc into each ch to end. 33 dc. **1st row** (wrong side): 1 ch, **working into back loop only** work 2 dc into first dc, 1 dc into each dc to last 2 dc, miss 1 dc, 1 dc into last dc (1 st increased at beg and 1 st decreased at end of row). **2nd row:** 1 ch, miss first dc, **working into back loop only** work 1 dc into each dc to last dc, 2 dc into last dc (1 st decreased at beg and 1 st increased at end of row).

These 2 rows form the pattern. Continue in pattern until band, **when slightly stretched,** fits round neck edge. Fasten off.

Cuffs (Make 2): Make 14 ch, work 1 dc into 2nd ch from hook, 1 dc into each ch to end. 13 dc.

Work in pattern as given for Neckband until cuff, **when slightly stretched,** fits round sleeve edge. Fasten off.

Join neckband into a ring and sew to neck edge stretching evenly. Roll neckband to right side. Join cuffs into a ring and sew to sleeve edges stretching evenly. Roll cuffs to right side. Slip stitch neckband and cuffs in place with sewing thread if required. Twist 1 strand of metallic thread round neckband and cuffs in every 3rd ridge as illustrated.

Family Sweaters

MEASUREMENTS

To fit chest or bust sizes 60(65/70-75-80/85-90-95/100-105-110) cms [24(26/28-30-32/34-36-38/40-42-44) ins]. Finished measurement 70(77-85-92-100-106-115-121) cms [28(31-34-37-40-42½-46-48½) ins]. Length to top of shoulder 47(56-60-68-73-76-78-80) cms [18½(22-23½-26¾-28¾-30-30¾-31½) ins]. Sleeve seam 29(34-38-44-45-46-47-47) cms [11½(13½-15-17¼-17¾-18-18½-18½) ins].

MATERIALS

Patons Promise Double Knitting 5(6-8-8-9-10-11-12) 40g balls. Pair needles each size 4mm (No 8) and 3¼mm (No 10).

TENSION

19 sts and 30 rows = 10 cms [4 ins] square measured over pattern using larger needles.

SPECIAL ABBREVIATION

K3B (Knit 3 Below) = knit into st 3 rows below next st dropping st above off needle, thus picking up loops of all 3 rows with the st.

V-Neck Sweater

BACK

Using smaller needles cast on 67(73-81-87-95-101-109-115) sts.

1st row (right side): K1, *p1, k1; rep from * to end.

2nd row: P1, *k1, p1; rep from * to end.

Rep the last 2 rows until rib measures 8(8-8-8-10-10-10-10) cms [3(3-3-3-4-4-4-4) ins] ending with a wrong side row.

Change to larger needles and work 2 rows in reversed st st, starting purl.

Commence Pattern

1st row: Purl.

2nd and every alt row: Knit.

3rd row: P3(3-1-1-2-2-3-3), *K3B (see Special Abbreviation), p5; rep from * to last 4(4-2-2-3-3-4-4) sts, K3B, purl to end.

5th row: Purl.

7th row: P6(6-4-4-5-5-6-6), *K3B, p5; rep from * to last 7(7-5-5-6-6-7-7) sts, K3B, purl to end.

8th row: Knit.

These 8 rows form the pattern.

Continue in pattern until back measures 30(37-39-45-47-48-48-48) cms [11¾(14½-15¼-17¾-18½-19-19-19) ins] or required length to armholes ending with a knit row.

Shape Raglan Armholes

★ Keeping pattern correct cast off 3(3-3-3-3-4-4-4) sts at beg of next 2 rows.

Work 2 rows straight.

5th row: P1, p2tog, work to last 3 sts, p2tog, p1.

6th row: Knit ★★.

Rep the last 4 rows until 49(53-61-65-71-71-79-85) sts remain, then the last 2 rows only until 25(27-29-31-33-35-37-37) sts remain ending with the knit row.

Next row: P1, p3tog, work to last 4 sts, p3tog, p1.

Next row: Knit to end decreasing 1 st at centre.

Break yarn and slip remaining 20(22-24-26-28-30-32-32) sts onto a holder for neckband.

SLEEVES

Using smaller needles cast on 35(37-39-41-43-45-47-49) sts and work 6(6-7-7-8-8-8-8) cms [2½(2½-2¾-2¾-3-3-3-3) ins] in k1, p1 rib as given for Back ending with a wrong side row.

Change to larger needles and work 2 rows in reversed st st, starting purl.

Commence Pattern

1st row: Purl.

2nd and every alt row: Knit.

3rd row: P2(3-1-2-3-1-2-3), *K3B, p5; rep from * to last 3(4-2-3-4-2-3-4) sts, K3B, purl to end.

5th row: Purl.

7th row: P5(6-4-5-6-4-5-6), *K3B, p5; rep from * to last 6(7-5-6-7-5-6-7) sts, K3B, purl to end.

Family Sweaters

8th row: Knit.

These 8 rows form the pattern. Keeping pattern correct and bringing extra sts into pattern inc 1 st at each end of next and every following 8th(9th-8th-9th-8th-7th-7th-6th) row until there are 49(53-59-63-67-73-77-81) sts. Work straight until sleeve measures 29(34-38-44-45-46-47-47) cms [11½(13½-15-17¼-17¾-18-18½-18½) ins], or required seam length ending with a knit row.

Shape Raglan Top

Work as given for Back from ★ to ★★.

Rep the last 4 rows until 29(31-37-39-37-39-41-43) sts remain, then the last 2 rows only until 7(7-7-7-9-9-9-9) sts remain ending with the knit row.

Break yarn and slip remaining sts onto a holder for neckband.

FRONT

Work as given for Back to start of raglan shaping.

Shape Raglan Armholes and Divide for Neck

1st row: Cast off 3(3-3-3-3-4-4-4) sts, work until there are 30(33-37-40-44-46-50-53) sts on right-hand needle, turn and complete this side first leaving remaining sts on a holder.

2nd row: Knit.

★★★ Work 2 rows straight.

5th row: P1, p2tog, work to last 3 sts, p2tog, p1.

6th row: Knit.

Rep the last 4 rows until 18(19-23-24-26-24-28-31) sts remain ending with the dec row. Now dec 1 st at raglan edge as before on every alt row, **at the same time** dec 1 st at neck edge as before on every following 6th(6th-6th-6th-8th-8th-8th-8th) row until 6(7-7-8-6-9-8-11) sts remain.

Keeping neck edge straight continue to dec 1 st at raglan edge as before on every alt row until 3 sts remain. Dec 1 st at neck edge only on following alt row. Cast off.

Slip next st at centre onto a safety pin for neckband. With right side of work facing rejoin yarn to neck edge of remaining sts and work to end.

2nd row: Cast off 3(3-3-3-3-4-4-4) sts, knit to end.

Complete as given for first side from ★★★ to end.

FINISHING AND NECKBAND

Press pieces according to instructions on ball band. Join front and left back raglan seams.

Neckband: Using smaller needles and with right side of work facing, knit across sts on holders at back neck and left sleeve top, pick up and k44(50-56-60-68-72-78-84) sts down left front slope, knit st from safety pin at centre front, pick up and k44(50-56-60-68-72-78-84) sts up right front slope and knit across sts on

holder at right sleeve top. 123(137-151-161-183-193-207-219) sts.

1st row: P1, *k1, p1; rep from * to 2 sts before centre front st, p2tog, p1, p2tog tbl, p1, *k1, p1; rep from * to end.

2nd row: *K1, p1; rep from * to 2 sts before centre front st, sl 1, k1, psso, k1, k2tog, *p1, k1; rep from * to end.

Rep the last 2 rows 2(2-2-3-3-3-4-4) times more. Cast off in rib decreasing on this row also.

Join remaining raglan seam and ends of neckband. Join side and sleeve seams.

Round Neck Sweater

BACK AND SLEEVES

Work as given for Back and Sleeves of V-Neck Sweater.

FRONT

Work as given for Back to ★★. Rep the last 4 rows until 49(53-61-65-71-71-79-85) sts remain, then the last 2 rows only until 35(37-41-45-47-51-55-55) sts remain ending with the dec row.

Shape Neck

Next row: K13(13-15-17-17-19-21-21), turn and complete this side first.

★★★★ Dec 1 st at raglan edge as before on next and every alt row, **at the same time** dec 1 st at neck edge on next 3(3-3-3-5-5-5-5) rows, then on following 2(2-3-4-2-3-4-4) alt rows. 4(4-4-4-5-5-5-5) sts remain.

Keeping neck edge straight continue to dec at raglan edge only until 3 sts remain. Dec 1 st at neck edge only on following alt row. Cast off.

Slip next 9(11-11-11-13-13-13-13) sts at centre onto a holder for neckband. With wrong side of work facing rejoin yarn to neck edge of remaining sts and knit to end. Complete as given for first side from ★★★★ to end.

FINISHING AND NECKBAND

Press pieces according to instructions on ball band. Join front and left back raglan seams.

Neckband: Using smaller needles and with right side of work facing, knit across sts on holders at back neck and left sleeve top, pick up and k10(10-12-14-14-16-18-18) sts down left front slope, knit across sts on holder at front neck, pick up and k10(10-12-14-14-16-18-18) sts up right front slope and knit across sts on holder at right sleeve top. 63(67-73-79-87-93-99-99) sts.

Work 7(7-8-8-8-9-9-9) cms [2¾(2¾-3-3-3-3½-3½-3½) ins] in k1, p1 rib as given for Back, starting with the 2nd row. Slip sts onto a length of yarn.

Join remaining raglan seam and ends of neckband. Fold neckband in half to inside and slip stitch **loosely** in place, allowing for stretch and taking care to catch every stitch. Join side and sleeve seams.

Man's Aran-Style Sweater

MEASUREMENTS

To fit chest sizes 90(95-100-105-110) cms [36(38-40-42-44) ins]. Finished measurement 101(105-110-115-120) cms [40½(42-44-46-48) ins]. Length to back of neck 67(68-69-70-71) cms [26½(26¾-27¼-27½-28) ins]. Sleeve length 47 cms [18½ ins].

MATERIALS

Coats 'Anchor' Knitting and Crochet Cotton No. 6 (50g) used double: 20(21-22-23-24) balls. Pair needles each size 4mm (No 8) and 3mm (No 11). Cable needle. Stitch holders. Coats Maxi 'Pellicano' Knitting and Crochet Cotton No. 5 (200g) used double: 5(6-6-6-6) balls. Pair needles each size 4½mm (No 7) and 3¼mm (No 10). Cable needle. Stitch holders.

TENSION

With yarn used double: 25 sts and 30 rows = 10 cms [4 ins] square measured over k1, p2 rib pattern using larger needles.

SPECIAL ABBREVIATIONS

T6B (Twist 6 Back) = slip next 3 sts onto cable needle and hold at back of work, p1, k1, p1 from left-hand needle, then knit sts from cable needle.

T6F (Twist 6 Front) = slip next 3 sts onto cable needle and hold at front of work, knit next 3 sts from left-hand needle, then k1, p1, k1 from cable needle.

C10B or C10F (Cable 10 Back or Cable 10 Front) = slip next 5 sts onto cable needle and hold at back (or front) of work, knit next 5 sts from left-hand needle, then knit sts from cable needle.

T12 (Twist 12) = slip next 6 sts onto cable needle and hold at back of work, [p1, k1] 3 times from left-hand needle, then [p1, k1] 3 times from cable needle.

T6L (Twist 6 Left) = slip next 3 sts onto cable needle and hold at front of work, knit next 3 sts from left-hand needle, then p1, k1, p1 from cable needle.

T6R (Twist 6 Right) = slip next 3 sts onto cable needle and hold at back of work, k1, p1, k1 from left-hand needle, then knit sts from cable needle.

PANEL A (Worked across 12 sts)

1st and 3rd rows: K3, [p1, k1] twice, p1, k4.
2nd and 4th rows: P3, [k1, p1] twice, k1, p4.
5th row: T6B, T6F.
6th row: K1, p1, k1, p7, k1, p1.
7th row: P1, k1, p1, k7, p1, k1.
Rep 6th and 7th rows 3 times more, then 6th row again.
15th row: T6L, T6R.
16th row: As 2nd row.
Rep 1st and 2nd rows twice more.
These 20 rows form Panel A.

PANEL B (Worked across 16 sts)

1st and 3rd rows: P3, k10, p3.
2nd and 4th rows: K3, p10, k3.
5th row: P3, C10B, p3.
6th row: As 2nd row.
Rep 1st and 2nd rows twice more.
These 10 rows form Panel B.

PANEL C (Worked across 20 sts)

1st and 3rd rows: K1, p4, k1, [p1, k1] 5 times, p3, k1.
2nd and 4th rows: P1, k4, p1, [k1, p1] 5 times, k3, p1.
5th row: K1, p3, T12, p3, k1.
6th row: As 2nd row.
Rep 1st and 2nd rows 4 times more.
These 14 rows form Panel C.

PANEL D (Worked across 16 sts)

Work as given for Panel B **but** working C10F instead of C10B.

SPECIAL NOTE

Yarn is used double throughout.

BACK

Using smaller needles cast on 102(110-114-122-126) sts.

1st row (right side): K2, *p2, k2; rep from * to end.

2nd row: P2, *k2, p2; rep from * to end.

Rep the last 2 rows until rib measures 5 cms [2 ins] ending with a right side row.

Next row (increase): Rib 2(9-8-6-5), *inc in each of next 2 sts, rib 3(3-3-4-4); rep from * to last 5(11-11-8-7) sts, inc in each of next 2 sts, rib to end. 142(148-154-160-166) sts.

Change to larger needles and commence pattern:

1st row: [K1, p2] 7(8-9-10-11) times, k1, p3, work 1st row of Panel A across next 12 sts, [p3, k1] twice, work 1st row of Panel B across next 16 sts, 1st row of Panel C across next 20 sts, 1st row of Panel D across next 16 sts, [k1, p3] twice, work 1st row of Panel A across next 12 sts, p3, k1, [p2, k1] 7(8-9-10-11) times.

2nd row: [P1, k2] 7(8-9-10-11) times, p1, k3, work 2nd row of Panel A, [k3, p1] twice, work 2nd row of Panels D, C and B, [p1, k3] twice, work 2nd row of Panel A, k3, p1, [k2, p1] 7(8-9-10-11) times.

These 2 rows form the rib pattern at each side and the pattern between panels. Keeping continuity of panels correct, continue in pattern until back measures 44 cms [17¼ ins] or required length to armholes ending with a wrong side row ★.

Shape Raglan Armholes

★★ Keeping pattern correct cast off 3(3-5-5-7) sts at beg of next 2 rows.

Man's Aran-Style Sweater

3rd row: [K1, p1] 3 times, sl 1, k1, psso, work in pattern to last 8 sts, k2tog, [p1, k1] 3 times.

4th row: [P1, k1] 3 times, p1, work to last 7 sts, p1, [k1, p1] 3 times ★★.

Rep the last 2 rows until 72(74-74-76-76) sts remain ending with the wrong side row.

Next row: [K1, p1] 3 times, sl 1, k2tog, psso, work to last 9 sts, k3tog, [p1, k1] 3 times.

Next row (decrease): Work 4(2-2-6-6) sts, *work 2tog, work 1 st; rep from * to last 7(5-5-9-9) sts, work 2tog, work to end.

Slip remaining 48(48-48-52-52) sts onto a holder for neckband.

FRONT

Work as given for Back to ★.

Shape Raglan Armholes and Divide for Neck

1st row: Cast off 3(3-5-5-7) sts, work until there are 67(70-71-74-75) sts on right-hand needle, turn and complete this side first.

Work 1 row.

3rd row: [K1, p1] 3 times, sl 1, k1, psso, work to last 2 sts, work 2tog.

4th row: Work 2tog, work to last 7 sts, p1, [k1, p1] 3 times.

1st(2nd-3rd-4th) sizes only

Rep the last 2 rows 4(3-2-1) times more.

All sizes: 52(58-62-68-72) sts remain. Dec 1 st at raglan edge as before on next and every alt row, **at the same time** dec 1 st at neck edge as before on next and every alt row until 8 sts remain, ending with the dec row. Dec 1 st at neck edge only on every alt row until 2 sts remain. Cast off.

Slip next 2 sts at centre onto a safety pin for neckband. With right side of work facing rejoin yarn to neck edge of remaining sts and work to end.

Cast off 3(3-5-5-7) sts at beg of next row.

3rd row: Work 2tog, work to last 8 sts, k2tog, [p1, k1] 3 times.

4th row: [P1, k1] 3 times, p1, work to last 2 sts, work 2tog.

Complete to match first side.

SLEEVES

Using smaller needles cast on 54(54-58-58-62) sts and work 5 cms [2 ins] in k2, p2 rib as given for Back ending with a right side row.

Next row (increase): Rib 5(5-4-4-3), *inc in each of next 2 sts, work 1 st; rep from * to last 7(7-6-6-5) sts, inc in each of next 2 sts, rib to end. 84(84-92-92-100) sts.

Change to larger needles and commence pattern:

1st row: K1, [p3, k1] 7(7-8-8-9) times, p7, work 1st row of Panel A across next 12 sts, p7, k1, [p3, k1] 7(7-8-8-9) times.

2nd row: P1, [k3, p1] 7(7-8-8-9) times, k7, work 2nd row of Panel A, k7, p1, [k3, p1] 7(7-8-8-9) times.

Keeping the 20 rows of panel correct throughout rep the last 2 rows twice more. Bringing extra sts into rib pattern inc 1 st at each end of next and every following 10th row until there are 108(108-116-116-124) sts. Work straight until sleeve measures 47 cms [18½ ins] or required sleeve length ending with a wrong side row.

Shape Raglan Top

Work as given for Back from ★★ to ★★. Rep the last 2 rows until 48(40-44-36-40) sts remain ending with the wrong side row.

Next row: [K1, p1] 3 times, sl 1, k2tog, psso, work to last 9 sts, k3tog, [p1, k1] 3 times.

Next row: As 4th row.

Rep the last 2 rows 5(3-4-2-3) times more. Slip remaining 24 sts onto a holder for neckband.

TO MAKE UP

Press each piece lightly on the wrong side using a warm iron and a damp cloth. Join front and left back raglan seams.

Neckband: Using smaller needles and with right side of work facing, knit across sts at back neck and left sleeve top (decreasing 4 sts evenly across sleeve top), pick up and k60(64-64-68-72) sts down left front slope, knit 2 sts from safety pin, pick up and k60(64-64-68-72) sts up right front slope, and knit across sts of right sleeve top decreasing 4 sts evenly. 210(218-218-230-238) sts.

1st row: P2, *k2, p2; rep from * to 2 sts before centre sts, k1, p2tog tbl, p2tog, k1, p2, *k2, p2; rep from * to end.

2nd row: K2, *p2, k2; rep from * to 1 st before centre sts, k2tog, sl 1, k1, psso, k2, *p2, k2; rep from * to end.

3rd row: *P2, k2; rep from * to 2 sts before centre sts, p1, p2tog tbl, p2tog, p1, *k2, p2; rep from * to end.

4th row: *K2, p2; rep from * to 1 st before centre sts, k2tog, sl 1, k1, psso, *p2, k2; rep from * to end.

Rep the last 4 rows once more. Cast off in rib decreasing on this row also.

Join remaining raglan seam and ends of neckband. Join side and sleeve seams. Press seams.

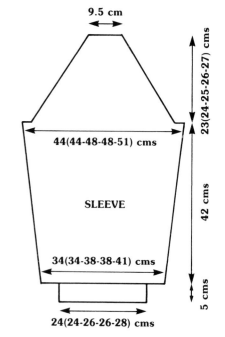

9.5 cm

23(24-25-26-27) cms

44(44-48-48-51) cms

42 cms

SLEEVE

34(34-38-38-41) cms

5 cms

24(24-26-26-28) cms

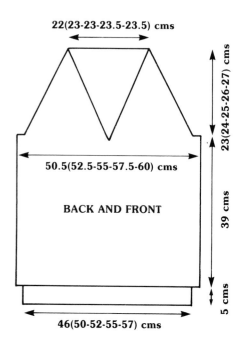

22(23-23-23.5-23.5) cms

23(24-25-26-27) cms

50.5(52.5-55-57.5-60) cms

BACK AND FRONT

39 cms

5 cms

46(50-52-55-57) cms

Cable and Lace Sweater

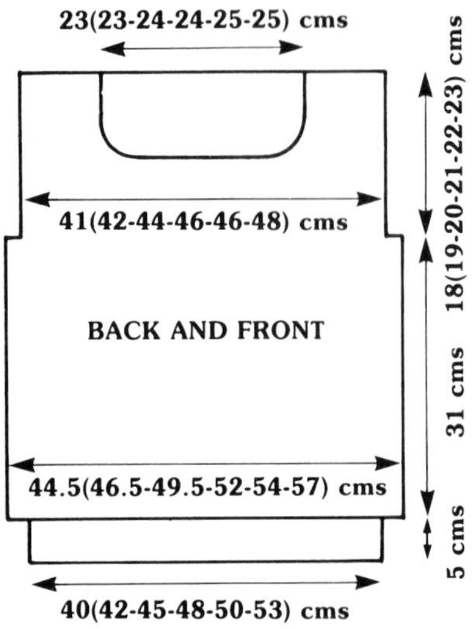

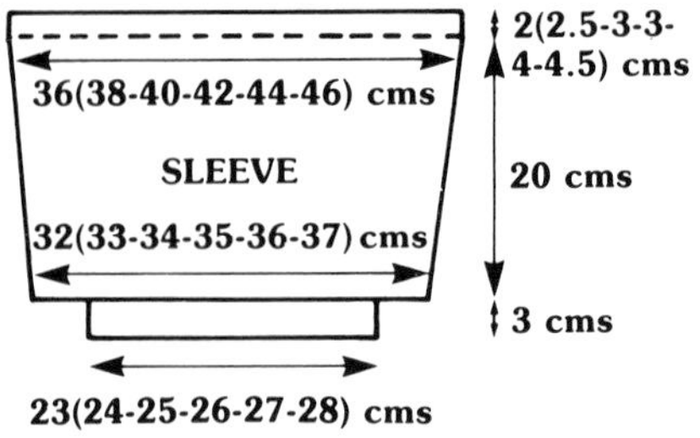

Figures

23(23-24-24-25-25) cms

18(19-20-21-22-23) cms

41(42-44-46-46-48) cms

BACK AND FRONT

31 cms

44.5(46.5-49.5-52-54-57) cms

5 cms

40(42-45-48-50-53) cms

2(2.5-3-3-4-4.5) cms

36(38-40-42-44-46) cms

SLEEVE

20 cms

32(33-34-35-36-37) cms

3 cms

23(24-25-26-27-28) cms

MEASUREMENTS

To fit bust sizes 80(85-90-95-100-105) cms [32(34-36-38-40-42) ins]. Finished measurement 89(93-99-104-108-114) cms [35½(37-39½-41½-43-45½) ins]. Length to shoulder 54(55-56-57-58-59) cms [21¼(21¾-22¼-22½-23-23¼) ins]. Sleeve length 23 cms [9 ins].

MATERIALS

Coats 'Anchor' Knitting and Crochet Cotton No. 6 (50g) used double: 10(11-12-13-14-15) balls. Pair needles each size 4½mm (No 7) and 3¼mm (No 10). Cable Needle. Stitch holders.

Coats Maxi 'Pellicano' Knitting and Crochet Cotton No. 5 (200g) used double: 3(3-3-4-4-4) balls. Pair needles each size 5mm (No 6) and 3¾mm (No 9). Cable needle. Stitch holders.

TENSION

With yarn used double: 21 sts and 28 rows = 10 cms [4 ins] square measured over st st using larger needles.

SPECIAL ABBREVIATIONS

PB1 = purl into back of next stitch.

C6B or C6F (Cable 6 Back or Cable 6 Front) = slip next 3 sts onto cable needle and hold at back (or front) of work, knit next 3 sts from left-hand needle, then knit sts from cable needle.

PANEL A (Worked across 10 sts)

1st and 3rd rows: P2, k6, p2.
2nd and 4th rows: K2, p6, k2.
5th row: P2, C6F, p2.
6th row: As 2nd row.
These 6 rows form Panel A.

PANEL B (Worked across 7 sts)

1st row: K1, [yf, k2tog] 3 times.
2nd row: P7.
Rep the last 2 rows 3 times more.
9th row: K7.
10th row: P7.
These 10 rows form Panel B.

PANEL C (Worked across 10 sts)

Work as given for Panel A **but** working C6B instead of C6F.

PANEL D (Worked across 5 sts)

1st row: K3, k2tog, yfrn.
2nd row: PB1, p4.
3rd row: K2, k2tog, yf, k1.
4th row: P1, PB1, p3.
5th row: K1, k2tog, yf, k2.
6th row: P2, PB1, p2.
7th row: K2tog, yf, k3.
8th row: P3, PB1, p1.
These 8 rows form Panel D.

PANEL E (Worked across 10 sts)

1st row: P7, yrn, p2tog, p1.
2nd and every alt row: K10.
3rd row: P5, p2tog, yrn, p3.
5th row: P4, p2tog, yrn, p4.
7th row: P3, p2tog, yrn, p5.
9th row: P2, p2tog, yrn, p6.
11th row: P1, p2tog, yrn, p7.
13th row: P3, yrn, p2tog, p5.
15th row: P4, yrn, p2tog, p4.
17th row: P5, yrn, p2tog, p3.
19th row: P6, yrn, p2tog, p2.
20th row: K10.
These 20 rows form Panel E.

PANEL F (Worked across 9 sts)

1st row: K9.
2nd and every alt row: P9.
3rd row: K3, C6B.
5th row: K9.
7th row: C6F, k3.
8th row: P9.
These 8 rows form Panel F.

PANEL G (Worked across 5 sts)

1st row: Yon, sl 1, k1, psso, k3.
2nd row: P4, PB1.
3rd row: K1, yf, sl 1, k1, psso, k2.
4th row: P3, PB1, p1.
5th row: K2, yf, sl 1, k1, psso, k1.
6th row: P2, PB1, p2.
7th row: K3, yf, sl 1, k1, psso.
8th row: P1, PB1, p3.
These 8 rows form Panel G.

Cable and Lace Sweater

SPECIAL NOTE

Yarn is used double throughout.

BACK

Using smaller needles cast on 85(89-95-101-105-111) sts.

1st row (right side): K1, *p1, k1; rep from * to end.

2nd row: P1, *k1, p1; rep from * to end.

Rep the last 2 rows until rib measures 5 cms [2 ins] ending with a right side row.

Next row (increase): Rib 6(2-5-4-6-2), *inc in each of next 2(1-1-2-2-1) sts, rib 5(3-3-7-7-4); rep from * to last 9(3-6-7-9-4) sts, inc in each of next 2(1-1-2-2-1) sts, rib to end. 107(111-117-123-127-133) sts.

Change to larger needles and commence pattern:

1st row: K7(9-12-15-17-20), *work 1st row of Panel A across next 10 sts, Panel B across next 7 sts, Panel C across next 10 sts*, Panel D across next 5 sts, Panel E across next 10 sts and Panel F across next 9 sts, work **11th** row of Panel E across next 10 sts, work 1st row of Panel G across next 5 sts, rep from * to * once more, k7(9-12-15-17-20).

2nd row: P7(9-12-15-17-20), work 2nd row of Panels C, B, A and G, work **12th** row of Panel E, work 2nd row of Panels F, E, D, C, B and A, p7(9-12-15-17-20).

These 2 rows form the st st at either side. Keeping continuity of panels correct rep the last 2 rows until back measures 36 cms [14¼ ins] or required length to armholes ending with a wrong side row.

Shape Armholes

Keeping pattern correct cast off 4(5-6-7-8-9) sts at beg of next 2 rows. 99(101-105-109-111-115) sts remain. Continue in pattern until armholes measure 18(19-20-21-22-23) cms [7(7½-8-8¼-8¾-9) ins] ending with a wrong side row.

Shape Shoulders

Cast off 22(23-24-26-26-28) sts at beg of next row.

Next row: Cast off 22(23-24-26-26-28) sts, work until there are 4(4-5-5-6-6) sts on right-hand needle, [work 2tog, work 7 sts] 5 times, work 2tog, work to end.

Slip remaining 49(49-51-51-53-53) sts onto a holder for neckband.

FRONT

Work as given for Back until front measures 10(10-11-11-12-12) cms [4(4-4¼-4¼-4¾-4¾) ins] less than back to shoulder ending with a right side row.

Shape Neck

Next row: Work 34(35-36-38-39-41) sts, turn and complete this side first.

★ Dec 1 st at neck edge on next 7 rows, then every alt row until 22(23-24-26-26-28) sts remain. Work straight until front measures same as back to shoulder ending with a right side row (work 1 row less here for 2nd side). Cast off.

Slip next 31(31-33-33-33-33) sts at centre onto a holder for neckband. With wrong side of work facing rejoin yarn to neck edge of remaining sts and work to end. Complete as given for first side from ★ to end reversing shaping where indicated.

SLEEVES

Using smaller needles cast on 49(51-53-55-57-59) sts and work 3 cms [1¼ ins] in k1, p1 rib as given for Back ending with a right side row.

Next row (increase): Rib 5(6-1-2-3-4), *inc in each of next 2(2-1-1-1-1) sts, work 1 st; rep from * to last 8(9-2-3-4-5) sts, inc in each of next 2(2-1-1-1-1) sts, rib to end. 75(77-79-81-83-85) sts.

Change to larger needles and commence pattern:

1st row: K1(2-3-4-5-6), work 1st row of Panel B across next 7 sts, Panel C across next 10 sts, Panel D across next 5 sts, Panel E across next 10 sts and Panel F across next 9 sts, work **11th** row of Panel E across next 10 sts, work 1st row of Panel G across next 5 sts, Panel A across next 10 sts and Panel B across next 7 sts, k1(2-3-4-5-6).

2nd row: P1(2-3-4-5-6), work 2nd row of Panels B, A and G, work **12th** row of Panel E, work 2nd row of Panels F, E, D, C and B, p1(2-3-4-5-6).

Keeping continuity of panels correct throughout work 2 more rows. Bringing extra sts into st st inc 1 st at each end of next and every following 10th(8th-7th-6th-5th-4th) row until there are 85(89-93-97-101-105) sts. Work straight until sleeve measures 23 cms [9 ins] or required sleeve length ending with a wrong side row. Tie a marker at each end of last row to mark end of sleeve seam. Work 5(7-8-9-11-12) more rows in pattern. Cast off.

TO MAKE UP

Press pieces according to instructions on ball band. Join left shoulder seam.

Neckband: Using smaller needles and with right side of work facing, knit across sts on holder at back neck, pick up and k24(24-26-26-30-30) sts down left front slope, knit across sts on holder at front neck decreasing 3 sts evenly, and pick up and k24(24-26-26-30-30) sts up right front slope. 125(125-133-133-143-143) sts.

Work 6 rows in k1, p1 rib as given for Back starting with the 2nd row. Cast off in rib.

Join right shoulder seam and ends of neckband. Join side seams and sleeve seams to markers. Insert sleeves. Press seams.

4-Colour Sweater

MEASUREMENTS

To fit bust sizes 80(85-90-95-100-105) cms [32(34-36-38-40-42 ins]. Length to shoulder (approximately) 52(53-54-55-56-57) cms [20¾(21¼-21½-22-22½-22¾) ins]. Width from wrist to wrist (approximately) 134(137-140-142-144-147) cms [53½(54¾-56-56¾-57½-58¾) ins].

MATERIALS

Patons Beehive Double Knitting 50g balls: 3 balls each in Colours A, B, C and D. Pair needles size 3¼mm (No 10). Circular needle size 4mm (No 8).

TENSION

22 sts and 30 rows = 10 cms [4 ins] square measured over st st using larger needles.

BACK

Using smaller needles and A cast on 87(93-99-103-109-115) sts.

1st row (right side): K1, *p1, k1; rep from * to end.

2nd row: P1, *k1, p1; rep from * to end.

Rep the last 2 rows until rib measures 10 cms [4 ins] ending with a right side row.

Next row (increase): Rib 5(6-6-6-6-7), *inc in next st, rib 14(15-16-17-18-19); rep from * to last 7(7-8-7-8-8) sts, inc in next st, rib to end. 93(99-105-109-115-121) sts.

Change to circular needle. Twisting yarns together on wrong side of work when changing colour to avoid making a hole and turning at end of every row, commence pattern ★:

1st row: Using A k1, [p1, k1] 23(24-26-27-28-30) times, using B knit to end.

2nd row: Using B p46(50-52-54-58-60), using A p1, *k1, p1; rep from * to end.

3rd row: Using A p1, [k1, p1] 23(24-26-27-28-30) times, using B *k1, p1; rep from * to end.

4th row: Using B p46(50-52-54-58-60), using

A k1, *p1, k1; rep from * to end.

★★ These 4 rows form the double moss st and fleck st patterns. Keeping patterns correct and bringing extra sts into pattern, inc 1 st at each end of next and every alt row until there are 117(123-129-133-139-145) sts. Inc 1 st at each end of every row until there are 199(205-211-215-221-227) sts, thus ending with a wrong side row. Break off A ★★.

Next row: Using C cast on 5 sts, knit these sts, then k100(102-106-108-110-114), using B knit to end.

Next row: Using B cast on 5 sts, purl these sts, then p99(103-105-107-111-113), using C p1, *k1, p1; rep from * to end.

Next row: Using C cast on 5 sts, knit these sts then k105(107-111-113-115-119), using B *k1, p1; rep from * to end.

Next row: Using B cast on 5 sts, purl these sts, then p104(108-110-112-116-118), using C *p1, k1; rep from * to end. 219(225-231-235-241-247) sts.

Keeping patterns correct and bringing extra sts into patterns, continue to cast on 5 sts at beg of every row until there are 264(270-276-280-286-292) sts, thus ending with a right side row. Break off B.

Next row: Using D cast on 5 sts, purl these sts, then p129(133-135-137-141-143), using C p1, *k1, p1; rep from * to end. 269(275-281-285-291-297) sts.

Next row: Using C k135(137-141-143-145-149), using D *k1, p1; rep from * to end.

Next row: Using D [k1, p1] 67(69-70-71-73-74) times, using C p1, *k1, p1; rep from * to end.

Next row: Using C k135(137-141-143-145-149), using D *p1, k1; rep from * to end.

Next row: Using D [p1, k1] 67(69-70-71-73-74) times, using C p1, *k1, p1; rep from * to end.

★★★ Keeping patterns correct as set work 23(25-29-31-35-37) rows straight, thus ending with a right side row.

4-Colour Sweater

Shape Neck

Next row: Work 119(122-124-126-128-131) sts, turn and complete this side first.

★★★ Dec 1 st at neck edge on next 7 rows, then following 2 alt rows. 110(113-115-117-119-122) sts remain. Work 5 rows straight. Cast off.

Slip next 31(31-33-33-35-35) sts at centre onto a holder for neckband. With wrong side of work facing rejoin yarn to neck edge of remaining 119(122-124-126-128-131) sts and work to end. Complete as given for first side from ★★★ to end.

FRONT

Work as given for Back to ★.

1st row: Using B k46(50-52-54-58-60), using A k1, *p1, k1; rep from * to end.

2nd row: Using A p1, [k1, p1] 23(24-26-27-28-30) times, using B purl to end.

3rd row: Using B [p1, k1] 23(25-26-27-29-30) times, using A p1, *k1, p1; rep from * to end.

4th row: Using A k1, [p1, k1] 23(24-26-27-28-30) times, using B purl to end.

Work as given for Back from ★★ to ★★.

Next row: Using B cast on 5 sts, knit these sts then k99(103-105-107-111-113), using C knit to end.

Next row: Using C cast on 5 sts, p1, *k1, p1; rep from * to colour change, using B purl to end.

Next row: Using B cast on 5 sts, k1, *p1, k1; rep from * to colour change, using C knit to end.

Next row: Using C cast on 5 sts, *k1, p1; rep from * to colour change, using B purl to end. 219(225-231-235-241-247) sts.

Keeping patterns correct and bringing extra sts into patterns, continue to cast on 5 sts at beg of every row until there are 264(270-276-280-286-292) sts, thus ending with a right side row. Break off B.

Next row: Using C cast on 5 sts, p1, *k1, p1; rep from * to colour change, using D purl to end.

Next row: Using D [k1, p1] 67(69-70-71-73-74) times, using C knit to end.

Next row: Using C p1, [k1, p1] 67(68-70-71-72-74) times, using D *k1, p1; rep from * to end.

Next row: Using D [p1, k1] 67(69-70-71-73-74) times, using C knit to end.

Next row: Using C p1, [k1, p1] 67(68-70-71-72-74) times, using D *p1, k1; rep from * to end.

Complete as given for Back from ★★★ to end.

FINISHING AND EDGINGS

Press pieces according to instructions on ball band. Join left shoulder seam.

Neckband: Using smaller needles and C and with right side of work facing, pick up and k14 sts down right back slope, knit across sts at back neck decreasing 1 st at centre, pick up and k14 sts up left back slope, 14 sts down left front slope, knit across sts at front neck and pick up and k14 sts up right front slope. 117(117-121-121-125-125) sts.

Work 10 rows in k1, p1 rib as given for Back starting with the 2nd row. Cast off in rib.

Join right shoulder seam and ends of neckband.

Left Cuff: Using smaller needles and D and with right side of work facing, pick up and k64(67-73-76-82-86) sts evenly along sleeve edge.

Next row (decrease): P4(4-1-1-5-5), *[p2tog] 1(1-1-1-2-2) times, p1; rep from * to last 6(6-3-3-7-6) sts, p2tog, purl to end. 45(47-49-51-53-55) sts remain.

Work 6 cms [2½ ins] in k1, p1 rib as given for Back. Cast off in rib.

Right Cuff: Work as given for Left Cuff **but** using C instead of D.

Join side and underarm seams and ends of cuffs. Press seams.

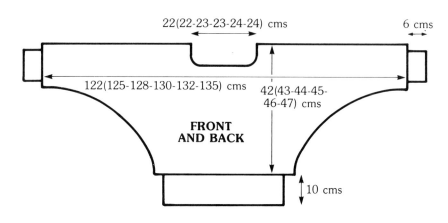

22(22-23-23-24-24) cms

6 cms

122(125-128-130-132-135) cms

42(43-44-45-46-47) cms

FRONT AND BACK

10 cms

Dolman Sweater

MEASUREMENTS

To fit bust sizes 80(85-90-95-100-105) cms [32(34-36-38-40-42) ins]. Finished measurement at bust 101(104-110-115-121-124) cms [40½(41½-44-46-48½-49½) ins]. Length to back of neck 56(57-58-60-62-63) cms [22(22½-22¾-23½-24½-24¾) ins]. Sleeve seam 16(16-16-16-16-16) cms [6¼(6¼-6¼-6¼-6¼-6¼) ins].

MATERIALS

Coats Maxi 'Pellicano' Knitting and Crochet Cotton No. 5 (200g) used double: 3(3-3-4-4-4) balls. Pair needles each size 3¾mm (No 9) and 4½mm (No 7). Stitch holders.

Coats 'Anchor' Knitting and Crochet Cotton No. 6 (50g) used double: 10(11-12-12-13-13) balls. Pair needles each size 3¼mm (No 10) and 4mm (No 8). Stitch holders.

TENSION

With yarn used double: 22 sts and 30 rows = 10 cms [4 ins] square measured over pattern using larger needles.

SPECIAL ABBREVIATION

Slip marker = make a slip knot in a short length of contrasting yarn and place on needle where indicated. On the following rows slip the marker from one needle to the other until the pattern is established and the marker is no longer required.

LACE PANEL (Worked across 25 sts between markers)

1st row: P2, k6, k3tog, yf, k1, yfrn, p1, yon, k1, yf, sl 1, k2tog, psso, k6, p2.

2nd and every alt row: K2, p10, k1, p10, k2.

3rd row: P2, k4, k3tog, k1, [yf, k1] twice, p1, k1, [yf, k1] twice, sl 1, k2tog, psso, k4, p2.

5th row: P2, k2, k3tog, k2, yf, k1, yf, k2, p1, k2, yf, k1, yf, k2, sl 1, k2tog, psso, k2, p2.

7th row: P2, k3tog, k3, yf, k1, yf, k3, p1, k3, yf, k1, yf, k3, sl 1, k2tog, psso, p2.

9th row: P2, k10, p1, k10, p2.

10th row: K2, p10, k1, p10, k2.

Rep the last 2 rows once more.

These 12 rows form the Lace Panel.

SPECIAL NOTE

Yarn is used double throughout.

BACK

Using smaller needles cast on 83(87-93-99-105-109) sts.

1st row (right side): K1, *p1, k1; rep from * to end.

2nd row: P1, *k1, p1; rep from * to end.

Rep the last 2 rows until rib measures 6 cms [2½ ins] ending with a right side row.

Next row (increase): Rib 2(4-2-5-2-4), *inc in next st, rib 6(6-7-7-8-8); rep from * to last 4(6-3-6-4-6) sts, inc in next st, rib to end. 95(99-105-111-117-121) sts.

Change to larger needles and commence pattern:

Work 3 rows in st st, starting knit.

4th row: P2(1-1-1-1-6), *k1, p5; rep from * to last 3(2-2-2-2-7) sts, k1, purl to end.

Work 3 rows in st st, starting knit.

8th row: P5(4-4-4-4-3), *k1, p5; rep from * to last 6(5-5-5-5-4) sts, k1, purl to end.

These 8 rows form the pattern. Bringing extra sts into pattern inc 1 st at each end of next and every following 4th row until there are 111(115-121-127-133-137) sts. Work straight until back measures 21 cms [8¼ ins] or required length to armholes ending with a wrong side row.

Shape Raglan Armholes

Cast off 2(3-3-3-3-3) sts at beg of next 2 rows. Knit 1 row.

4th row: P2, work to last 2 sts, p2.

5th row: K1, sl 1, k1, psso, knit to last 3 sts, k2tog, k1.

6th row: P2, work to last 2 sts, p2 ★.

Rep the last 4 rows until 91(93-99-105-111-115) sts remain, then rep the last 2 rows only until 21(21-23-23-25-25) sts remain ending with the wrong side row.

Next row: K1, sl 1, k2tog, psso, knit to last 4 sts, k3tog, k1.

Next row: P2, work to last 2 sts, p2.

Slip remaining 17(17-19-19-21-21) sts onto a holder for neckband.

FRONT

Work as given for Back to ★.

Rep the last 4 rows until 95(97-103-109-115-119) sts remain ending with the dec row. Work 1 row.

Divide for Neck

1st row: K47(48-51-54-57-59), turn and complete this side first, leaving remaining sts on a holder.

★★ **2nd row:** P2, work to last 2 sts, p2.

3rd row: K1, sl 1, k1, psso, knit to last 3 sts, k2tog, k1.

Continue to dec 1 st at raglan and neck edges on every following 4th row until 39(40-43-46-49-51) sts remain. Now dec 1 st at raglan edge on every alt row, **at the same time** dec 1 st at neck edge on every following 4th row 8(8-9-9-10-10) times, 15(16-16-19-19-21) sts remain, then every following 6th row twice. 7(8-8-11-11-13) sts remain.

146

Dolman Sweater

Keeping neck edge straight continue to dec at raglan edge only until 3 sts remain. Dec 1 st at neck edge only on following alt row. Cast off.

Slip next st at centre onto a safety pin for neckband. With right side of work facing rejoin yarn to neck edge of remaining sts and knit to end.

Complete as given for first side from ★★ to end.

RIGHT SLEEVE

Using smaller needles cast on 55(57-59-61-63-65) sts and work 3 cms [1¼ ins] in k1, p1 rib as given for Back ending with a wrong side row.

Next row (increase): K1(2-3-4-5-6), *inc in each of next 2 sts, k1; rep from * to last 3(4-5-6-7-8) sts, inc in each of next 2 sts, knit to end. 91(93-95-97-99-101) sts.

Change to larger needles and purl 1 row. Commence pattern:

1st row: K33(34-35-36-37-38), slip marker, work 1st row of Lace Panel across next 25 sts, slip marker, knit to end.

2nd row: P33(34-35-36-37-38), work 2nd row of Lace Panel, purl to end.

3rd row: As 1st row but working 3rd row of Lace Panel.

4th row: P1(2-3-4-5-6), [k1, p5] 5 times, k1, p1, work 4th row of Lace Panel, p1, k1, [p5, k1] 5 times, p1(2-3-4-5-6).

5th row: As 1st row but working 5th row of Lace Panel.

6th row: As 2nd row but working 6th row of Lace Panel.

7th row: As 1st row but working 7th row of Lace Panel.

8th row: P4(5-6-1-2-3), [k1, p5] 4(4-4-5-5-5) times, k1, p4, work 8th row of Lace Panel, p4, k1, [p5, k1] 4(4-4-5-5-5) times, p4(5-6-1-2-3).

These 8 rows form the pattern either side of Lace Panel. Keeping the 12 rows of lace panel correct on sts between markers and bringing extra sts into pattern, inc 1 st at each end of next and every alt row until there are 115(117-119-121-123-125) sts. Work straight until sleeve measures 16 cms [6¼ ins] or required seam length ending with a wrong side row.

Shape Raglan Top

Keeping pattern correct cast off 2(3-3-3-3-3) sts at beg of next 2 rows. Work 1 row.

4th row: P2, work to last 2 sts, p2.

5th row: K1, sl 1, k1, psso, work to last 3 sts, k2tog, k1.

6th row: P2, work to last 2 sts, p2.

Rep the last 4 rows 1(2-3-5-6-7) times more, 107(105-105-103-103-103) sts remain, then rep the last 2 rows only until 21 sts remain ending with the dec row ★★★.

Next row: Work 11 sts, turn and slip remaining 10 sts onto a holder for neckband.

Next row: K2tog tbl, work to last 3 sts, k2tog, k1.

Next row: Work to end.

Rep the last 2 rows twice more. 5 sts remain.

Next row: K2tog tbl, k2tog, k1. 3 sts remain. Work 1 row.

Next row: K2tog, k1. 2 sts remain. Cast off.

LEFT SLEEVE

Work as given for Right Sleeve to ★★★.

Next row: Work 10 sts, slip these sts onto a holder for neckband, work to end. 11 sts remain.

Next row: K1, sl 1, k1, psso, work to last 2 sts, k2tog.

Next row: Work to end.

Rep the last 2 rows twice more. 5 sts remain.

Next row: K1, sl 1, k1, psso, k2tog. 3 sts remain.

Work 1 row.

Next row: K1, sl 1, k1, psso. 2 sts remain. Cast off.

TO MAKE UP

Press pieces according to instructions on ball band. Join front and left back raglan seams.

Neckband: Using smaller needles and with right side of work facing knit across sts on holder at back neck decreasing 1 st at centre, pick up and k8 sts evenly across left sleeve slope, knit across sts on holder at front of left sleeve top, pick up and k61(63-67-71-75-79) sts down left front slope, knit st from safety pin at centre front, pick up and k61(63-67-71-75-79) sts up right front slope, knit across sts on holder at front of right sleeve top and pick up and k8 sts evenly across right sleeve slope. 175(179-189-197-207-215) sts.

1st row: P1, *k1, p1; rep from * to 2 sts before centre front st, p2tog, p1, p2tog tbl, p1, *k1, p1; rep from * to end.

2nd row: *K1, p1; rep from * to 2 sts before centre front st, sl 1, k1, psso, k1, k2tog, *p1, k1; rep from * to end.

Rep the last 2 rows 3 times more. Cast off in rib decreasing on this row also.

Join remaining raglan seam and ends of neckband. Join side and sleeve seams.

Square Patterned Tabard

MEASUREMENTS

To fit bust sizes 81/86(91/96) cms [32/34(36/38) ins]. Finished bust measurement at underarm 96(107) cms [38½(43) ins]. Length 75(76.5) cms [29½(30) ins].

MATERIALS

Patons Beehive Knits as 4 Ply 50g balls: 5 balls Main colour (M), 2 balls each in Colours A and B. Pair needles size 3¼mm (No 10). Circular knitting needles each size 2¾mm (No 12) and 3¼mm (No 10), 80 cms [29 ins] long. Four oblong novelty buttons.

TENSION

28 sts and 26 rows = 10 cms [4 ins] over colourwork pattern using 3¼mm needles.
30 sts and 30 rows = 10 cms [4 ins] over twisted rib pattern using 3¼mm needles.

NOTES

When working colourwork pattern, use a separate bobbin of yarn for colours A and B and carry colours not in use **loosely** on wrong side to keep proper tension.

When changing colours, twist yarns on wrong side to prevent holes. To avoid excessively long strands or 'floats' at back of work, weave or twist yarns not in use around working yarn every 4 or 5 sts.

Body of tabard is made in rounds on circular needle above lower edge rib.

BODY

Lower Edge Rib: Starting at lower edge of back, using 3¼mm needles and M cast on 145(160) sts.

Work Twisted Rib as follows:

1st row (wrong side): *P1, k1 tbl; rep from *, ending p1(0).

2nd row: K1(0) tbl, *p1, k1 tbl; rep from * to end.

Rep 1st and 2nd rows for twisted rib for 20.5 cms [8 ins] from beg, ending with a wrong side row.

Slip sts onto a holder to be worked later.

Work lower edge rib for front in same way, but do not slip sts onto a holder.

Join Front and Back

Change to 3¼mm circular needle. Knit across 145(160) sts of front rib, decreasing 10 sts evenly spaced, continue to knit across 145(160) sts of back rib, decreasing 10 sts evenly spaced. 270(300) sts. Join and place marker for beg of round.

1st round: Starting as indicated for chosen size, work in colourwork pattern following 1st row of chart, a total of 9(10) pattern block repeats.

Continuing to work in rounds, rep 1st to 25th pattern rows until piece measures 46 cms [18 ins] from beg.

Divide for Armholes

Work pattern across first 135(150) sts (for front), slip remaining sts onto a holder to be worked later (for back). Continue in pattern as set and working back and forth in rows, work straight until armhole measures 19(20.5) cms

Square Patterned Tabard

[7½(8) ins], ending with a wrong side row.

Shape Neck

Next row (right side): Work first 59(65) sts, join 2nd ball of yarn and cast off centre 17(20) sts, work to end.

Working both sides at the same time with separate balls of yarn, cast off 4 sts from each neck edge every alt row 4 times, dec 1 st every row 10 times. 33(39) sts each side. Work straight in pattern until armhole measures approximately 26.5(28) cms [10½(11) ins], ending with a wrong side row.

Next row (right side): Slip first 33(39) sts onto a holder (for left shoulder), work pattern on 33(39) sts for right shoulder.

Continue in pattern on right shoulder sts only until armhole measures approximately 29(30.5) cms [11½(12) ins], ending with an M row. Slip sts onto a holder (to be woven later for shoulder) or cast off.

Rejoin yarn to sts for back and work back armhole and neck as for front, being sure to reverse working of right and left shoulders.

FINISHING

Press according to instructions on ball band. Sew or weave right shoulder seam.

Right Armhole Edging: Using 2¾mm circular needle and M and starting at back armhole edge, pick up and k66(69) sts to shoulder, pick up and k66(69) sts along front edge. 132(138) sts. Do **not** join. Work back and forth in twisted rib for 2 rows.

Commence short rows:

1st row (wrong side): Rib to last 3 sts, leave these sts unworked, turn.

2nd row: Sl 1, rib to last 3 sts, leave these sts unworked, turn.

3rd row: Sl 1, rib to 5 sts before last unworked sts, leave these sts unworked, turn.

Rep last row 11 times more.

15th row: Sl 1, rib to 10(11) sts before last unworked sts, leave these sts unworked, turn.

Rep last row 3 times more.

19th row: Sl 1, rib to 11(12) sts before last unworked sts, leave these sts unworked, turn.

Rep this row once more.

21st row: Rib across all sts to end, closing holes at each short-row interval as follows: rib to short-row interval, insert tip of left-hand needle from front to back into centre of st 2 rows below last st on right-hand needle, slip st to left-hand needle and k2tog, rib in this way to end. Cast off all sts loosely, closing holes as before. Edging measures aproximately 5.5 cms

[2¼ ins] at widest point.

Left Armhole Edging: Using 2¾mm circular needle and M and starting left front armhole edge, pick up and k60(63) sts to top of armhole edge. Work back and forth in twisted rib for 2 rows.

Commence short rows:

1st row (wrong side): Rib to last 3 sts, leave these sts unworked, turn.

2nd row: Sl 1, rib to end.

Continue to work short row shaping at end of wrong side rows only (and working right side rows straight) leaving 5 sts unworked at armhole edge 6 times, 11 sts twice. Cast off, closing holes as before.

Starting at left shoulder edge, pick up and k60(63) sts to armhole edge. Being sure to work short row shaping at armhole edge only

(end of right side rows), work to correspond to left front armhole edging.

Left Back Shoulder Rib: Slip 33(39) sts from back left holder onto 2¾mm circular needle, then with M pick up and k16 sts from top of armhole edging. 49(55) sts. Work in twisted rib for 4 cms [1½ ins]. Cast off loosely in rib.

Work left front shoulder rib to correspond.

Neckband: Using 2¾mm circular needle and M and starting at top of left front shoulder rib, pick and k8 sts along side of shoulder rib, 72(75) sts around front neck edge, 80(83) sts around back neck edge and shoulder rib. 160(166) sts. Work back and forth in rows of twisted rib for 2.5 cms [1 inch]. Cast off loosely in rib.

Overlap left front shoulder over back shoulder. Sew buttons evenly spaced through both thicknesses.

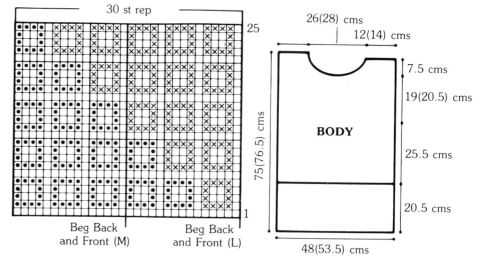

□ = M
☒ = A
▣ = B

Medium (M) = 81/86 cms [32/34 ins] bust
Large (L) = 91/96 cms [36/38 ins] bust

Oversized Slipover

MEASUREMENTS

To fit bust/chest sizes 86/91(96/101-106/112) cms [34/36(38/40-42/44) ins]. Finished bust/chest measurement at underarm 112(120-130) cms [44(48-52) ins]. Length 68.5(71-73.5) cms [27(28-29) ins].

MATERIALS

13(15-17) 50g balls of Scheepjeswool Superwash Zermatt in colour 4836 green or 4802 grey. Pair needles each size 5½mm (No 5) and 6½mm (No 3). 5½mm (No 5) circular knitting needle, 60 cms [24 ins] long. Cable needle.

TENSION

14 sts and 18 rows = 10 cms [4 ins] over st st using size 6½mm needles and 2 strands of yarn.

NOTES

For easier working of pattern sts, keep careful count of rows.

Use 2 strands of yarn held tog throughout.

BACK

Using smaller needles and 2 strands of yarn cast on 76(82-88) sts. Work in k2, p2 rib for 5 cms [2 ins].

Change to larger needles.

Next row: Purl, increasing 2 sts across row. 78(84-90) sts.

Commence Diagonal and St St Patterns

1st row (right side): K1, with right-hand needle behind left-hand needle miss next st on left-hand needle and k into 2nd st in back loop, then k the missed st in front loop and slip both sts from left-hand needle — left twist made over 2 sts (LT), p3, LT over next 2 sts, k to end.

2nd row: P until 7 sts remain, k4, p3.

3rd row: K2, LT, p3, LT, k to end.

4th row: P until 8 sts remain, k4, p4.

5th row: K3, LT, p3, LT, k to end.

6th row: P until 9 sts remain, k4, p5.

Continue to work diagonal and st st patterns, having 1 more knit st at beg of each right side row and 1 more purl st at the end of each wrong side row for 21 rows more.

28th row (wrong side): Knit first 30 sts, work remaining sts in set patterns.

29th row (right side): Work in patterns to last 30 sts, p30.

30th to 53rd rows: Continue in diagonal and st st patterns only.

54th row (wrong side): Continue to work diagonal and st st patterns to last 18 sts, k2, p16.

55th row (right side): K16, p2, work in patterns to last 18 sts, p2, k16.

56th row (wrong side): P16, k2, work in patterns to last 18 sts, k2, p16.

Rep 55th and 56th rows 7 times more.

71st row (right side): K16, p2, work in patterns to last 18 sts, p18.

72nd row: K18, work in patterns to last 18 sts, k2, p16.

73rd row: K16, p2, work in diagonal and st st patterns to end.

74th row: Work in patterns to last 18 sts, k2, p16.

Rep 73rd and 74th rows 6 times more, ending with 86th row.

Continue in diagonal and st st patterns only for 12(16-22) rows more.

99th(103rd-109th) row (right side): K13, work 1st row of Chart 1 over next 8 sts, work to end.

Work in set patterns working Chart 1 for next 12 rows. Work 1 row more in diagonal and st st patterns. Piece measures approximately 68.5(71-73.5) cms [27(28-29) ins] from beg. Cast off.

FRONT

Work as given for Back until rib measures 5 cms [2 ins]. Change to larger needles.

Next row: Purl, increasing 2 sts across row. 78(84-90) sts.

Work 2 rows in st st.

3rd row (right side): K44(47-50), p1, k6, p1, knit to end.

4th row: P26(29-32), k1, p6, k1, p to end.

5th row: K44(47-50), p1, slip next 3 sts to cable needle and hold to **front** of work, knit next 3 sts, k3 sts from cable needle — cable twist made (CT), p1, knit to end.

6th row: As 4th row.

7th and 9th rows: As 3rd row.

8th row: As 4th row.

Work 16 rows in st st.

26th row (wrong side): P15, *k4, p2; rep from * ending k3.

27th row: P3, *k2, p4; rep from * to last 15 sts, k15.

Work 7 rows in st st.

35th row (right side): K to last 12 sts, work 1st row of Chart 2 over next 9 sts, k3.

36th row (wrong side): P3, work 2nd row of Chart 2 over next 9 sts, purl to end.

Continue in st st and work Chart 2 for remaining 7 rows of chart as set. Continue in st st until 44 rows have been worked above rib, approximately 30.5 cms [12 ins] from beginning.

Shape Neck

45th row (right side): K39(42-45) sts, place remaining sts on a holder for right front.

Working on left front only, dec 1 st at neck edge on the next right side row and every 4th row 9(11-11) times more, then every 6th row 4 times, **at the same time** on 63rd row (right side) p all sts and on 64th row knit all sts. Continue in st st on all sts for 14 rows more.

79th row (right side): Continuing neck decs, k15, p1, k6, p1, knit to end.

80th row: P to last 23 sts, k1, p6, k1, p15.

81st row: K15, p1, work CT over next 6 sts, p1, knit to end.

82nd row: As 80th row.

83rd and 84th rows: As 79th and 80th rows.

85th row: As 81st row.

86th and 88th rows: As 80th row.

87th row: As 79th row.

Work in st st until same length as back. Cast off 25(26-29) sts for shoulder. Slip sts from holder to needle, and working in st st only, work neck decs to correspond to left front. When same length as back, cast off 25(26-29) sts for shoulder.

FINISHING

Press pieces according to instructions on ball band. Sew shoulder seams.

V-Neckband: With right side facing, circular needle and 2 strands of yarn and beg at left shoulder edge, pick up and k58(60-62) sts along left neck edge to neck centre, place marker, pick up and k58(60-62) sts along right neck edge and 26(30-30) sts along back neck edge. 142(150-154) sts. Join.

Next round: K2(0-2), *p2, k2; rep from * to 2 sts before centre marker, ending p2; k2tog through back loops, slip marker, k2tog, *p2, k2; rep from * to end of round.

Rep last round (working dec sts into rib pattern) until neckband measures 5 cms [2 ins]. Cast off loosely knitwise.

Place markers on front and back 28(30.5-33) cms [11(12-13) ins] down from shoulder seams. Sew side seams from lower edge to markers.

Armhole Bands: With right side facing, circular needle and 2 strands of yarn, pick up and k88(92-96) sts around armhole edge. Join. Work in rounds of k2, p2 rib for 5 cms [2 ins]. Cast off loosely knitwise.

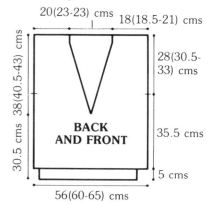

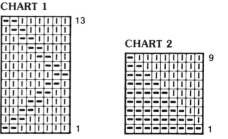

[ ] = knit on right side, purl on wrong side

[ ] = purl on right side, knit on wrong side

Beach and Sportswear

6 Super Styles for Fun in the Sun

Sun Top

MEASUREMENTS

To fit bust sizes 81(86-91-96) cms [32(34-36-38) ins]. Finished bust measurement at underarm 78(82-88-92) cms [31(33-35-37) ins]. Length 53(53-54-54) cms [21(21-21¼-21¼) ins].

MATERIALS

4(4-5-5) 100g balls of Anny Blatt Flirt'Anny in colour 1223 grey. Pair of needles size 4½mm (No 7). Cable needle. Stitch markers.

TENSION

16 sts and 24 rows = 10 cms [4 ins] over moss stitch using size 4½mm needles.

FRONT

Cast on 70(74-78-82) sts.

1st row (right side): K1 *p1, k1; rep from * until 29(31-33-35) sts have been worked, place marker on right-hand needle, p2, k8, p2, place 2nd marker on right-hand needle, k1, **p1, k1, rep from ** across remaining 29(31-33-35) sts.

2nd row: K1, *p1, k1; rep from * to first marker, slip marker onto right-hand needle, k2, p8, k2 to 2nd marker, slip marker onto right-hand needle, k1 **p1, k1; rep from ** to end of row.

3rd row: K1, *p1, k1; rep from * to first marker, slip marker onto right-hand needle, p2, slip 4 sts onto cable needle and hold at back of work, knit next 4 sts, k4 sts from cable needle (cable twist made), p2, slip marker onto right-hand needle, k1 **p1, k1; rep from ** to end of row.

4th, 6th, 8th, 10th and 12th rows: As 2nd row.

5th, 7th, 9th and 11th rows: As 1st row.

13th row: As 3rd row (cable twist row).

Rep 4th to 13th rows working moss st on two outer panels and cable in centre panel between markers, until front measures 7.5 cms [3 ins] from beg, ending with a wrong side row.

Keeping to pattern dec 1 st at each end of next row, then dec 1 st at each end of row every 7.5 cms [3 ins] 4 times in all. 62(66-70-74) sts.

Work straight in pattern until front measures 33 cms [13 ins], ending with a 4th pattern row.

Shape Armhole

Keeping to pattern cast off 2(3-4-5) sts at beg of next 2 rows. Dec 1 st at each end of every alt row 7 times. 44(46-48-50) sts.

Shape Neck

Next row (right side): Keeping to pattern work across 16(16-17-17) sts, join a 2nd ball of yarn, cast off next 12(14-14-16) sts, work to end.

Continue in moss st and working both sides at same time with separate balls of yarn, dec 1 st at each armhole edge on next and then on every 4th row and **at the same time** as shaping armhole, dec 1 st at each neck edge on every alt row until 4(4-5-5) sts remain on each side.

1st and 2nd sizes only

Next row (right side): Dec 1 st at each neck edge.

3rd and 4th sizes only

Next row (right side): Dec 1 st at each end neck edge and armhole edge.

Straps
All sizes

Work straight in moss st on 3 remaining sts for each side until straps measure 16.5(16.5-18-18) cms 6½(6½-7-7) ins slightly stretched. Cast off in moss st.

BACK

Cast on 69(73-77-81) sts. Work in moss st as given for front (omitting cable), shaping sides as for front until back measures 33 cms [13 ins] from beg, ending with a wrong side row. 61(65-69-73) sts.

Shape Armhole

Keeping moss st pattern correct, cast off 8(10-10-12) sts at beg of next 2 rows. 45(45-49-49) sts. Cast off 4 sts at beg of next 4 rows. 29(29-33-33) sts. Dec 1 st at each end of every row 8(8-10-10) times. 13 sts.

Work straight in pattern on 13 sts until back measures 47 cms [18½ ins] from beg. Cast off in moss st.

FINISHING

Press pieces according to instructions on ball band. Sew side seams. Sew straps to back.

Crochet Sun Top

MEASUREMENTS

To fit bust sizes 81(86-91-96) cms [32(34-36-38) ins]. Finished bust measurement at under-arm 83(88-93-98) cms [33(35-37-39½) ins]. Length 48(49-49-49.5) cms [19¼(19½-19½-19¾) ins].

MATERIALS

Patons Cotton Perlé 50g balls: 5(5-6-6) balls Main colour (M), 1(1-2-2) balls Contrast colour (C). 5.00mm crochet hook.

TENSION

15 dc and 21 rows = 10 cms [4 ins] over stripe pattern using size 5.00mm crochet hook.

BACK

Using M make 63(67-71-75) ch.

1st row (right side): 1 dc in 2nd ch from hook, 1 dc into each ch to end, turn. 62(66-70-74) dc.

2nd row 1 ch, 1 dc into each dc to end, turn.

3rd to 6th rows: As 2nd row.

7th row: Change to C and work as for 2nd row.

Continue in dc and stripe pattern, working 6 rows in M and 1 row in C, until back measures 30 cms [12 ins] from beg or required length to armhole.

Shape Armhole

Next row: Keeping stripe pattern correct, work 1 sl st into each of first 2(3-4-5) dc, 1 ch, 1 dc into each of next 58(60-62-64) dc, turn.

Continuing in stripe pattern, dec 1 st each end of every alt row 10 times in all. 38(40-42-44) dc remain. Fasten off.

FRONT

Work as given for Back to armhole.

Shape Neck and Armhole

Next row: Keeping stripe pattern correct, work 1 sl st into each of first 2(3-4-5) dc, 1 ch, 1 dc into each of next 29(30-31-32) dc, turn.

Continuing in stripe pattern, dec 1 st at neck edge on every row 17(18-19-20) times in all, and **at the same time** as shaping neck, dec 1 st at armhole edge on every alt row 10 times in all. 2 sts remain.

Using M only, work straight on 2 remaining sts until strap measures 16(18-18-19) cms [6½(7-7-7½) ins]. Fasten off.

Work second side in same way as first side reversing shaping.

FINISHING

Press pieces according to instructions on ball band. Sew side seams. Adjust straps to fit and sew to back neckline flush with edges of armholes.

Using M work 1 row of dc evenly around armholes and neck edge including straps.

Crochet Tank Top

MEASUREMENTS

To fit bust sizes 81(86-91-96) cms [32(34-36-38) ins]. Finished bust measurement at underarm 94(100-106-109) cms [38(40-42-43½) ins]. Length 58(58-59-59) cms [23(23-23½-23½) ins].

MATERIALS

Patons Cotton Perlé 6(6-7-7) 50g balls. Pair needles size 4mm (No 8). 3.00mm crochet hook.

TENSION

22 sts and 28 rows = 10 cms [4 ins] over st st using size 4mm needles.

BACK

Cast on 104(110-116-120) sts. Work in st st until back measures 25.5 cms [10 ins] from beg, ending with a wrong side row.

Shape Neck and Armhole

Next row: Continuing in st st, k2tog, knit next 48(51-54-56) sts, k2tog, join a second ball of yarn and k2tog, knit next 48(51-54-56) sts, knit last 2 sts tog.

There are 50(53-56-58) sts on each side of neck opening.

Working both sides at same time with separate balls of yarn, dec 1 st at each neck edge on every row 3 times more, then dec 1 st at each neck edge on every alt row 15(15-18-18) times, then every 3rd row 8(8-7-7) times, and **at the same time** as shaping neck edge, dec 1 st at each armhole edge on every alt row 1(2-2-7) times, then every 3rd row 1(11-12-9) times, then every 4th row 13(5-5-5) times.

When all neck and armhole decreases are completed 9 sts remain on each shoulder.

Work straight until back measures 33(33-34-34) cms [13(13-13½-13½) ins] from beg of neck and armholes. Slip sts onto holders.

FRONT

Work as given for Back.

FINISHING

Press pieces according to instructions on ball band. Graft front and back shoulder straps tog. Sew side seams.

Lower Edging: Work a crochet edging around lower edge as follows:

1st round: With right side facing work 1 dc in side seam at lower edge, then keeping edge flat, dc evenly around entire lower edge. Join with sl st to first dc.

2nd round: Working loosely, sl st in each dc around. Fasten off.

Designed by Patricia Marks
Photographed by Arthur Elgort

Sleeveless Top

MEASUREMENTS

To fit bust sizes 81(86-91-96) cms [32(34-36-38) ins]. Finished measurement at underarm 97(100-103-106) cms [39(40-41-42) ins]. Length 46.5(47.5-48-48.5) cms [18½(18¾-19-19¼) ins].

MATERIALS

Copley Sandpiper 8(9-9-10) 50g balls. Pair needles size 5½mm (No 5). Row counter.

TENSION

14 sts and 21 rows = 10 cms [4 ins] over st st using 2 strands' of yarn and size 5½mm needles.

NOTES

Use 2 strands of yarn held tog throughout.
Use a row counter to keep track of rows.

BACK

Using 2 strands of yarn cast on 68(70-72-74) sts and knit 2 rows.

Commence pattern st as follows:

1st and 3rd rows (wrong side): Purl.

2nd row: K9(10-11-12), k2tog, yo, k57(58-59-60).

4th row: K11(12-13-14), k2tog, yo, k22, cast off next 2 sts, knit to end.

5th row: P31(32-33-34), [yo] 3 times, p2tog, p33(34-35-36).

6th row: K34(35-36-37), p1, k1, p1, k20, k2tog, yo, k9(10-11-12).

7th row: Purl.

8th row: K24(25-26-27), cast off next 3 sts, knit to end.

9th row: P39(40-41-42) p2tog, [yo] 5 times, p2tog, p22(23-24-25).

10th row: K23(24-25-26), [p1, k1] twice, p1, k40(41-42-43).

11th and 13th rows: Purl.

12th row: Knit.

14th row: K5(6-7-8), k2tog, [yo] twice, sl 1, k1, psso, k36, k2tog, [yo] twice, sl 1, k1, psso, k19(20-21-22).

15th row: P20(21-22-23), p1, k1, p38, p1, k1, p6(7-8-9).

16th to 27th rows: Work straight in st st.

28th row: K53(54-55-56), cast off next 3 sts, knit to end.

29th row: P10(11-12-13), p2tog, [yo] 5 times, p2tog, p51(52-53-54).

30th row: K52(53-54-55), [p1, k1] twice, p1, k11(12-13-14).

31st to 35th rows: Work straight in st st.

36th row: K15(16-17-18), cast off next 4 sts, knit to end.

37th row: P49(50-51-52), cast on 4 sts, p15(16-17-18).

38th and 39th rows: Work straight in st st.

40th to 45th rows: As 2nd to 7th rows.

46th row: K44(45-46-47), cast off next 4 sts, knit to end.

47th row: P20(21-22-23), cast on 4 sts, p44(45-46-47).

48th to 51st rows: Work straight in st st.

52nd row: K24(25-26-27), cast off next 3 sts, knit to end.

53rd row: P39(40-41-42), p2tog, [yo] 5 times, p2tog, p22(23-24-25).

54th row: K23(24-25-26), [p1, k1] twice, p1, k40(41-42-43).

55th row: Purl.

Back measures approximately 27 cms [10¾ ins] from beginning.

Shape Armhole

Note: Purl 2nd and next to last st on all following knit rows to prevent rolling of armhole edge.

Working in st st cast off 3(3-4-4) sts at beg of next 2 rows.

58th row: K2tog, p1, k4, k2tog, yo, k27(29-29-31), k2tog, yo, k14, k2tog, yo, k5, p1, k2tog.

59th, 61st and 63rd rows: Purl.

60th row: K2tog, p1, k7, k2tog, yo, k11, k2tog, yo, k25(27-27-29), k2tog, yo, k5, p1, k2tog.

62nd row: K2tog, p1, knit to last 3 sts, p1, k2tog.

64th row: K2tog, p1, k3, cast off next 4 sts, k21, k2tog, [yo] twice, sl 1, k1, psso, k8(10-10-12), k2tog, [yo] twice, sl 1, k1, psso, k6, p1, k2tog.

65th row: P10, k1, p10(12-12-14), p1, k1, p22, cast on 4 sts, p5.

66th, 68th, 70th and 72nd rows: As 62nd row.

67th, 69th and 71st rows: Purl.

4th size only

73rd row: Purl.

74th row: As 62nd row.

All sizes: 46(48-48-48) sts remain.

Work straight in st st until armhole measures 12(12.5-13.5-14) cms [4¾(5-5¼-5½) ins], ending with a wrong side row.

Shape Neck

Next row (right side): K1, p1, k12, slip 14 sts on right-hand needle onto a holder, cast off centre 18(20-20-20) sts, knit to last 2 sts, p1, k1.

Working right side of neck only, shape neck as follows:

Next row: Purl.

Next row: K2tog, k3, k2tog, yo, k5, p1, k1.

Next row: Purl.

Next row: K2tog, k4, k2tog, yo, k3, p1, k1.

Working in st st, dec 1 st at beg of every knit row until 7 sts remain.

Work straight in st st until armhole measures 19.5(20.5-21-21.5) cms [7¾(8-8¼-8½) ins]. Cast off.

Slip 14 sts of left side of neck back onto needle.

Next row: With wrong side facing, purl.

Next row: K1, p1, knit to last 2 sts, k2tog.

Next row: Purl.

Next row: K1, p1, k2, cast off next 4 sts, knit to last 2 sts, k2tog.

Next row: Purl to cast off sts, cast on 4 sts, purl to end.

Working in st st, dec 1 st at end of every knit row until 7 sts remain.

Work straight until left side of neck measures same as right side. Cast off.

FRONT

Work as given for Back.

FINISHING

Press pieces according to instructions on ball band. Sew shoulder and side seams.

Lacy Sleeveless Top

MEASUREMENTS

To fit bust sizes 86/91(96/101) cms [34/36(38/40) ins]. Finished measurement at underarm 95(109) cms [37(43) ins]. Length 51 cms [20¼ ins].

MATERIALS

Patons Cotton Ribbon 5(6) 50g balls. Pair needles size 5½mm (No 5).

TENSION

16 sts = 11.5 cms [4½ ins] and 18 rows = 10 cms [4 ins] over seafoam pattern st using size 5½mm needles. (**Note:** For best results when making a tension piece for seafoam pattern cast on 26 sts and work 34 rows. Cast off. Wet and block piece. Take measurements over entire piece).

SEAFOAM PATTERN ST (multiple of 10 sts plus 6 extra)

1st and 2nd rows: Knit.

3rd row (right side): K6, *yo, k1, [yo] twice, k1, [yo] 3 times, k1, [yo] twice, k1, yo, k6; rep from * to end.

4th row: Knit dropping all yo's off needle.

5th and 6th rows: Knit.

7th row: K1, rep from * of 3rd row, ending last rep k1 instead of k6.

8th row: As 4th row.

Rep 1st to 8th rows for seafoam pattern st.

BACK

Using size 5½mm needles cast on 66(76) sts. Knit 6 rows (garter st border). Starting seafoam pattern st with 1st row work 4 complete pattern repeats. (32 rows). Work measures approx 20 cms [7¾ ins] from beg.

Shape Armholes

Knit next 2 rows casting off 4(5) sts at beg of each row. 58(66) sts.

3rd pattern row: K2tog, k0(9), rep from * of 3rd row, ending last rep k0(9), k2tog (1 dec each side). 56(64) sts.

4th pattern row: Work straight in pattern.

5th pattern row: K2tog, knit to last 2 sts, k2tog. 54(62) sts.

6th pattern row: Knit.

7th pattern row: K2tog, k3(2), rep from * of 3rd row, ending last rep k3(2), k2tog. 52(60) sts.

8th pattern row: Knit dropping off all yo's.

1st pattern row: K2tog, knit to last 2 sts, k2tog. 50(58) sts.

2nd pattern row: Knit.

1st size only

3rd pattern row: K8, rep from * of 3rd row, ending last rep k8. 50 sts.

2nd size only

3rd pattern row: K2tog, k5, rep from * of 3rd row, ending last rep k5, k2tog. 56 sts.

Both sizes

4th, 5th and 6th pattern rows: Work straight in pattern.

7th pattern row: K3(1), rep from * of 3rd pattern row, ending last rep k3(1).

8th pattern row: Work straight in pattern.

1st and 2nd pattern rows: Work straight in pattern.

3rd pattern row: K8(6), rep from * of 3rd row, ending last rep k8(6).

Continuing to work in pattern as set, rep last 8 rows until armhole measures 31 cms [12½ ins] (approx 7 pattern reps), ending with a 2nd or 6th pattern row.

Cast off.

FRONT

Work as given for Back.

FINISHING

Press pieces according to instructions on ball band. Sew shoulder 4 cms [1½ ins] from each edge. Sew side seams.

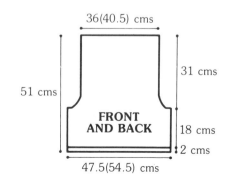

Designed by Nancy J. Thomas
Photographed by Naomi Kaltman

Patterned Cotton Sweater

MEASUREMENTS

To fit bust sizes 80(85-90-95-100) cms [32(34-36-38-40) ins]. Finished measurement 96(100-106-110-116) cms [$38\frac{1}{2}$(40-$42\frac{1}{2}$-44-$46\frac{1}{2}$) ins]. Length to shoulder 60(61-61-62-62) cms [$23\frac{1}{2}$(24-24-$24\frac{1}{2}$-$24\frac{1}{2}$) ins]. Sleeve seam 40 cms [$15\frac{3}{4}$ ins].

MATERIALS

Coats Maxi 'Pellicano' Knitting and Crochet Cotton No. 5 (200g) used double: 5(5-5-5-6) balls. Pair needles each size $4\frac{1}{2}$mm (No 7) and $3\frac{1}{4}$mm (No 10). Cable needle. Stitch holders.

Coats 'Anchor' Knitting and Crochet Cotton No. 6 (50g) used double: 17(18-19-20-21) balls. Pair needles each size 4mm (No 8) and 3mm (No 11). Cable needle. Stitch holders.

TENSION

With yarn used double: 30 sts and 30 rows = 10 cms [4 ins] square measured over rib pattern using larger needles.

SPECIAL ABBREVIATIONS

T3B (Twist 3 Back) = slip next st onto cable needle and hold at back of work, knit next 2 sts from left-hand needle, then purl st from cable needle.

T3F (Twist 3 Front) = slip next 2 sts onto cable needle and hold at front of work, purl next st from left-hand needle, then knit sts from cable needle.

T3L (Twist 3 Left) = slip next st onto cable needle and hold at front of work, purl next 2 sts from left-hand needle, then knit st from cable needle.

T3R (Twist 3 Right) = slip next 2 sts onto cable needle and hold at back of work, knit next st from left-hand needle, then purl sts from cable needle.

T2B (Twist 2 Back) = slip next st onto cable needle and hold at back of work, knit next st from left-hand needle, then purl st from cable needle.

T2F (Twist 2 Front) = slip next st onto cable needle and hold at front of work, purl next st from left-hand needle, then knit st from cable needle.

MB (Make Bobble) = purl into front, back, front, back and front of next st, turn and k5, turn and p2tog, p1, p2tog, turn and k3tog, turn and sl 1.

DIAGONAL PANEL A (Worked across 23 sts)

1st row: P16, T2B, p1, T2B, p2.
2nd row: K3, T2B, k1, T2B, k15.
3rd row: P14, T2B, p1, T2B, p4.
4th row: K5, T2B, k1, T2B, k13.
5th row: P9, MB, p2, T2B, p1, T2B, p6.
6th row: K7, T2B, k1, T2B, k11.
7th row: P10, T2B, p1, T2B, p8.
8th row: K9, T2B, k1, T2B, k9.
9th row: P8, T2B, p1, T2B, p10.
10th row: K11, T2B, k1, T2B, k7.
11th row: P3, MB, p2, T2B, p1, T2B, p12.
12th row: K13, T2B, k1, T2B, k5.
13th row: P4, T2B, p1, T2B, p14.
14th row: K15, T2B, k1, T2B, k3.
15th row: P2, T2B, p1, T2B, p16. .
16th row: [K2, p1] twice, k11, [p1, k2] twice.
These 16 rows form Diagonal Panel A.

DIAGONAL PANEL B (Worked across 23 sts)

1st row: P2, T2F, p1, T2F, p16.
2nd row: K15, T2F, k1, T2F, k3.
3rd row: P4, T2F, p1, T2F, p14.
4th row: K13, T2F, k1, T2F, k5.
5th row: P6, T2F, p1, T2F, p2, MB, p9.
6th row: K11, T2F, k1, T2F, k7.
7th row: P8, T2F, p1, T2F, p10.
8th row: K9, T2F, k1, T2F, k9.

Patterned Cotton Sweater

9th row: P10, T2F, p1, T2F, p8.
10th row: K7, T2F, k1, T2F, k11.
11th row: P12, T2F, p1, T2F, p2, MB, p3.
12th row: K5, T2F, k1, T2F, k13.
13th row: P14, T2F, p1, T2F, p4.
14th row: K3, T2F, k1, T2F, k15.
15th row: P16, T2F, p1, T2F, p2.
16th row: [K2, p1] twice, k11, [p1, k2] twice.
These 16 rows form Diagonal Panel B.

ZIG-ZAG PANEL (Worked across 20 sts)

1st row: P3, k1, p2, k1, p8, T3B, p2.
2nd row: K3, T3R, k7, p1, k2, p1, k3.
3rd row: P3, k1, p2, k1, p6, T3B, p4.
4th row: K5, T3R, k5, p1, k2, p1, k3.
5th row: P3, k1, p2, k1, p4, T3B, p6.
6th row: K3, p1, k3, T3R, k3, p1, k2, p1, k3.
7th row: P3, [k1, p2] twice, T3B, p4, k1, p3.
8th row: K3, [p1, k2] twice, T3R, k1, p1, k2, p1, k3.
9th row: P3, k1, p3, T3B, p3, k1, p2, k1, p3.
10th row: K3, p1, k2, p1, k4, T3R, k2, p1, k3.
11th row: P5, T3B, p5, k1, p2, k1, p3.
12th row: K3, p1, k2, p1, k6, T3R, k4.
13th row: P3, T3B, p7, k1, p2, k1, p3.
14th row: P3, p1, k2, p1, k8, T3R, k2.
15th row: P2, T3F, p8, k1, p2, k1, p3.
16th row: K3, p1, k2, p1, k7, `T3L, k3.

17th row: P4, T3F, p6, k1, p2, k1, p3.
18th row: K3, p1, k2, p1, k5, T3L, k5.
19th row: P6, T3F, p4, k1, p2, k1, p3.
20th row: K3, p1, k2, p1, k3, T3L, k3, p1, k3.
21st row: P3, k1, p4, T3F, [p2, k1] twice, p3.
22nd row: K3, p1, k2, p1, k1, T3L, [k2, p1] twice, k3.
23rd row: P3, k1, p2, k1, p3, T3F, p3, k1, p3.
24th row: K3, p1, k2, T3L, k4, p1, k2, p1, k3.
25th row: P3, k1, p2, k1, p5, T3F, p5.
26th row: K4, T3L, k6, p1, k2, p1, k3.
27th row: P3, k1, p2, k1, p7, T3F, p3.
28th row: K2, T3L, k8, p1, k2, p1, k3.
These 28 rows form the Zig-Zag Panel.

SPECIAL NOTE

Yarn is used double throughout.

BACK AND FRONT ALIKE

Using smaller needles cast on 98(102-110-114-122) sts.
1st row (right side): K2, *p2, k2; rep from * to end.
2nd row: P2, *k2, p2; rep from * to end.
Rep the last 2 rows until rib measures 4 cms [1½ ins] ending with a right side row.

Next row (increase): Rib 1(1-4-3-5), *inc in next st, work 1 st, inc in next st, rib 2; rep from * to last 2(6-6-6-7) sts, [inc in next st, rib 1(1-2-2-6)] 1(3-2-2-1) times. 137(143-152-158-167) sts.

Change to larger needles and commence pattern:

1st row: [P2, k1] 4(5-6-6-7) times, work 1st row of Diagonal Panel A across next 23 sts, k1, [p2, k1] 2(2-2-3-3) times, work 1st row of Zig-Zag Panel across next 20 sts, k1, [p2, k1] 4(5-5-5-6) times, work 15th row of Zig-Zag Panel across next 20 sts, k1, [p2, k1] 2(2-2-3-3) times, work 1st row of Diagonal Panel B across next 23 sts, [k1, p2] 4(5-6-6-7) times.

2nd row: [K2, p1] 4(5-6-6-7) times, work 2nd row of Diagonal Panel B, p1, [k2, p1] 2(2-2-3-3) times, work 16th row of Zig-Zag Panel, p1, [k2, p1] 4(5-5-5-6) times, work 2nd row of Zig-Zag Panel, p1, [k2, p1] 2(2-2-3-3) times, work 2nd row of Diagonal Panel A, [p1, k2] 4(5-6-6-7) times.

These 2 rows form the rib pattern at each side and between panels. Keeping the 28 rows of zig-zag panels and 16 rows of diagonal panels correct, rep the last 2 rows until piece measures 53(54-54-55-55) cms [20¾(21¼-21¼-21¾-21¾) ins], or 7 cms [2¾ ins] less than required length to shoulder ending with a right side row.

Shape Neck

Next row: Work 42(45-48-51-54) sts, turn and complete this side first.

★ Keeping pattern correct cast off 4(4-4-5-5)

sts at beg of next row. Work 1 row. Cast off 3(4-4-4-4) sts at beg of next row, then 3(3-3-4-4) sts at beg of following alt row. (Work 1 extra row straight here for 2nd side). Dec 1 st at neck edge on next 9 rows. 23(25-28-29-32) sts remain. Work 6 rows straight, thus ending with a wrong side row. Cast off.

Slip next 53(53-56-56-59) sts at centre onto a holder for neckband. With wrong side of work facing rejoin yarn to neck edge of remaining 42(45-48-51-54) sts and complete as given for first side from ★ to end reversing shaping by working 1 row more where indicated.

SLEEVES

Using smaller needles cast on 62(62-66-66-70) sts and work 4 cms [1½ ins] in k2, p2 rib as given for Back and Front ending with a right side row.

Next row (increase): Rib 4(4-7-1-4), *inc in next st, work 1 st; rep from * to last 6(6-9-3-6) sts, inc in next st, rib to end. 89(89-92-98-101) sts.

Change to larger needles and commence pattern:

1st row: [P2, k1] 6(6-6-7-7) times, work 1st row of Zig-Zag Panel across next 20 sts, k1, [p2, k1] 4(4-5-5-6) times, work 15th row of Zig-Zag Panel across next 20 sts, [k1, p2] 6(6-6-7-7) times.

2nd row: [K2, p1] 6(6-6-7-7) times, work 16th row of Zig-Zag Panel, p1, [k2, p1] 4(4-5-5-6) times, work 2nd row of Zig-Zag Panel, [p1, k2] 6(6-6-7-7) times.

Keeping continuity of panels correct and bringing extra sts into rib pattern, inc 1 st at each end of next and every following 4th row until there are 109(103-104-110-109) sts, then every alt row until there are 167(173-178-184-191) sts. Work straight until sleeve measures 40 cms [15¾ ins] or required sleeve length ending with a wrong side row. Cast off.

TO MAKE UP

Press pieces according to instructions on ball band. Join left shoulder seam.

Neckband: Using smaller needles and with right side of work facing, pick up and k26(27-27-27-29-29) sts down right back slope, work across sts on holder at back neck as follows: k3(3-5-5-3), *k2tog, k7(7-9-9-8); rep from * to last 5(5-7-7-6) sts, k2tog, knit to end, pick up and k26(27-27-29-29) sts up left back slope, 26(27-27-29-29) sts down left front slope, work across sts on holder at front neck as given for back neck, then pick up and k26(27-27-29-29) sts up right front slope. 198(202-210-218-222) sts.

Work 8 rows in k2, p2 rib as given for Back and Front starting with the 2nd row. Cast off in rib.

Join right shoulder seam and ends of neckband. Fold sleeves in half lengthways and mark centre of cast off edge. Sew sleeve to side edge placing centre at shoulder seam. Note: armhole should measure approximately 28(29-30-31-32) cms [11(11½-11¾-12¼-12½) ins]. Join side and sleeve seams.

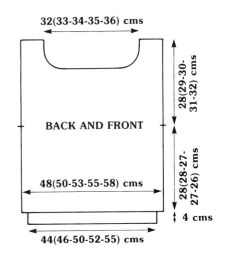

32(33-34-35-36) cms

28(29-30-31-32) cms

BACK AND FRONT

28(28-27-27-26) cms

48(50-53-55-58) cms

4 cms

44(46-50-52-55) cms

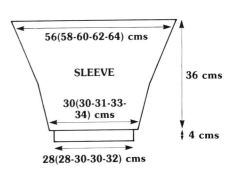

56(58-60-62-64) cms

SLEEVE

36 cms

30(30-31-33-34) cms

4 cms

28(28-30-30-32) cms

Evening Specials

4 Sophisticated Styles
for Night-Time Elegance

V-Back Evening Sweater

MEASUREMENTS

To fit bust sizes 81(86-91-96) cms [32(34-36-38) ins]. Width across front at underarm 41(43.5-46-48.5) cms [16¼(17¼-18¼-19¼) ins]. Length (including scallops) 55.5(57-58-58) cms [22(22½-23-23) ins]. Sleeve width at upper arm 33.5(34-35-36) cms [13¼(13¾-14-14¼) ins].

MATERIALS

Berger du Nord Angora 70% 10(11-12-13) 20g balls Main colour (M), Berger du Nord Moonlight 1 100m spool. 1 ball of double knitting 'waste' yarn in contrasting colour for cast on rows. Pair needles size 3¾mm (No 9). Crochet hook size 4.50mm. Shoulder pads (optional).

TENSION

24 sts and 32 rows = 10 cms [4 ins] over st st using M and size 3¾mm needles.

NOTES

The stitches for the front, back and sleeves are all cast on with waste yarn that is discarded later when the M stitches are picked up to work the scalloped lower edges.

When increasing on the first row of the scalloped edgings, make increases by lifting the thread between 2 sts onto the left-hand needle and knitting into the back of the loop to cross the stitch.

FRONT

With waste yarn cast on 94(100-106-112) sts. Knit 1 row, purl 1 row.

Change to M and work in st st decreasing 1 st at each end of row every 2.5 cms [1 inch] twice. 90(96-102-108) sts.

Work straight until front measures 12.5 cms [5 ins]. Inc 1 st at each end of row every 4 cms [1½ ins] 4 times. 98(104-110-116) sts.

Work straight until front measures 29 cms [11½ ins] from beg, ending with a purl row.

Shape Armholes

Continuing in st st, cast off 3(3-3-4) sts at beg of next 2 rows, 2(2-3-3) sts at beg of next 2 rows, then dec 1 st at each end of every alt row 1(2-3-3) times. 86(90-92-96) sts.

Work straight in st st until armhole measures 11.5(12.5-14-14) cms [4½(5-5½-5½) ins], ending with a purl row.

Shape Neck

Next row (right side): Knit first 35(36-36-37) sts, join 2nd ball of yarn and cast off centre 16(18-20-22) sts, knit remaining 35(36-36-37) sts.

Working both sides at same time with separate balls of yarn cast off 3 sts at each neck edge once, 2 sts at neck edge once, then dec 1 st at neck edge twice. 28(29-29-30) sts on each side of neck.

Work straight until armhole measures 19(20.5-21.5-21.5) cms [7½(8-8½-8½) ins]. Cast off.

BACK

Work as given for Front until back measures 18 cms [7 ins] from beg, ending with a purl row.

Shape Neck and Armhole

Divide sts in half on 2 needles. Working both sides at same time with separate balls of yarn, dec 1 st at each neck edge on first row, then on every 6th(6th-5th-5th) row 4 times, then on every 6th row 10(11-12-13) times, and **at the same time** shape side edges and armholes as for front. After all decreases are completed, work straight until back measures same as front to shoulder. Cast off.

SLEEVES

With waste yarn cast on 46(48-50-52) sts. Knit 1 row, purl 1 row.

Change to M and working in st st, inc 1 st at each end of every 6th row 17 times. 80(82-84-86) sts.

Work straight until sleeve measures 34(35.5-36-37) cms [13½(14-14¼-14½) ins] from beg or required length to underarm excluding scalloped edging, ending with a purl row.

Shape Cap

Continuing in st st, cast off 3(3-3-4) sts at beg of next 2 rows, then 2(2-3-3) sts at beg of next 2 rows, then dec 1 st at each end of every alt row 2(2-1-1) times. 66(68-70-70) sts.

Work straight until cap measures 18(19-20.5-20.5) cms [7(7½-8-8) ins], ending with a purl row.

Next row (right side): *K2tog; rep from * to end. 33(34-35-35) sts.

Next row: *P2tog; rep from * ending p1(0-1-1). 17(17-18-18) sts.

Cast off, knitting 2 tog while casting off.

FINISHING

Do not press.

Back Scalloped Edging: With wrong side facing pick up 94(100-106-112) sts of first row of M along lower back and discard waste yarn. With right side facing and M, knit increasing 46(48-42-40) sts evenly across row. 140(148-148-152) sts. Work 3 rows straight in st st, thus ending with a purl row.

Work 4 scallops separately as follows:

Next row (right side): K2tog, k31(33-33-34) sts, k2tog for first scallop, slip remaining 105(111-111-114) sts onto a holder.

Continuing on first scallop sts only, dec 1 st at each end of every alt row 9 times more. 15(17-17-18) sts. Cast off decreasing 1 st at each end of row while casting off.

Work 3 more scallops in same way.

Front Scallop Edging: Work as for Back Scalloped Edging.

Scalloped Cuffs: With wrong side facing pick up 46(48-50-52) sts of first row of M along lower edge of sleeve and discard waste yarn. With right side facing and M, knit increasing 14(16-14-16) sts evenly across row. 60(64-64-68) sts. Purl 1 row.

Work 4 scallops separately as follows:

Next row (right side): K2tog, k11(12-12-13) sts, k2tog for first scallop, slip remaining 45(48-48-51) sts onto holder. Continuing on first scallop sts only, dec 1 st each end of every alt row 3 times more. 7(8-8-9) sts. Cast off decreasing 1 st at each end of row while casting off.

Work 3 more scallops in same way.

Sew shoulder, side and sleeve seams. Set in sleeves easing in fullness at shoulders.

Crochet Edging: With right side facing, crochet hook and 2 strands of C held tog, work one row of dc evenly around neck edge and around scalloped edges of front, back and sleeves. Fasten off.

Designed by Lylia de Brevanne
Photographed by Eric Boman

Cardigan with Back Button Fastening

MEASUREMENTS

To fit bust sizes 81(86-91-96) cms [32(34-36-38) ins]. Finished bust measurement at underarm 101(106-111-115) cms [40(42-44-46) ins]. Length 48.5(48.5-49.5-49.5) cms [19(19-19½-19½) ins]. Sleeve width at upper arm 51(51-53-53) cms [20(20-21-21) ins].

MATERIALS

2(2-3-3) 50g balls of Berger du Nord Kid Mohair each in colour 7988 khaki (A) and 8455 blue (B), 2 balls each of colour 8450 light blue (C), 7989 light brown (D) and 8443 beige (E). Pair needles each size 4mm (No 8) and and 4½mm (No 7). 4 buttons.

TENSION

17 sts and 24 rows = 10 cms [4 ins] over st st using 4½mm needles.

24 sts and 28 rows = 10 cms [4 ins] over k1, p1 rib using 4mm needles.

Note: When changing colours, twist yarns together on wrong side to prevent holes.

FRONT

Using smaller needles and B cast on 43(45-47-49) sts, then using A cast on 43(45-47-49) sts. 86(90-94-98) sts.

1st rib row (right side): Using A p2(0-2-0), *k2, p2; rep from * across first 42(44-46-48) sts, k1, with B k1, **p2, k2; rep from **, ending p2(0-2-0).

2nd rib row: Knit the knit sts and purl the purl sts, matching colours.

Rep last 2 rows until rib measures 4 cms [1½ ins] from beg, ending with a 2nd row.

Change to larger neeedles. Continuing to match colours, work straight in st st (1 row knit, 1 row purl) until front measures 23 cms [9 ins] from beg, or required length to underarm. Mark each end of last row for beg of armhole. Continue in st st until armhole measures 18(18-19-19) cms [7(7-7½-7½) ins], ending with a wrong side row.

Shape Neck

Next row (right side): K36(37-38-39), join 2nd ball of A and cast off centre 14(16-18-20) sts for neck (being sure to match colours), knit to end.

Working both sides at same time with separate balls of yarn, cast off 2 sts from each neck edge once, then dec 1 st at each neck edge every row 10 times, then every alt row once more. 23(24-25-26) sts each side.

Work straight until armhole measures 25.5(25.5-26.5-26.5) cms [10(10-10½-10½) ins]. Cast off sts each side for shoulders.

RIGHT BACK

Using smaller needles and B cast on 40(42-44-46) sts.

1st rib row (right side): *K2, p2; rep from *, ending k0(2-0-2).

2nd rib row: Knit the knit sts and purl the purl sts.

Rep last 2 rows for 4 cms [1½ ins], ending with a 2nd row.

Change to larger needles. Work straight in st st until right back measures same as front to armhole markers. Mark beg of next right side row for beg of armhole.

Continue in st st until armhole measures 1.5 cms [½ inch], ending with wrong side row.

Shape Neck

Next row (right side): Knit to last 3 sts, k2tog, k1.

Continue to dec 1 st at neck edge in this way alltternately every 2nd and 4th row (therefore 2 sts are decreased every 6 rows) until there are 23(24-25-26) sts. Work straight until same length as front to shoulder. Cast off.

LEFT BACK

Using A work to correspond to right back reversing all shaping.

SLEEVES

Note: Make one sleeve with C and one sleeve with D.

Using smaller needles cast on 38(38-42-42) sts. Work in k2, p2 rib for 4 cms [1½ ins] increasing 6(6-4-4) sts evenly spaced across last wrong side row. 44(44-46-46) sts.

Change to larger needles. Work straight in st st increasing 1 st each end every 4th row (21(21-22-22) times. 86(86-90-90) sts. Work straight until sleeve measures 40.5(40.5-43-43) cms [16(16-17-17) ins] from beg, or required sleeve length. Cast off.

COLLAR

Using smaller needles and E cast on 203(207-215-219) sts. Work in k1, p1 rib for 2 rows. Work first point of collar in short rows as follows:

1st row (right side): *K1, p1; rep from * across first 8 sts, turn work.

2nd and all wrong side rows: Sl 1 wyib, rib to end.

3rd row: Rib across first 16 sts, turn.

Continue in this way to work 8 more rib sts from left-hand needle every alt row twice more. On next right side row, rib across all 203(207-215-219) sts.

Work 2nd point of collar to correspond to first point, beg short rows on next wrong side row.

When all short rows have been worked, work straight in rib on all sts until depth of collar at centre measures 10 cms [4 ins] from beg. Cast off loosely in rib.

FINISHING

Button Band: With right side facing, smaller needles and A pick up and k46 sts along left back inside edge. Work in k2, p2 rib for 7 rows. Cast off loosely in rib.

Buttonhole Band: With right side facing, smaller needles and B pick up and k46 sts along right back inside edge. Work in k2, p2 rib for 3 rows.

Next row (right side): Rib 4 sts, cast off 2 sts, [rib 10 sts, cast off 2 sts] 3 times, rib last 4 sts.

Next row: Rib, casting on 2 sts over each set of cast off sts. Rib for 2 more rows. Cast off loosely in rib.

DO NOT PRESS. Sew shoulder seams. With centre cast on edge of collar at centre front neck edge, sew collar around front and back neck edges. Sew top of sleeves to front and back between armhole markers. Sew side and sleeve seams. Sew on buttons opposite buttonholes.

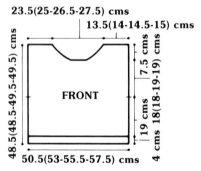

23.5(25-26.5-27.5) cms
13.5(14-14.5-15) cms
7.5 cms
FRONT
48.5(48.5-49.5-49.5) cms
19 cms
18(18-19-19) cms
4 cms
50.5(53-55.5-57.5) cms

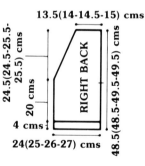

13.5(14-14.5-15) cms
24.5(24.5-25.5-25.5) cms
20 cms
4 cms
RIGHT BACK
48.5(48.5-49.5-49.5) cms
24(25-26-27) cms

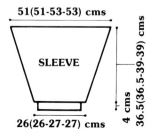

51(51-53-53) cms
SLEEVE
36.5(36.5-39-39) cms
4 cms
26(26-27-27) cms

Cable Crochet Top

MEASUREMENTS

To fit bust sizes 81/86(91-96) cms [32/34(36-38) ins]. Finished measurement at underarm 101(109-116) cms [39(42-45) ins]. Length 63(63-66) cms [25(25-26) ins].

MATERIALS

13(14-15) 50g balls of Berger du Nord Rabane in colour 8862 tan. 5.00mm and 6.00mm crochet hooks.

TENSION

16 sts (4 cables) and 12 rows = 15.5 cms [6 ins] over cable pattern using size 6.00mm crochet hook.

BACK

Using larger hook make 54(58-62) ch.

Commence Cable Pattern

1st row (right side): Dc into 2nd ch from hook and in each ch to end. 53(57-61) dc. 3 ch, turn.

2nd row: Miss first dc, *tr in each of next 3 dc, yo hook, insert hook from front to back into missed st, draw loop through loosely to height of row, complete tr (1 cable st made), miss next dc; rep from * ending tr into last dc. 13(14-15) cable sts. 1 ch, turn.

3rd row: Dc into each tr. 53(57-61) dc. 3 ch, turn.

Rep 2nd and 3rd rows for cable pattern until piece measures 38 cms [15 ins] from beg, or required length to underarm, ending with a 3rd pattern row. Do not ch at end of last row. Turn.

Shape Armhole

Next row (wrong side): Sl st across first 4 dc, 3 ch, *miss next dc, tr into next 3 dc, work cable; rep from * to last 5 sts, tr into next st, leave remaining 4 sts unworked. 11(12-13) cable sts. 1 ch, turn.

Next row: Dc into each tr. 45(49-53) dc.

Continue to work straight in cable pattern until armhole measures 25(25-28) cms [10(10-11) ins], ending with a 3rd pattern row. Fasten off.

FRONT

Work as given for Back until armhole measures 15(15-18) cms [6(6-7) ins], ending with a 2nd pattern row.

Note: When working dec over 2nd row of cable st, do not work cable over less than 3 sts and work these sts in tr only.

Shape Neck

Dc across first 14(16-17) sts, miss next 17(17-19) sts, join 2nd ball of yarn, dc to end.

Working both sides at same time with separate balls of yarn, dec 1 st at neck edge (working dec sts into pattern) every cable row 4 times. 10(12-13) sts each side. Work straight, if necessary, until same length as back. Fasten off sts each side for shoulders.

FINISHING

Press according to instructions on ball band. Sew shoulder and side seams.

Armhole Band

1st row: With right side facing and smaller hook, work 62(62-68) dc around armhole edge, 1 ch, turn.

2nd to 4th rows: Dc into each dc, 1 ch, turn.

Fasten off. Sew side edges of band to sl sts at underarm.

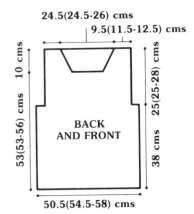

24.5(24.5-26) cms
9.5(11.5-12.5) cms
10 cms
53(53-56) cms
25(25-28) cms
38 cms
BACK AND FRONT
50.5(54.5-58) cms

Lacy Sweater

MEASUREMENTS

To fit bust sizes 80(85-90-95-100) cms [32(34-36-38-40) ins]. Finished measurement 89(95-101-107-113) cms [35½(38-40½-43-45) ins]. Length to shoulder (approximately) 57(57-59-59-61) cms [22¾(22¾-23½-23½-24¼) ins]. Sleeve seam (approximately 45 cms [18 ins].

MATERIALS

Patons Promise Double Knitting 7(7-8-9-9) 40g balls. Pair needles each size 4mm (No 8) and 3¼mm (No 10). Approximately 300 small pearl beads if required.

TENSION

20 sts and 30 rows = 10 cms [4 ins] square measured over pattern using larger needles.

BACK

Using smaller needles cast on 89(95-101-107-113) sts.

1st row (right side): K1, *p1, k1; rep from * to end.

2nd row: P1, *k1, p1; rep from * to end.

Rep the last 2 rows until rib measures 8 cms [3 ins], ending with a wrong side row.

Change to larger needles and commence pattern:

1st row: K6(9-6-9-6), yf, sl 1, k1, psso, yf, sl 1, k2tog, psso, yf, *k7, yf, sl 1, k1, psso, yf, sl 1, k2tog, psso, yf; rep from * to last 6(9-6-9-6), knit to end.

2nd and every alt row: Purl.

3rd row: K7(10-7-10-7), [yf, sl 1, k1, psso] twice, *k8, [yf, sl 1, k1, psso] twice; rep from * to last 6(9-6-9-6), knit to end.

5th row: K5(8-5-8-5), k2tog, yf, k1, [yf, sl 1, k1, psso] twice, *k5, k2tog, yf, k1, [yf, sl 1, k1, psso] twice; rep from * to last 5(8-5-8-5) sts, knit to end.

7th row: K4(7-4-7-4), *[k2tog, yf] twice, k1, [yf, sl 1, k1, psso] twice, k3; rep from * to last 1(4-1-4-1), knit to end.

9th row: K3(6-3-6-3), *[k2tog, yf] twice, k3, [yf, sl 1, k1, psso] twice, k1; rep from * to last 2(5-2-5-2), knit to end.

11th row: K2(5-2-5-2), [k2tog, yf] twice, k5, *yf, sl 1, k1, psso, yf, k3tog, yf, k2tog, yf, k5; rep from * to last 6(9-6-9-6), [yf, sl 1, k1, psso] twice, k2(5-2-5-2).

13th row: K1(4-1-4-1), [k2tog, yf] twice, k7, *yf, k3tog, yf, k2tog, yf, k7; rep from * to last 5(8-5-8-5), [yf, sl 1, k1, psso] twice, knit to end.

15th row: K1(4-1-4-1), [yf, sl 1, k1, psso] twice, k7, *[k2tog, yf] twice, k8; rep from * to last 5(8-5-8-5), [k2tog, yf] twice, knit to end.

17th row: K2(5-2-5-2), [yf, sl 1, k1, psso] twice, k5, *[k2tog, yf] twice, k1, yf, sl 1, k1, psso, k5; rep from * to last 6(9-6-9-6) sts, [k2tog, yf] twice, knit to end.

19th row: K3(6-3-6-3), *[yf, sl 1, k1, psso] twice, k3, [k2tog, yf] twice, k1; rep from * to last 2(5-2-5-2) sts, knit to end.

21st row: K4(7-4-7-4), *[yf, sl 1, k1, psso] twice, k1, [k2tog, yf] twice, k3; rep from * to last 1(4-1-4-1), knit to end.

23rd row: K5(8-5-8-5), yf, sl 1, k1, psso, yf, sl 1, k2tog, psso, yf, k2tog, yf, *k5, yf, sl 1, k1, psso, yf, sl 1, k2tog, psso, yf, k2tog, yf; rep from * to last 5(8-5-8-5) sts, knit to end.

24th row: Purl.

These 24 rows form the pattern. Rep these 24 rows twice more, then work the first 14 rows again.

Shape Armholes

1st row: Cast off 5 sts (1 st on right-hand needle), k6(9-6-9-6), *[k2tog, yf] twice, k8; rep from * to last 5(8-5-8-5) sts, [k2tog, yf] twice, knit to end.

2nd row: Cast off 5 sts, purl to end.

3rd row: K2tog tbl, k4(7-4-7-4), [k2tog, yf] twice, k1, yf, sl 1, k1, psso, *k5, [k2tog, yf] twice, k1, yf, sl 1, k1, psso; rep from * to last 6(9-6-9-6) sts, k4(7-4-7-4), k2tog.

4th row: P2tog, purl to last 2 sts, p2tog tbl.

5th row: K2tog tbl, k1(4-1-4-1), [k2tog, yf] twice, k1, [yf, sl 1, k1, psso] twice, *k3, [k2tog, yf] twice, k1, [yf, sl 1, k1, psso] twice; rep from * to last 3(6-3-6-3), k1(4-1-4-1), k2tog.

6th row: As 4th row.

1st(3rd-5th) sizes only

7th row: K2tog tbl, k2tog, yf, k3, *[yf, sl 1, k1, psso] twice, k1, [k2tog, yf] twice, k3; rep from * to last 4 sts, yf, sl 1, k1, psso, k2tog.

2nd(4th) sizes only

7th row: K2tog tbl, k1, *[k2tog, yf] twice, k3, [yf, sl 1, k1, psso] twice, k1; rep from * to last 2 sts, k2tog.

5th size only

8th row: As 4th row.

9th row: K2tog tbl, k4, *yf, sl 1, k1, psso, yf, sl 1, k2tog, psso, yf, k2tog, yf, k5; rep from * to last 13 sts, yf, sl 1, k1, psso, yf, sl 1, k2tog, psso, yf, k2tog, yf, k4, k2tog.

All sizes

Next row: Purl.

Keeping pattern correct dec 1 st at each end of next and following 1(1-4-4-5) alt rows. 65(71-71-77-77) sts remain ★.

Keeping pattern correct work straight until armholes measure 20(20-22-22-24) cms [8(8-8¾-8¾-9½) ins], measured straight from start of armhole shaping and ending with a purl row.

Shape Shoulders

Cast off 6(7-7-7-7) sts at beg of next 4 rows, then 6(6-6-8-8) sts at beg of following 2 rows. Slip remaining 29(31-31-33-33) sts onto a holder for neckband.

FRONT

Work as given for Back to ★. Work straight until front is 19(19-21-21-23) rows shorter than back to start of shoulder shaping thus ending with a right side row.

Shape Neck

1st row: P25(27-27-29-29), turn and complete this side first.

★★ Dec 1 st at neck edge on next 5 rows, then following 2 alt rows. 18(20-20-22-22) sts remain. Work 10(10-12-12-14) rows straight (work 1 row less here for 2nd side) thus ending at armhole edge.

Shape Shoulder

Cast off 6(7-7-7-7) sts at beg of next and following alt row. Work 1 row. Cast off remaining 6(6-6-8-8) sts.

Slip next 15(17-17-19-19) sts at centre onto a holder for neckband. With wrong side of work facing rejoin yarn to neck edge of remaining sts and purl to end.

Complete to match first side from ★★ to end reversing shaping by working 1 row less where indicated.

SLEEVES

Using smaller needles cast on 45(47-49-51-53) sts and work 8 cms [3 ins] in k1, p1 rib as given for Back ending with a right side row.

Next row (increase): Rib 3(5-3-5-3), *inc in next st, p1; rep from * to last 4(8-4-8-4) sts, inc in next st, rib to end. 65(65-71-71-77) sts.

Change to larger needles and work 24 rows in pattern as given for 1st(1st-2nd-2nd-1st) size of Back. Rep these 24 rows 3 times more, then work the first 14 rows again.

Shape Top

Keeping pattern correct cast off 5 sts at beg of next 2 rows. Dec 1 st at each end of next 3(3-5-5-5) rows, then every following 4th row until 33(33-33-33-37) sts remain. Dec 1 st at each end of next 5 rows, then cast off 5(5-5-5-6) sts at beg of following 2 rows. Cast off remaining 13(13-13-13-15) sts.

FINISHING AND NECKBAND

Press pieces according to instructions on ball band. Join left shoulder seam.

Neckband: Using smaller needles and with right side of work facing knit across sts on holder at back neck increasing 1 st at centre, pick up and k21(21-23-23-25) sts down left front slope, knit across sts on holder at centre front and pick up and k21(21-23-23-25) sts up right front slope. 87(91-95-99-103) sts.

Work 7 cms [2¾ ins] in k1, p1 rib as given for Back starting with the 2nd row. Slip sts onto a length of yarn.

Join right shoulder seam and ends of neckband. Fold neckband in half to inside and slip stitch **loosely** in place allowing for stretch and taking care to catch every st. Join side and sleeve seams. Insert sleeves.

Sew beads to centre of diamonds as illustrated if required.

Quick and Easy Knits

5 Fashionable Designs
for Easy Knitting

Short-Waisted Casual

MEASUREMENTS

To fit bust sizes 81(86-91-96) cms [32(34-36-38) ins]. Finished measurement at underarm 90(96-100-104) cms [36(38-40-42) ins]. Length 50.5 cms [20 ins]. Sleeve width at upper arm 60 cms [24 ins].

MATERIALS

Berger du Nord Sport 3(4-4-4) 100g balls each in Colours A and B. Pair of needles each size 5mm (No 6) and 5½mm (No 5).

TENSION

16 sts and 20 rows = 10 cms [4 ins] over st st using 5½mm needles.

NOTE

Sweater is designed with A sections on left side and B sections on right side.

BACK

SECTION A

Using smaller needles and A cast on 36(38-40-42) sts. Work in garter st (every row knit) for 4 cms [1½ ins], ending with a wrong side row. Change to larger needles and st st (1 row knit, 1 row purl) as follows:

1st row (right side): Knit.

2nd row (wrong side): K1 (selvage st), purl to last st, k1 (selvage st).

Rep 1st and 2nd rows until back section A measures 20.5 cms [8 ins] from beg, or required length to underarm, ending with a right side row. Mark end of last row for beg of armhole.

Work straight until armhole measures 30 cms [12 ins], ending with a wrong side row. Cast off.

SECTION B

Using B work as given for Back Section A, placing armhole marker at beg instead of end of row.

FRONT

Work as given for Back Sections.

SLEEVES

Note: Make one sleeve in colour A and one sleeve in colour B.

Using smaller needles cast on 34(36-36-38) sts. Work in garter st for 2.5 cms [1 inch], ending with a wrong side row.

Change to larger needles and st st. Inc 1 st at each end of every alt row 31(30-30-29) times. 96 sts.

Work straight in st st until sleeve measures 40.5 cms [16 ins] from beg, or required sleeve length ending with wrong side row. Cast off.

FINISHING

Press pieces according to instructions on ball band. With wrong side of pieces together, sew Back Section A and B together at centre as follows:

With side A facing, back st by using colour B and yarn needle. **Note:** Be sure to work very loosely.

Starting at approx 3mm down from neck edge bring needle through both sections inside selvage st, *then insert needle back 3mm behind where the needle came through and bring the needle out 3mm in front of where needle came through; rep from * along centre front of section A.

With side B of same piece facing and colour A, rep back st as for A section.

Sew front sections A and B as for back sections. Sew front to back at shoulders 14(14-15-16.5) cms [5½(5½-6-6½) ins] from side edge. Sew sleeves to front and back between markers. Sew side and sleeeve seams.

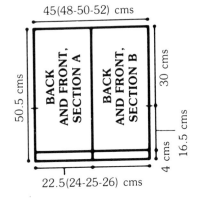

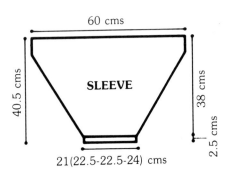

Dropped Shoulder Sweater

MEASUREMENTS

To fit bust sizes 81/86(91/96) cms [32/34(36/38) ins]. Finished bust measurement at underarm 100(106) cms [40(42) ins]. Length 65.5 cms [26 ins]. Sleeve width at upper arm 60 cms [24 ins].

MATERIALS

Patons Solo 7 50g balls in Colour A, Copley Light 'n' Bright 4 50g balls Colour B, Jaeger Cotton Flammé 3 50g balls Colour C. Pair needles size 5mm (No 6).

TENSION

16 sts and 28 rows = 10 cms [4 ins] over pucker st pattern using 5mm needles.

BACK

Using A cast on 80(84) sts.

Foundation rows 1-12

Work in st st (1 row knit, 1 row purl) for 6 rows. Change to B and work in st st for 6 rows.

Commence pucker st pattern:

1st row (right side): Using A k0(2), *k3, **with right-hand needle in back of work, pick up next A st 6 rows below and knit this st together with next st on needle; rep from ** once more — pucker st made over 2 sts — called work pucker st (wps), k6, wps, k4, wps*; rep from * to *, ending k4(6).

Using A work 5 rows more in st st.

7th row (right side): Using C k0(2), *k8, wps, k6, wps; rep from *, ending k8(10).

Using C work 5 more rows in st st.

13th row (right side): Using A k0(2), *k2, wps, k8, wps, k4; rep from *, ending k2, wps, k4(6).

Using A work 5 more rows in st st.

19th row (right side): Using B k0(2), *k6, wps, k3, wps; rep from *, ending k2(4).

20th - 24th rows: Using B work in st st.

Rep 1st — 24th rows for pucker st pattern until back measures 35.5 cms [14 ins] from beg, ending with a wrong side row. Mark each end of last row for beg of armhole.

Continue in pattern until armhole measures 30 cms [12 ins] from marker ending with 6 rows in colour A. Cast off all sts loosely.

FRONT

Work as given for Back.

SLEEVES

Using A cast on 36 sts. Work 12 foundation rows as for Back and **at the same time** inc 1 st each end of every 4th row 30 times, working pattern st as follows:

Commence pucker st pattern:

1st row (right side): With A, k1, make one (m1), [k5, wps] 5 times, k3, m1, k1. 42 sts.

Using A work 5 more rows in st st.

Note: Always work 5 rows st st after each pucker st row, using same yarn as previous row and be sure to work increases on appropriate st st rows.

7th row: Using C [k6, wps, k8, wps] twice, k8.

13th row: Using A k1, m1, k3, wps, k8, wps, k7, wps, k5, wps, k8, wps, k3, m1, k1. 48 sts.

19th row: Using B k8, [wps, k4, wps, k6] 3 times.

25th row: Using A k1, m1, k4, wps, [k5, wps] 6 times, k2, m1, k1. 54 sts.

31st row: Using C k4, wps, [k6, wps, k8, wps] twice, k6, wps, k6.

37th row: Using A k1, m1, k2, [wps, k5, wps, k8, wps, k7] twice, k2, m1, k1. 60 sts.

43rd row: Using B k6, [wps, k6, wps, k4] 4 times.

49th row: Using A k1, m1, k3, [wps, k5] 8 times, wps, k1, m1, k1. 66 sts.

55th row: Using C k10, [wps, k6, wps, k8] 3 times, wps, k2.

61st row: Using A k1, m1, k8, [wps, k5, wps, k8, wps, k7] twice, wps, k6, m1, k1. 72 sts.

67th row: Using B [k6, wps, k4, wps] 5 times, k4.

73rd row: Using A k1, m1, k2, [wps, k5] 10 times, k2, m1, k1. 78 sts.

79th row: Using C [k6, wps, k8, wps] 4 times, k8.

85th row: Using A k1, m1, k5, [wps, k7, wps, k5, wps, k8] twice, wps, k7, wps, k5, wps, k5, m1, k1. 84 sts.

91st row: Using B [k4, wps, k6, wps] 6 times, k2.

97th row: Using A k1, m1, k1, wps, [k5, wps] 11 times, k6, m1, k1. 90 sts.

103rd row: Using C k4, [wps, k6, wps, k8] 4 times, wps, k6, wps, k6.

109th row: Using A k1, m1, k1, [wps, k8, wps, k7, wps, k5] 3 times, wps, k8, wps, k1, m1, k1. 96 sts.

Using A work straight in st st for 5 more rows. Sleeve should measure approx 46 cms [18 ins] from beg. Cast off all sts loosely.

FINISHING

Press pieces according to instructions on ball band. Sew first and last 22(24) sts of front and back tog for shoulder seams, leaving centre 36 sts open for neck.

Sew top of sleeves to front and back between markers. Sew side and sleeve seams.

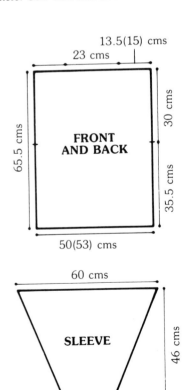

13.5(15) cms

23 cms

65.5 cms

FRONT AND BACK

30 cms

35.5 cms

50(53) cms

60 cms

SLEEVE

46 cms

22.5 cms

Designed by Ethel Seftel
Photographed by Gordon Munro

Basketweave Sweater

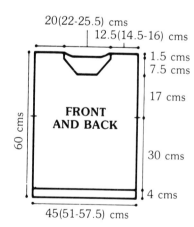

20(22-25.5) cms

12.5(14.5-16) cms

1.5 cms

7.5 cms

17 cms

FRONT AND BACK

30 cms

60 cms

4 cms

45(51-57.5) cms

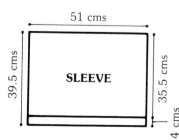

51 cms

39.5 cms

SLEEVE

35.5 cms

4 cms

MEASUREMENTS

To fit bust sizes 76/81(86/91-96) cms [30/32(34/36-38) ins]. Finished bust measurement at underarm 90(102-115) cms [36(41-46) ins]. Length 60 cms [23¾ ins]. Sleeve width at upper arm 51 cms [20½ ins].

MATERIALS

Patons Moorland Tweed Double Knitting 14(15-16) 50g balls. Pair needles each size 4½mm (No 7) and 5mm (No 6).

TENSION

16 sts and 24 rows = 10 cms [4 ins] over pattern st using 5mm needles.

NOTES

For ease in working basketweave pattern circle the numbers that pertain to the size you are making.

As basketweave pattern tends to pull in, block test piece before checking tension for a more accurate measurement.

BACK

Using smaller needles cast on 72(82-92) sts. Work in garter st (every row knit) for 13 rows.

Next row (wrong side): Purl.

Change to larger needles and commence basketweave pattern:

1st row (right side): K6(11-7), *p2, k2, p2, k12; rep from *, ending last rep k6(11-7) instead of k12.

2nd row: K4(9-5), *[p2, k2] twice, p2, k8; rep from *, ending last rep k4(9-5), instead of k8.

3rd row: P4(9-5), *[k2, p2] twice, k2, p8; rep from *, ending last rep p4(9-5).

4th row: P6(11-7), *k2, p2, k2, p12; rep from *, ending last rep p6(11-7).

5th — 8th rows: As 1st — 4th rows.

9th row: Knit.

10th row: P1(2-2), [k2, p2] 1(2-1) times, *p10, [k2, p2] twice; rep from *, ending last rep k2, p1(2-2).

11th row: K1(2-2), [p2, k2] 1(2-1) times, *p8, [k2, p2] twice, k2; rep from *, ending last rep [k2, p2] 1(2-1) times, k1(2-2).

12th row: P1(2-2), [k2, p2] 1(2-1) times, *k8, [p2, k2] twice, p2; rep from *, ending last rep [p2, k2] 1(2-1) times, p1(2-2).

13th row: K1(2-2) [p2, k2] 0(1-0) times, p2, *k12, p2, k2, p2; rep from *, ending last rep [p2, k2] 0(1-0) times, p2, k1(2-2).

14th — 17th rows: As 10th — 13th rows.

18th row: Purl.

Rep 1st — 18th rows for pattern st until back measures 34 cms [13½ ins] from beg, or required length to underarm. Mark each end of last row for beg of armholes.

Work straight in pattern until armhole measures 24.5 cms [9¾ ins], ending with a wrong side row.

Shape Neck

Next row (right side): Work 26(29-32) sts, join 2nd ball of yarn, cast off centre 20(24-28) sts for back of neck, work to end.

Working both sides at same time with separate balls of yarn, cast off 3 sts at each neck edge twice. 22(23-26) sts each side. Cast off remaining sts for shoulders.

FRONT

Work as given for Back until armhole measures 17 cms [6¾ ins], ending with a wrong side row.

Shape Neck

Next row (right side): Work 29(32-35) sts, join 2nd ball of yarn, cast off centre 14(18-22) sts for neck, work to end.

Working both sides at same time with separate balls of yarn, dec 1 st at each neck edge every alt row 9 times. 20(23-26) sts each side.

Work straight until armhole measures same as back to shoulders. Cast off.

SLEEVES

Using smaller needles cast on 82 sts and work in garter st for 13 rows.

Next row (wrong side): Purl.

Change to larger needles and commence basketweave pattern:

1st row (right side): K11, *p2, k2, p2, k12; rep from *, ending last rep k11 instead of k12.

Continue in this way to work pattern as for Back, working as for **2nd size,** until piece measures 39.5 cms [15½ ins] from beg or required sleeve length. Cast off.

FINISHING

Press pieces according to instructions on ball band. Sew right shoulder seam.

Neckband: With right side facing and smaller needles, pick up and k80(90-100) sts around entire neck edge. Work in garter st for 12 rows. Cast off all sts on wrong side.

Sew side of neckband and left shoulder seam. Sew top of sleeves to back and front between markers. Sew side and sleeve seams.

Patch Pocket Jacket

MEASUREMENTS

To fit bust sizes 81/86(91/96) cms [32/34(36/38) ins]. Finished bust measurement at underarm 105(112) cms [42(45) ins]. Length 70.5 cms [28 ins]. Sleeve width at upper arm 75 cms [30 ins].

MATERIALS

Patons Parade 16(17) 50g balls. Pair of needles size 5½mm (No 5). Crochet hook size 5.00mm. Sticks for closing coat.

TENSION

12 sts and 19 rows = 10 cms [4 ins] over reverse st st using size 5½mm needles.

BACK

Cast on 63(67) sts. Work in garter st (every row knit) for 6 rows.

Next row (right side): Purl.

Next row (wrong side): Knit.

Rep last 2 rows for reverse st st until back measures 33 cms [13 ins] from beg, or required length to underarm. Mark each end of last row for beg of armhole.

Work straight until armhole measures 35 cms [14 ins], ending with a wrong side row. Work in garter st for 6 rows. Cast off.

RIGHT FRONT

Cast on 44(46) sts. Work in garter st for 6 rows.

Next row (right side): Knit first 5 sts (front edge), purl to end.

Next row: Knit.

Rep the last 2 rows until right front measures same as back to armhole, ending with a wrong side row. Mark end of last row for beg of armhole.

Work straight until armhole measures 35 cms [14 ins], ending with a wrong side row. Work in garter st for 6 rows. Cast off.

LEFT FRONT

Cast on 34(36) sts. Work in garter st for 6 rows.

Next row (right side): Purl first 29(31) sts, k5 sts (front edge).

Next row: Knit.

Complete left front to correspond to right front, placing armhole marker at beg of row.

SLEEVES

Cast on 28 sts. Work in garter st for 6 rows. Working in reverse st st, inc 1 st each end of every alt row 31 times. 90 sts.

Work straight until sleeve measures 43 cms [17 ins] from beg, or required sleeve length. Cast off.

POCKETS (Make 2)

Cast on 24 sts. Work in reverse st st for 21.5 cms [8½ ins], ending with a wrong side row. Work in garter st for 6 rows (top edge). Cast off.

FINISHING

Press pieces according to instructions on ball band.

Sew first and last 22 sts of fronts and back tog for shoulders seams. Sew top of sleeves to fronts and back between markers. Sew side and sleeve seams.

Outside Edging: With right side and crochet hook, join yarn at lower left back side seam, 1 ch, dc in joining, work dc evenly spaced along lower edge of back and right front, work 3 dc in corner, dc along right front edge to neck edge, 3 dc in corner, dc around neck edge, 3 dc in corner, dc along left front edge, 3 dc in corner, dc along lower edge of left front. Join with sl st to first dc. Fasten off.

Sew one pocket on right front, 5 cms [2 ins] from lower edge and 2.5 cms [1 inch] from side seam. Sew other pocket 5 cms [2 ins] from lower edge on left front overlapping to back so that centre of pocket lies over side seam.

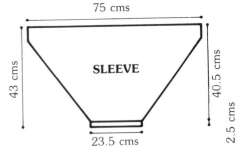

75 cms

SLEEVE

43 cms

40.5 cms

2.5 cms

23.5 cms

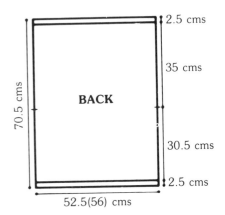

2.5 cms

35 cms

BACK

70.5 cms

30.5 cms

2.5 cms

52.5(56) cms

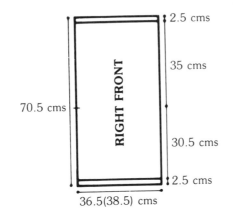

2.5 cms

35 cms

RIGHT FRONT

70.5 cms

30.5 cms

2.5 cms

36.5(38.5) cms

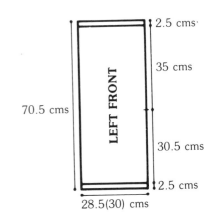

2.5 cms

35 cms

LEFT FRONT

70.5 cms

30.5 cms

2.5 cms

28.5(30) cms

Slipover with Cable

MEASUREMENTS

To fit bust sizes 81(86-91-96) cms [32(34-36-38) ins]. Finished bust measurement at underarm 86(90-96-100) cms [34(36-38-40) ins]. Length 71(71-72-72) cms [28(28-28½-28½) ins]. Armhole depth 33(33-34-34) cms [13(13-13½-13½) ins].

MATERIALS

Patons Diploma for Aran Knitting 10(11-12-13) 50g balls. Pair needles each size 4mm (No 8) and 5mm (No 6). Cable needle.

TENSION

18 sts and 24 rows = 10 cms [4 ins] over reverse st st using 5mm needles.

NOTES

Cable is worked on opposite sides on front and back to line up when pieces are sewn tog.

Back and Front of vest is worked in reverse st st (1 row purl, one row knit).

CABLE PATTERN (over 6 sts)

1st row (right side): Knit.

2nd row: Purl.

3rd and 5th rows: As 1st row.

4th and 6th rows: As 2nd row.

7th row: Slip first 3 sts to cable needle and hold at back of work, knit next 3 sts, k3 sts from cable needle (cable twist made).

8th row: As 2nd row.

Rep these 8 rows for cable pattern.

BACK

Using smaller needles cast on 74(78-82-86) sts.

1st row: *K1, p1; rep from * to end.

Rep this row for 10 cms [4 ins], increasing 4(4-5-5) sts evenly spaced across last row. 78(82-87-91) sts.

Change to larger needles. Commence cable pattern:

1st row (right side): P59(62-66-69), work 1st row of cable pattern over next 6 sts, p13(14-15-16).

2nd row (wrong side): K13(14-15-16), work 2nd row of cable pattern over next 6 sts, k59(62-66-69).

Continue working in reverse st st and cable pattern as set until back measures 38 cms [15 ins] from beg, ending with a wrong side row.

Shape Armhole

Cast off 5 sts at beg of next 2 rows. 68(72-77-81) sts.

★ **Next row:** Dec 1 st at beg and end of row. Work straight for 6(5-6-5) rows ★.

Rep from ★ to ★ 4(5-5-6) times more. 58(60-65-67) sts. Work straight until armhole measures 25.5(25.5-26-26) cms [10(10-10¼-10¼) ins], ending with a wrong side row.

Shape Neck

Next row (right side): Work in pattern across first 22(23-25-26) sts, join 2nd ball of yarn and cast off centre 14(14-15-15) sts, work to end.

Working both sides at the same time with separate balls of yarn, dec 1 st at each neck edge **every** row 4(5-5-6) times. 18(18-20-20) sts each side. Now dec 1 st at each neck edge every 3rd row 6 times. 12(12-14-14) sts each side.

Work straight in pattern until armhole measures same as back. Cast off sts each side for shoulders.

FRONT

Cast on and work rib as given for Back, increasing 4(4-5-5) sts evenly spaced across last row. 78(82-87-91) sts.

Change to larger needles. Commence cable pattern:

1st row (right side): P13(14-15-16), work 1st row of cable pattern over next 6 sts, p59(62-66-69).

2nd row (wrong side): K59(62-66-69), work 2nd row of cable pattern over next 6 sts, k13(14-15-16).

Continue working in reverse st st and cable pattern to correspond to back, with reversing cable placement, until armhole measures 20.5(20.5-21-21) cms [8(8-8¼-8¼) ins], ending with a wrong side row.

Shape Neck

Next row (right side): Work in pattern across first 22(23-25-26) sts, join 2nd ball of yarn and cast off centre 14(14-15-15) sts, work to end.

Working both sides at the same time with separate balls of yarn, dec 1 st at each neck edge **every** row 4(5-5-6) times. 18(18-20-20) sts each side. Now dec 1 st at each neck edge every 3rd row 6 times. 12(12-14-14) sts each side.

Work straight in pattern until armhole measures same as back. Cast off sts each side for shoulders.

FINISHING

Press pieces according to instructions on ball band. Sew left shoulder seam matching cables.

Note: Bands do not need to be sewn in place as they roll naturally to outside.

Rolled Neckband: With right side facing, smaller needles and starting at right shoulder, pick up and k60(62-63-65) sts along back neck and 80(82-83-85) sts along front neck. 140(144-146-150) sts.

1st row (wrong side): Purl.

2nd row (right side): Knit.

Rep 1st and 2nd rows until band measures 5 cms [2 ins], ending with a purl row. Cast off all sts loosely.

Sew right shoulder seam including neckband.

Rolled Armhole Bands: With right side facing, smaller needles and starting at left front underarm, pick up and k5 sts across cast off sts, 65(65-68-68) sts evenly spaced along front armhole to shoulder, 65(65-68-68) sts evenly spaced along back armhole to cast off sts, and 5 sts across cast off sts. 140(140-146-146) sts. Work band same as for neckband. Work right armhole band to correspond to left armhole band.

Sew side seams, including armhole bands.

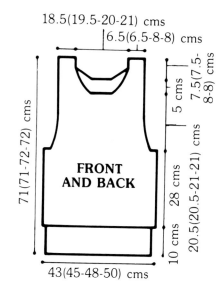

18.5(19.5-20-21) cms
6.5(6.5-8-8) cms
7.5(7.5-8-8) cms
5 cms
71(71-72-72) cms
20.5(20.5-21-21) cms
28 cms
10 cms
43(45-48-50) cms

FRONT AND BACK